# Canadian Books for Children

## A Guide to Authors & Illustrators

*Jon C. Stott / Raymond E. Jones*

**HBJ**

Harcourt Brace Jovanovich Canada
Toronto Orlando San Diego London Sydney

**Canadian Cataloguing in Publication Data**

Stott, Jon C., 1939–
    Canadian books for children

Bibliography: p.
Includes index.
ISBN 0-7747-3081-1

1. Children's literature, Canadian — Bio-bibliography. 2. Authors, Canadian.
3. Illustrators — Canada. 4. Children's literature, Canadian.
I. Jones, Raymond E. II. Title.

PS8081.S86 1988      C810'.9'9282      C88-093694-0
PR9186.2.S86 1988

Cover: from an original painting by Ann Blades

Publisher: David Dimmell
Editor: Heather McWhinney
Publishing Services Manager: Karen Eakin
Editorial Co-ordinator: Edie Franks
Copy Editor: Tilly Crawley
Production Assistant: Barbara Sherman

Interior and Cover Design: Landgraff Design
Typesetting and Assembly: Vellum Print & Graphic Services Inc.
Printing & Binding: Alger Press Ltd.

Printed and bound in Canada
1 2 3 4 5    92 91 90 89 88

For Anne D. Jordan and Norma Youngberg
Guides and Pathfinders
—JCS

For Maryam, Mark, and Sara
—REJ

# *P* reface

The recent rapid growth in the quantity and quality of Canadian books for children has been a mixed blessing for many adults. On the one hand, they have been delighted by the array of good material available for use with children. On the other, they have felt frustrated because this very profusion has complicated their choices. Faced with this abundance, they have sought help in choosing and using Canadian books. Unfortunately, information about Canadian authors, illustrators, and their books is scattered. Until now, no single work has offered a comprehensive and timely treatment of the field. Furthermore, no single work has brought together biographical information, critical assessment of the literature, factual data on book awards, and practical advice on using Canadian books with children. This guide to Canadian English-language books for children meets the need for information in all four areas.

As the authors of this guide, we have developed our understanding of these needs and of ways of satisfying them through practical experience. Individually, we have conducted numerous workshops for teachers and librarians all across Canada, addressed professional and lay groups, taught university and college courses on children's literature, and worked frequently with teachers and students in elementary and junior high classrooms. As a consequence, we have come to understand especially well the needs of teachers and librarians who want to use Canadian books in the Language Arts curriculum.

*Canadian Books for Children: A Guide to Authors & Illustrators* is not, however, exclusively for teachers and librarians. Part I is designed to introduce adults — parents, grandparents, students of childhood and children's literature, all those interested in Canadian culture or Canadian children's books, as well as teachers and librarians — to the authors and illustrators who have created children's literature in Canada, a literature only now receiving the respect it deserves. In the 105 bio-critical articles in Part I, we have provided a few biographical notes; an overview of the individual's career; an introduction to the major themes, character types, and techniques; and a more detailed look at their major works. The focus is on the person as author and/or illustrator, rather than on the author/illustrator as person. Each of the articles is designed to give adult readers factual and critical information that will enable them to read specific books with greater understanding and enjoyment.

At the conclusion of each of these articles, we have included a short list of secondary references that readers wishing to engage in further study may consult. Because of space limitations, we have used an abbreviated form of bibliographical notation, an explanation of which precedes the individual entries in Part I. Within the articles, we have, because of space limitations, indicated by a shortened title the major awards won by specific writers and artists. Part III, Major English-Language Children's Book Awards, provides the full titles of these awards and a complete list of their winners.

The entry for each author or illustrator in Part I, to the best of our knowledge, lists or discusses all works published prior to July 1, 1987. In some cases we have been able to include information on works published after that date before sending this book to the printer.

To aid teachers and librarians, many of whom have asked us for practical advice on integrating Canadian texts into the Language Arts curriculum, we discuss in Part II some of the ways they can make meaningful use of Canadian children's books in the classroom. We also provide a starting point for the study of Canadian books, "Recommended Canadian Books for Elementary and Junior High: A Graded Reading List." The selections and grade recommendations in this list are neither arbitrary nor absolute. Many books not included are worthy of attention by children in and out of the classroom. Inclusion on the list signals that the text may be an especially good one for classroom purposes. Although teachers may follow the grade level recommendations with confidence, they should not consider them to be rigid, inflexible rules for selection. Many works are suitable for more than one grade. As we indicate elsewhere, those seeking to make the best use of a book must not only know the book thoroughly but must also know the child or the class. Finally, although we stress the use of the list for classroom teachers, we must also note that librarians, parents, and grandparents — anyone seeking to bring together the right book and the right child — may find this book a useful place to begin.

Although we take responsibility for the analyses and evaluations of the writers and illustrators discussed in this book, we also wish to acknowledge the enormous debt to many people and organizations who have assisted us during the writing of the book or whose own writings have provided valuable information. All students of Canadian children's literature must acknowledge the pioneering work of Sheila Egoff, whose *The Republic of Childhood* is a starting point for any critical study of the field. The work of Irma McDonough, for many years the editor of *In Review* and the driving force behind the formation of the Children's Book Centre, and of Elizabeth Waterston, Mary Rubio, and John Sorfleet, founding editors of the journal, *Canadian Children's Literature*, cannot be overestimated.

Over the years, we have interviewed dozens of Canadian authors, illustrators, and publishers, who freely discussed their works and creative processes. We have frequently drawn on these interviews in writing our bio-critical articles. During the writing of the book, Kathy Lowinger and her staff at the Children's Book Centre in Toronto and Lynne Bernard and other members of the Edmonton Public Library have provided invaluable assistance. Adele Kostiak, David Booth, and Helen Langford read portions of the manuscript in its earlier stages and offered useful criticism. We also owe a large debt of gratitude to Heather McWhinney, our editor. Her enthusiastic support encouraged us from the very beginning, and her sound professional judgments aided in the preparation of the manuscript.

Finally, Jon C. Stott wishes to acknowledge the assistance of the University of Alberta, whose provision of a year's Study Leave gave the needed time for research and writing.

Jon C. Stott<br>
Raymond E. Jones<br>
May 1988

# *I* ntroduction

"Canadians don't buy Canadian books. It's a proven fact. And if they won't, who will?"
Quoted by Thomas H. Raddall, *Dalhousie Review* 34 (Summer 1954): 144

Although the gentleman quoted by Thomas Raddall was not speaking of children's books, his question was as applicable to Canadian children's literature as to Canadian adult literature. Aside from such staples as L.M. Montgomery's "Anne of Green Gables" books and the animal stories of Sir Charles G.D. Roberts and Ernest Thompson Seton, Canadian works for young readers have until recently been neglected both at home and abroad. For the most part, British and American books, or, unfortunately, American television programs supplied stories for Canadian children. The few Canadian books for children that were published were printed in small quantities, and were therefore expensive and soon out of print.

As recently as ten years ago, a print run of only one or two thousand copies was the norm. Now, print runs of new children's books by major Canadian authors and illustrators range from ten to twenty-five thousand. In addition, because many publishers now have strong backlists, they frequently reprint older titles, and, so do not have to depend solely on the success of three or four new books to maintain financial health. Nor is the interest in Canadian children's books limited to the domestic market. Our best-known books are now regularly reprinted in Great Britain and the United States and are frequently translated into European languages. In fact, in 1987, a new work by a well-known Canadian illustrator interested so many British publishers that it was necessary to hold an auction for the reprint rights.

It is probably impossible to cite all the reasons for the tremendous growth of Canadian children's books over the last two decades, but several major factors are apparent. The success of Dennis Lee's *Alligator Pie*, published in 1974, showed that it was possible for a Canadian children's book to be a best-seller. During the late 1970s, the formation of the Children's Book Centre; the publication of the journal *Canadian Children's Literature*; the creation of such children's publishing firms as Groundwood Books, Kids Can Press, and Annick Press; the opening of specialized children's bookstores in various parts of the country; the establishment of a number of awards for Canadian children's books; and the increase in provincial and federal government support for children's literature — all have created a climate conducive to writers, illustrators, and publishers.

Without favourable conditions, it is doubtful whether many of the writers and illustrators would have developed; conversely, without strong imaginative talent to create good children's books, the publishers would not have been able to develop the healthy lists they enjoy today. Even the most casual reader of the Canadian children's books that have appeared in the last decade will be aware that this strong imaginative talent exists — and in abundance.

Because more and more fine authors and illustrators are publishing children's books and interest in earlier Canadian children's books is quickly increasing, we would have liked to include in this book a far greater number of bio-critical articles than we had space for. We have, therefore, selected entries to provide readers with an accurate sense of both the development of Canadian children's literature and its current state. Our focus is exclusively on English-language books. We have, however, included entries on several French-Canadian authors and illustrators whose works have been widely read in English editions. The growing body of French-Canadian children's literature is definitely worthy of study on its own merits, but is beyond the scope of this work.

Our first criterion for selection has been artistic excellence, either literary or graphic. We have thus included writers and illustrators, no matter how few their books, who have produced work that meets the most discriminating tests of merit — artists who have shown that they are worthy of inclusion in any discussion of children's literature, not just a discussion of Canadian books. Next, we have attempted to include studies of all those earlier and contemporary writers and illustrators whose work has achieved sufficient critical acclaim and popular approval to earn them the vague adjective "major." These are the artists whose names are or were familiar to a large body of readers. Some of these writers do not currently enjoy a wide readership, but their work provides us with an understanding of attitudes towards both children and literature in Canada at various times, and helps us to appreciate the ways in which children's literature has developed over the last century. We have also included shorter articles on earlier and contemporary writers and illustrators whose works illustrate developments in specific genres or, more generally, trends and patterns within children's publishing at a given time. These are the "popular" writers and illustrators, either because they have many readers or because they practise forms that attract large numbers of children. Such writers and illustrators help us to understand the literary milieu in which major works appear and help us to gauge the originality or conventionality of given works. Finally, although the focus of this book is on imaginative literature, we have included, at the request of some librarians who read an early draft, entries on non-fiction writers who have achieved popularity, and thus have drawn attention to the power of Canadian children's books to educate as well as entertain.

Undoubtedly, we will have omitted personal favourites of some readers. However, we hope that we will have included studies of some writers and illustrators not familiar to our readers and thus will have encouraged them to re-evaluate writers and illustrators they had not known well. We also hope that this book will lead adults not only to discover for themselves some of the rich pleasures offered by Canadian books for children, but also will encourage them to share these pleasures with children, whether in the library, the classroom, or the home.

# C ontents

# Part I:
# A Guide to Canadian
# Children's Literature

# A bbreviations for Secondary References

The following chart explains the abbreviations used in the Secondary Reference list that follows most entries. Reference works vary in the way they are organized. In the case of reference works published in more than one volume but organized alphabetically within each volume, numerals following an abbreviation indicate volume numbers. Thus, *CA* 97–100 indicates that material on an author appears alphabetically in *Contemporary Authors*, volumes 97–100. (These volumes are physically one book.) In the case of journals, numerals indicate volume or issue number and relevant pages. Thus, *CCL* 21: 8–16 indicates that material related to an entry appears in *Canadian Children's Literature* issue 21, pages 8–16. In instances where bibliographic convention dictated or where we could prevent confusion by doing so, we also cite parenthetically a journal's month and year of publication. *QQ* 51 (June 85): 26 directs the reader to page 26 of the June, 1985 issue, which can be found in volume 51 of *Quill and Quire*.

| | |
|---|---|
| *BIC* | *Books in Canada* |
| *CA* | *Contemporary Authors* |
| *CAFR* | *Contemporary Authors First Revision Series* |
| *CANR* | *Contemporary Authors New Revision Series* |
| *CCL* | *Canadian Children's Literature* |
| *ChL* | *Children's Literature* |
| *ChLQ* | *Children's Literature Quarterly* |
| *CL* | *Canadian Literature* |
| *CLC* | *Contemporary Literary Criticism* |
| *CLR* | *Children's Literature Review* |
| *Junior 1* | *Junior Book of Authors* |
| *Junior 2* | *More Junior Authors* |
| *Junior 3* | *Third Book of Junior Authors* |
| *Junior 4* | *Fourth Book of Junior Authors and Illustrators* |
| *Junior 5* | *Fifth Book of Junior Authors and Illustrators* |
| *OCCL* | *Oxford Companion to Canadian Literature* |
| *OCChL* | *Oxford Companion to Children's Literature* |
| *Ocean* | *One Ocean Touching: Papers from the First Pacific Rim Conference on Children's Literature*, ed. Sheila Egoff (Metuchen, N.J. and London: Scarecrow, 1979) |
| *Profiles* | *Profiles*, rev. ed., ed. Irma McDonough (Ottawa: Canadian Library Association, 1975) |
| *Profiles 2* | *Profiles 2*, ed. Irma McDonough (Ottawa: Canadian Library Association, 1982) |
| *QQ* | *Quill and Quire* |
| *SATA* | *Something About the Author* |
| *TCCW 1* | *Twentieth-Century Children's Writers*, 1st ed. |
| *TCCW 2* | *Twentieth-Century Children's Writers*, 2nd ed. |

# B io-Critical Articles on Authors and Illustrators

## Alderson, Sue Ann (1940–    )

A love of word play, careful observation of the antics of her two children, and an understanding of child and family psychology are the major elements that Sue Ann Alderson has used in the creation of her seven books for children. The daughter of psychologists, Alderson was born and raised in New York City. She received a Bachelor of Arts from Antioch College and a Master's degree in English from Ohio State University. She did further graduate work at the University of California, Berkeley, before moving to Vancouver in the late 1960s. Since 1980 Alderson has taught creative writing at the University of British Columbia. Her poetry has appeared in a number of journals, and her Bonnie McSmithers books have become minor Canadian classics. When *Bonnie McSmithers You're Driving Me Dithers* appeared in 1975, it was enthusiastically reviewed, and she wrote two sequels, *Hurry Up, Bonnie!* (1977) and *Bonnie McSmithers Is at It Again* (1979). Two fairy-tale stories, *The Finding Princess* (1977) and *Prince Paul's Adventures* (1977), were written for her children. *Comet's Tale* (1983) and *The Not Impossible Summer* (1983) are novels for the middle elementary grades.

Each Bonnie McSmithers book focuses on the relationship between the title heroine and her mother, who are either in conflict with each other or separated by their different personalities or interests. In *Bonnie McSmithers You're Driving Me Dithers*, the little girl keeps getting into trouble — using a banana peel as a hat, washing the walls with toothpaste, cutting the dog's hair. After each episode the mother begins her despairing refrain, "Bonnie McSmithers, you're driving me dithers...," and sends the child either outside or to her room. The resolution occurs when Bonnie asks her mother to join her in an activity, and the mother realizes that she has been as responsible as her child for the conflict. This summary reveals the psychological basis of the story and its careful observation of children and parents. The popularity of the story comes not only from the humour of the situations but also from the rhythmic poetic prose in the refrain concluding each episode. Young children can easily learn the words and say them along with an adult reader. In *Hurry Up, Bonnie!* and *Bonnie McSmithers Is at It Again*, mother and child once more share activities and reach a reconciliation.

Alderson's two novels also deal with relationships between children and adults, but include a larger number of characters. *Comet's Tale* is about Wanda, Willy, and Walter II; their father, Max, a painter whose favourite subjects include "poached eggs" and "mermaids" and "long woolen underwear"; their mother, Vanessa, a poet who writes such

Alderson, Sue Ann. BONNIE McSMITHERS YOU'RE DRIVING ME DITHERS. Ill.
by Fiona Garrick. Edmonton: Tree Frog, 1974. Reprinted
by permission from Tree Frog Press Ltd.

lines as "there's a rose in every cabbage"; Aunt Tweedle, who forces cream of rosehip soup on everyone; and Theodore Rexford Fripple, the local poundkeeper, who spends much of his time standing on his head. The plot involves two sinister characters who wish to close the pound and who kidnap the baby, a dreaded visit from Aunt Tweedle, and the appearance of Hartley's comet, supposedly the cause of the unusual events of the novel. Underlying the humourous plot is a serious theme: the need for individuals to feel special and to belong to a loving group. At the end of the story, everyone realizes that, as Max says, "We have a pretty special family."

*The Not Impossible Summer*, intended for older readers, is more serious in tone. Jenny and her mother are spending a summer vacation on one of the Gulf Islands of British Columbia. The mother, busy writing an historical article, has little time for her daughter, who feels somewhat antagonistic, but wants to please her mother. During the vacation Jenny achieves a sense of self-worth, gains her mother's admiration and respect, and is able to let go of Debra, an imaginary friend she had turned to in times of loneliness and rejection.

Alderson's books are noteworthy for their memorable characters and humorous episodes. Bonnie, Jenny, and the siblings of *Comet's Tale* have strong personalities. During their adventures they display an independence of spirit, and they grow in their understanding of the people close to them. This underlying portrayal of character growth gives added dimensions to Alderson's books, making them more than merely humorous and entertaining stories; for children they are significant examinations of their relationships to the worlds in which they live.

SECONDARY REFERENCE: *Profiles 2.*

## *Allinson, Beverley (1936–      )*

Born in Melbourne, Australia, Beverley Allinson grew up enjoying such writers of fantasy as C.S. Lewis, E.B. White, and Lucy Boston. Before and after her move to Toronto in 1968, she worked as a language arts teacher and curriculum developer. She has been involved in several textbook projects, including Nelson's "Language Stimulus" series, Heath's "Women at Work" series, and Methuen's "Kids Like Us" series. She has also collaborated with Barbara O'Kelly and Judith Lawrence on *The Dog Power Tower* (1977), a Mr. Dressup Adventure, and with Barbara O'Kelly on *"All Aboard!" A Cross-Canada Adventure* (1979). Allinson's two stories written for the trade market are *Mandy and the Flying Map* (1973) and *Mumbles and Snits* (1975), both illustrated by Ann Powell. In the former, a little girl rides on a map above her town. In the latter, Mift, a Mumble who, unlike the rest of her species, likes playing at night, meets a Snit, a Stumble who looks very much like her but has never heard of Mumbles. Together, the two of them teach their respective communities to become friends. Both books emphasize the individual's right to take independent action in exploring beyond the secure confines of her world. In addition, individuals must learn to understand others who may be different. The fantasies are quite simple, but are told with humour; the underlying messages are evident, but are not forced upon readers.

SECONDARY REFERENCES: *CANR* 4; *Profiles; Canada Writes!*

## Allison, Rosemary (1953–        )

Born in Jamaica, Rosemary Allison attended school in England before moving to Canada to study at the Ontario College of Art. After graduating in 1974, she helped to found Kids Can Press. In her first story, *The Travels of Ms Beaver* (1973), the restless heroine leaves her country home for adventures and misadventures in Toronto. In a sequel, *Ms Beaver Travels East* (1979), she is again on the road, this time in Nova Scotia, where she helps a group of villagers rebuild a fish plant that has burned down. *The Green Harpy at the Corner Store* (1976) tells about a kindly grocer who rescues a grumpy, unruly harpy who injured her wing when she flew into Toronto's CN Tower. *The Pillow* (1979) recounts the unhappiness of a little girl who has recently immigrated from Italy. In *Chito* (1981), a Guatemalan boy and his grandfather fly their own kite during an All Saints' Day festival. Allison's other books are *I Never Met a Monster I Didn't Like* (1973), *Yak* (1974), *Yaay Crickets!* (1975), and translations of Christiane Duchesne's *The Lonely Dragon* (1977) and *Lazarus Laughs* (1977). Allison's stories are noted for their portrayal of strong female characters in the central roles, for their sense of the importance of the family, and for their themes of self-worth.

SECONDARY REFERENCES: *CANR* 11; *Profiles 2*.

## Andersen, Doris (1909–        )

Born in Tanana, Alaska, Doris Andersen grew up in Victoria, British Columbia, and studied at the University of British Columbia and the University of Washington before beginning a career as a librarian. In the 1960s, after her three children had grown up, she began writing for children: "My library supervisor kept telling me that I could write a good children's book. Then, I discovered that some of my husband's forebears had been part of the great trek of Norwegians from Minnesota to Bella Coola. I did some research on the trek, on Bella Coola in the 1890s, and the relationships between whites and Indians." The result was *Blood Brothers* (1969), the story of the friendship between a white and a Native boy. Her second children's book, *Slave of the Haida* (1974), is set in precontact times, and tells of the escape of a Salish boy from his northern captors.

*Blood Brothers* clearly portrays three groups of Indians: the young generation symbolized by Qwata, who expresses bewilderment at the changes and tensions he experiences; those like the shaman Askankots, who jealously defends the old ways against the whites; and the old leaders, represented by Qwata's grandfather, who tells the boy: "Keep the old laws, but learn the white man's ways."

In *Slave of the Haida* Kim-ta, a captured Salish boy, has failed to follow the sacred rituals of the bear hunt and feels responsible for the disasters that befall him and his people. The book is notable for its presentation of cultural relativity. In his contacts with the Kwakiutl, Haida, and Tsimsham, Kim-ta comes to learn and to appreciate the differences between his group and other groups.

Although Andersen has been criticised for introducing somewhat improbable and coincidental incidents into her plots and for the stereotyping of characters, she has been praised for the knowledge of traditional cultures and the fairness with which she treats them. In the era when the arrival of white people had begun to alter West Coast life drastically, the greatest difficulty lay in the opposing groups' inability or unwillingness to understand others. Each of the novels ends with an uneasy peace; there is no promise of lasting harmony among the Indian peoples of the West Coast or between them and the newly arrived Europeans.

SECONDARY REFERENCES: *Profiles 2; TCCW 2.*

## *Atwood, Margaret (1939–        )*

Margaret Atwood is an internationally acclaimed poet and novelist for adults. She was born in Ottawa and did not attend a full year of school until the eighth grade because her father, an entymologist, took his family with him when doing research in the bush. Atwood received a BA from the University of Toronto and an MA from Radcliffe College, Harvard. Although she has said that she has written a number of books for children, Atwood has published only two. Both treat a theme prominent in her adult work, the relationship between people and nature, but her children's books treat it with much more lightness.

Because of economic constraints, Atwood herself drew the illustrations and hand-lettered the text for her first children's book, *Up in the Tree* (1978). The limitations of the two-colour pictures create such elements as a blue tree and a red sun. The accompanying poem shows that nature can both frustrate and satisfy people. Two children, stranded in their tree home when two porcupines chew their ladder, are rescued by a bird (a motif no doubt developed from the tales of Grimm, which Atwood avidly read as a child).

Atwood collaborated with Joyce Barkhouse, her aunt, on her second book, *Anna's Pet* (1980), for which Ann Blades provided colourful illustrations. An educational tale with a controlled vocabulary, it tells of a lonely girl who searches for a pet, catching in turn a toad, a worm, and a snake. Each of Anna's mistaken efforts to make her pets happy produces an overtly didactic speech about that pet's habitat and needs, but her efforts are mildly amusing.

SECONDARY REFERENCES: *CL* 78: 13–15; *CCL* 42: 9–16.

# Aubry, Claude (1914–1984)

"I began writing for children because I wanted to keep the poetical side of myself alive and the freshness of the child I knew was within me. One needs to have a poet within to write well for children." In this way the late Claude Aubry described his beginnings as a children's writer; he also discussed the influences of his childhood and teenage years. Born in Morin Heights, in rural Quebec, he used to exercise his imagination on the two-mile walk to and from school, creating exciting adventures involving savage Indians and wild animals. After receiving his Bachelor of Library Science degree from McGill University, Aubry worked at a variety of library jobs. From 1953 to 1979 he was Director of the Ottawa Public Library.

Aubry wrote several radio and television plays, but it was not until 1960 that his first children's book, *Îles du roi Maha Mah II (The King of the Thousand Islands)*, was published. It won the CACL Award for French books, as did his second book, *Le loup de Noël (The Christmas Wolf)*, published in 1962. *Le violon magique et autres légendes du Canada français (The Magic Fiddler and Other Legends of French Canada)*, which appeared in 1968, is for teenage and adult readers. *Agouhanna* (1972) is a novel for children. Aubry also translated into French James Houston's *River Runners*, Tony German's *Tom Penny*, and Brian Doyle's *You Can Pick Me Up at Peggy's Cove*. In 1974 he was made a member of the Order of Canada.

*The King of the Thousand Islands*, a literary folktale set along the St. Lawrence River hundreds of years before the coming of the Europeans, is about the Yellow Ant people, a mound-building culture that, at the beginning of the story, is "prosperous and respected and peaceful." However, because an evil and ambitious counsellor gives the king bad advice, the happiness is shattered. Enamoured of a mysterious siren, the king follows his counsellor's advice and orders his people to build a beautiful garden of islands. But, in so doing, he loses "the most precious thing in the world, the affection of my people." Now, only the islands remain, monuments to human foolishness. Aubry combined extensive research on pre-Columbian cultures, an understanding of the literary folktale, and wry satire of human nature to create one of Canada's few modern *pourquoi* legends.

Aubry created *The Christmas Wolf* to recapture the fast-disappearing festivals of rural Quebec and to encompass in a story the celebrations that brightened the hard lives of the people. During the harsh Laurentian winter, Maître Greboux, an ageing wolf who was once the terror of the north, is reduced to creeping into the village to find food. It is Christmas Eve, and slinking into the church during midnight Mass, he is surrounded by angry, yet fearful people. The priest saves him, reminding the people that it is a time of love and mercy and that they, too, have been guilty of wolf-like behaviour. The story is a combination of three genres, the animal story, the Christmas miracle, and the satire on human behaviour.

*The Magic Fiddler* contains ten French-Canadian legends, many dealing with the intrusion of extraordinary events and beings into the lives of ordinary people. In "The Magic Fiddler" and "Rose Latulippe," the Devil wins the souls of the unsuspecting. "La Courriveau" is about a witch who confronts a lonely traveller. In "Le Loup garou," a werewolf comes to live with a miller. The narrator often casts doubt upon the marvellous adventures he recounts. For example, at the conclusion of "The Witch Canoe," we are left wondering whether excessive drinking had anything to do with the supposed adventures. Three of the stories, "The Caughnawaga Bell," "The Legend of Percé Rock," and "Pilotte," are historical legends. In his preface Aubry drew attention to his "somewhat ironical tone," and indeed one is often aware in the stories of the sardonic tone and satirical view of human nature.

Aubry wrote his final children's book, *Agouhanna*, "because I wanted to see the Iroquois as they were, not as they'd been shown in movies. I'd done a great deal of background research, and wanted to combine it with a story about a young person who embodied the creative, poetic side of life." The timid chief's son, whose name means "brave among the braves," is afraid of being alone in the forest during his initiation rites. His closest friend, Little Doe, a girl to whom he is betrothed at the end of the story, is his direct opposite and wishes to become a great warrior. Although the story portrays the cultural details accurately and sensitively, aspects of plot and characterization are sometimes forced, and the blend of historical facts and adventure story conventions is only partially successful.

Discussing the role of the creator of literature for Canadian children, Aubry frequently stressed the necessity of integrating Native, British, or French folklore with the harsh, rugged landscape. His greatest achievement was in writing stories that do this. He was, in a sense, a modern "myth-maker" drawing on legends, motifs, and character types frequently found in traditional literature, which he wove into his original stories. He wrote for two audiences, children and adults. While his younger audience responds to the adventures and the human emotions of a story, older readers can enjoy the witty, ironic satire of human weakness.

SECONDARY REFERENCES: *CA* 106; *CCL* 4: 14–19; *Ocean*, 197–201; *Profiles; SATA* 29.

# Ballantyne, Robert Michael (1825–1894)

"Ballantyne the brave," as Stevenson called him in the introductory poem to *Treasure Island* (1883), is best known for his tropical survival story, *The Coral Island* (1858). Because of him, however, generations of English boys grew up with a romantic view of Canada as an endlessly challenging land of wild animals and wilder Indians, a land in which boys used to Victorian restraint could enjoy endless adventures. Born in Edinburgh to a family associated with the publishing of Sir Walter Scott's romances, Ballantyne was enlisted in the Hudson's Bay Company at the age of sixteen, serving at a number of posts in Canada from 1841 to 1847.

Ballantyne's first book, *Hudson's Bay; or, Everyday Life in the Wilds of North America* (1848), was a nonfiction record of his life in Canada. This material also provided the basis for *Snowflakes and Sunbeams; or, The Young Fur Traders* (1856), the novel that launched his career as the foremost writer of romances for boys. Assembled by scenes rather than skilfully plotted, richly detailed in its descriptions of the exotic Canadian North, filled with scenes of exciting adventure, it set the pattern for the children's books he later wrote — over a hundred of them. Characterization is somewhat rudimentary and stereotypical. The young white heroes who prove their manhood in the wilderness are Christians who never swear or drink. There is a Native who converts to Christianity and works with a missionary, as well as a bloodthirsty, cowardly devil who slaughters a woman without thought. Behind all of this romance of wish fulfillment, however, is something else: an authentic picture of the northern landscape and a small glimpse of life in the wilderness forts.

Ballantyne used his Canadian experience as background in a number of other works, including *Ungava: A Tale of the Esquimaux Land* (1858), *The Wild Man of the West: A Tale of the Rocky Mountains* (1863), *Away in the Wilderness; or, Life Among the Red Indians and Fur Traders of North America* (1869), *The Pioneers: A Tale of the Western Wilderness Illustrative of the Adventures of Sir Alexander Mackenzie* (1872), *The Red Man's Revenge: A Tale of the Red River Flood* (1880), and *The Buffalo Runners: A Tale of the Red River* (1891).
SECONDARY REFERENCES: *TCCW* 2; *OCCL*; *SATA* 24.

# Bellingham, Brenda (1931– )

Born in Liverpool, England, Brenda Bellingham came to Canada in 1958. She was a social worker and a teacher before she took up writing. Although she has said that she has no special reason for her choices of plots, all of Bellingham's novels focus on the problems of single-parent children. In each book a young girl must come to terms with her situation and, by so doing, accept or discover her own identity.

Bellingham's first novel, *Joanie's Magic Boots* (1979), is a tale of wish fulfillment within a realistic setting. Joanie, accused of shoplifting some boots, must endure the label of thief until she dramatically proves her integrity by capturing an actual thief. Joanie then discovers that her boots are "magic": she gets her deepest wish, a father, when the policeman who had handled her shoplifting charge marries her mother.

*Two Parents Too Many* (1985) portrays the feeling of rejection children develop because of divorce. In the first part of the novel, two sisters conduct an amusing campaign to prevent their mother from remarrying. A somewhat darker note, however, sounds underneath the light surface tones: Jenny, the older girl, is developing anorexia because she believes that her father has divorced not only her mother but her, too. The novel is careful to show that both of the divorced parents love their children in spite of new marriages.

Bellingham's best book is *Storm Child* (1985), a soundly researched historical novel. She uses a common historical situation, the abandonment of a Native wife and her children by a white trader, as the basis for contrasting white and Indian cultures and for exploring the question of Metis identity. Isobel Macpherson, a Metis who finds all white ways hateful after her Scots father deserts her mother, takes her Indian name, Storm Child, and goes to live with her Peigan grandparents. She discovers, however, that she is neither white nor Indian but "part Isobel, part Storm Child — a country-born girl."

Bellingham's limitations are in her endings; her books too rapidly wind up with somewhat facile and optimistic conclusions. Her strength is in characterization; with just a few strokes, she draws convincing psychological portraits of girls seeking a secure place within a family to establish a satisfying and secure identity for themselves.

## *Berton, Pierre (1920–        )*

Like many well-known authors of adult books, Pierre Berton wrote his only children's book, *The Secret World of Og* (1971), for his own children: "I had at that time five children just growing up, and I put them into a fantasy situation to see what would happen." The book, the author's favourite, has become a Canadian classic. It is, however, just one of the many accomplishments of this journalist, TV personality, social critic, and historian.

Born in Dawson City in the Yukon, Berton is an officer of the Order of Canada and the holder of several honorary doctorates. He now lives in Toronto. Berton has published over thirty titles, three of which, *The Mysterious North* (1956), *Klondike: the Life and Death of the Last Great Gold Rush* (1958), and *The Last Spike* (1971), received the Governor General's Medal for nonfiction.

Many of Berton's historical books are good reading for young adults.

Critic Sheila Egoff has written of *The Golden Trail: the Story of the Klondike Gold Rush*: "the triumph of the book is due to Berton's judgment in selecting evocative details from the sources." His monumental histories of the building of the Trans-Canada railroad (*The National Dream* [1970] and *The Last Spike* [1971]), and of the War of 1812 (*The Invasion of Canada, 1812–1813* [1980] and *Flames Across the Border, 1813–1814* [1981]) present a gallery of vivid portraits, interesting anecdotes, and direct quotations from original participants, all of which give immediacy to the presentation. Two books of short biographies, *My Country: the Remarkable Past* (1976) and *The Wild Frontier: More Tales from the Remarkable Past* (1978) also contain readable portrayals of unique Canadians.

In *The Secret World of Og*, Penny, Pamela, Patsy, Peter, and Pollywog climb through a trapdoor they have found in their playhouse and down a long tunnel into the subterranean world of Og, which is inhabited by small green people. There they not only escape several threatening situations, but help the Ogians to live more fulfilling lives.

Berton's interest, he has said, was "to see how the characters of my kids would develop.... At the end, two of them grow up. The baby stands on his own two feet and for the first time realizes that he's not a dog. And the eldest daughter realizes that she's an adult." In portraying the children, Berton was influenced by one of his favourite childhood fantasists, Edith Nesbit, whose characters are ordinary children who have extraordinary adventures in which they discover inner strengths.

Berton includes jokes "which I think kids will get but which are really there for the adults." Many of these jokes are satirical jibes at elements of the adult world: conventional notions of how children should be educated, the quality of mass-appeal television programs, and, most important, the pressure towards conventionality and imitation in contemporary society.

In 1974 the book was reprinted in a new edition illustrated by the author's daughter, Patsy. It remains very popular with Canadian children. Although somewhat slow starting, it contains humour and action, along with an accurate portrayal of children's views both of themselves and of the adults who often try to restrict their lives. Like Mordecai Richler's *Jacob Two-Two Meets the Hooded Fang*, it is not only an outstanding adventure-fantasy but also a strong portrayal of life as children see it.

SECONDARY REFERENCES: *CCL* 7: 21–27; *CCL* 23/24: 4–19; *OCCL*.

## Bice, Clare (1908–1976)

Clare Bice, who was born in Durham, Ontario, and educated at the University of Western Ontario, the New York Art Students' League, and the Grand Central School of Art in New York, is primarily known for his work as an artist. Curator of the London Art Museum from 1940 to 1972, he exhibited his landscape and portrait paintings widely. His illustrations for seventeen children's books, including Catherine Anthony Clark's *The Sun Horse* (1951), made him one of Canada's most important illustrators of the 1940s and 1950s. He also wrote five children's books of his own. Three of these — *Jory's Cove* (1941), *The Great Island* (1954), and *Hurricane Treasure* (1965) — are mystery-adventure stories set in small fishing villages on the Atlantic coast. *A Dog for Davie's Hill* (1956), a story about sheep stealers, takes place in the Scottish Highlands. *Across Canada: Stories of Canadian Children* (1949) contains realistic stories of everyday life from eight regions of the country.

The books are fairly conventional. There are plenty of red herrings in the mysteries, some near escapes from the elements, individuals who are misjudged by the young heroes, and wise old helpers. The main characters do not undergo any real struggles or development. The stories' greatest successes are their presentations of daily life. Critic Mary Rubio has called Bice's stories "a pastoral vision of Canadian rural life." In reading them, contemporary children will gain a fuller understanding of Canada as it was three decades ago.
SECONDARY REFERENCES: *Profiles; TCCW 1; SATA 22.*

## Bilson, Geoffrey (1938–1987)

Many authors of historical novels for children focus on major events of the past and place their heroes in the midst or on the edge of these events. History professor and children's novelist Geoffrey Bilson does not. In *Goodbye Sarah* (1981), *Death Over Montreal* (1982), and *Hockeybat Harris* (1985), he takes lesser known but nonetheless important events and shows how they influence the lives of young teenagers.

Born in Cardiff, Wales, Bilson studied at the University of Wales and later at Stanford University, California, where he earned a doctorate in American history. In 1967 he began teaching at the University of Saskatchewan. Although he had often made up stories for his children, it was not until the late 1970s, while they were away on summer holidays, that he sat down to write them a novel. *Death Over Montreal* made use of his studies in Canadian medical history to tell the story of Jamie Douglas, who arrived in Montreal early in the nineteenth century in the middle of a cholera epidemic. *Goodbye Sarah*, set in Winnipeg during the General Strike of 1919, is the account of a young girl's struggles with friendship and family. Saskatoon is the scene of *Hockeybat Harris*, the story of David Harris, who was among those evacuated from England early in World War II.

The central character in each novel is cut off from a secure past and, essentially alone, must face his or her major crisis. Jamie Douglas has come with his family from Scotland, reluctantly accepting his father's hope that Canada will provide their "big break." When the father dies of cholera after giving all his money to a swindler, Jamie must fend for himself. He proves his heroism working for Dr. Ayres, a naturalistic healer, whose faith in him gives the boy courage and self-confidence.

Mary Jarrett's security is destroyed by the General Strike, of which her father is an organizer. Not only does the family find itself in severe financial difficulties, but Mary's friendship with Sarah is destroyed by the tensions generated by the conflict. At the conclusion, Mary is able to accept the fact that Sarah is no longer her friend and that she will never be able to say goodbye to her in person.

Like Jamie Douglas, David Harris is an unwilling immigrant. Worried about his mother back in bomb-ravaged England and his father on active duty in Egypt, he is hostile to his adoptive Canadian family, especially his new "brother," Bob Williams. He steals from the family cookie jar, blames Bob for a number of bed-wetting incidents, and refuses to help with family chores. The patience of the adult members of the Williams family and his growing skill at hockey, using what he calls his "hockey bat," help him to overcome his unhappiness and belligerence.

Ordinary kids in extraordinary circumstances: this phrase captures the essence of Geoffrey Bilson's novels. Readers will gain knowledge of little-known events of Canadian history; but they will be most interested in the conflicts of the main characters, coming to understand and respect the difficulties of their lives and the strengths they develop in confronting them.

# Blades, Ann (1947– )

"During Easter vacation when I was teaching at Mile 18, I felt quite isolated and lonely. So I began to think of a story about one of the children in my class and started to paint some watercolours to go with it. None of the books the children had at school related to them at all, and I thought it would be nice for them to have a story about something familiar." From that week's vacation came one of Canada's most famous picture books, *Mary of Mile 18* (1971), winner of the CACL Award; the book has since been translated into several languages.

Born in Vancouver, Ann Blades began painting when she was eleven; but she never gave any thought to professional art until she began publishing books. She taught a year at Mile 18 and another at Taché, both in northern British Columbia, studied for her Registered Nurse's degree, and worked in hospitals for several years before devoting herself full time to painting and to illustrating books. In addition to *Mary of Mile 18*, she has written *A Boy of Taché* (1973), *The Cottage at Crescent Beach* (1977), and *By the Sea: An Alphabet Book* (1985). She illustrated Michael Macklem's *Jacques the Woodcutter* (1977), Betty Waterton's *A Salmon for Simon* (1978) and *Pettranella* (1980), Margaret Laurence's *Six Darn Cows* (1979), Margaret Atwood's *Anna's Pet* (1980), and Jean Speare's *A Candle for Christmas* (1986). For her illustrations for *A Salmon for Simon*, Blades received the Howard-

Blades, Ann. MARY OF MILE 18. Montreal: Tundra, 1971.
Reprinted with permission from Tundra Books Inc.

Gibbon Medal and the Canada Council Prize for illustration. *By the Sea* won the first Elizabeth Mrazik-Cleaver Award for illustration.

The story of *Mary of Mile 18* is a simple one. Awakening in the middle of a $-40°$ winter night, Mary Fehr watches the Northern Lights and sees in them the promise of something special the next day. The promise seems to have come true when, on the way home from school, she discovers a lost half-wolf pup. However, her father tells her that she cannot keep it because "our animals must work for us or give us food," and she is forced to abandon the pup in the woods. Late that night the whines of the pup warn the family that a wolf is breaking into the hen house, and now that he has proved his worth, the pup is brought into Mary's bedroom by her father.

The simplicity of the plot may lead some to categorize *Mary of Mile 18* as just another dog story. The book, however, is really a tribute to the Fehr family. This Mennonite family moved north in response to the government's promise of title to land they clear. They live a hard life without plumbing, taps, electricity, or telephones; they obtain water by melting snow; and their nearest neighbours are two miles away. But the family works and plays together, older children helping younger ones, and all helping their mother who is soon to have a baby. Mr. Fehr suffers emotional hardships, for he must often refuse to give the children what they want, concealing his sorrow in anger.

The artistry of the illustrations makes up a large part of the greatness of this book. Blades' watercolours capture the bleak quality of the northern wilderness against which the family lives its life. In contrast to the pale blues, drab greys, and dull browns of the landscape are the rich colours of human tools: the warm yellows of the lanterns, the vivid scarlet of the tractor.

Particularly effective are the illustrations that reveal Mary's changing emotions. When she first discovers the pup, she kneels before it, extending her bright yellow mittens, a faint smile on her lips. The horizon appears distant, the slender trunks of the bare trees less overwhelming than in other pictures. However, as she walks into the woods to abandon the pup, the grey and brown tree trunks dominate. There is no brightness on the page, just as there is no happiness in Mary's heart. When Mary is finally given the pup, warmth radiates from the illustration. Sitting up in her bed, she cradles the dog in her arms. Her rich, golden hair is down, a full smile plays on her face, and her eyes twinkle. On her bed is a gaily coloured quilt; the browns of the bedstead and walls are rich and warm in colour.

Like *Mary of Mile 18, A Boy of Taché* draws on people Blades knew while teaching in northern British Columbia. She has said that, although the story was based on an actual event in which a teenaged boy brought help for his sick grandfather, "I made the boy much younger, so that he'd be about the age of the children who'd be reading it. The events, however, are very true to the experiences of Native children. Their lives are much less protected than those of children growing up in the city; they see violence and death at an early age." *A Boy of Taché* is more than a rescue story; it is the account of a boy's growth to maturity, his development of an understanding of ageing and death in a rugged and demanding environment.

In the illustrations, Blades contrasts the harsh elements with the courageous but vulnerable human beings. There are no people in the opening picture; bare, black tree trunks are silhouetted against a cold, blue-grey, early spring sky. Several illustrations, however, do emphasize human warmth: Charlie looks admiringly at Za as the old man talks to him about trapping; both crouch before a campfire roasting a grouse; and in the concluding picture, the old man, recovered from his illness, puts his arm on Charlie's shoulder as the two of them look at the bright red hues of the setting sun. The two face not only the horizon but also the future that awaits the boy who has proved his courage and love.

*The Cottage at Crescent Beach* and *By the Sea* are simple accounts of children's everyday experiences on the beaches near White Rock, British Columbia. In the former, Blades describes the summer activities of two girls: collecting pop bottles, exploring a "haunted house," swimming, roasting wieners, and listening to an uncle's scary stories. In the latter, she uses the letters of the alphabet as the structure for a small girl's play at the beach. In addition to illustrating the various activities, she gives a strong sense of the colours and details of the seashore and sea. Green is the dominant colour of *The Cottage at Crescent Beach*: the rich foliage of the trees and the bottle-green underwater areas the girls explore. Blue dominates *By the Sea*; it is as if one were looking at a hazy West Coast summer day. In both, one senses the security of the children as they play in a familiar environment.

Not surprisingly, five of the six books Blades has illustrated for other writers portray children engaged in realistic activities and aware of the support of loving families. In fact, the success of Blades' art is in its communication of both adventure and security. At the beginning of *A Salmon for Simon*, the hero of the title fishes alone, a pensive expression on his face. At the end, he has moved to the wharf; again he is fishing, but now he is grinning. His rescue of a trapped salmon has given him greater confidence and a sense of accomplishment, and it has made him feel like the others in the village, all of whom are successful fishermen. His unhappiness early in the story, when he cannot catch a fish, is emphasized in an illustration of him hunched over a tidal pool, gazing at the small sea creatures. The page is designed around a series of downward curves — his hairline, eyebrows, mouth, shoulders, and the hill on which he slouches, all reinforce the frown on his face. Later, when he has freed the fish, he leans contentedly on his shovel, a small smile on his face. In the distance, a bright sun casts a cheery glow.

From the time she leaves her old world home to the time when she discovers the seeds her grandmother gave her blooming in the Manitoba

Copyright Ann Blades 1986 from A CANDLE FOR CHRISTMAS by Jean Speare.
Illustrated by Ann Blades, a Groundwood Book, Douglas and McIntyre.

wilderness, the heroine of *Pettranella* feels many emotions, all of which are communicated clearly by the illustrations. At first, the prospect of a voyage to the new world thrills the child, and she smiles radiantly; but the enthusiasm fades as she sits slouched on her family's trunk in a dingy waiting room. When she loses her grandmother's gift, she slumps dejectedly, looking sadly down at the empty seed bag. She is surrounded by yellow birch trees without leaves. In contrast, when she discovers the flowers, she holds them in her hands and smiles, surrounded by the pale green spring grass, delicately coloured blossoms, a powder blue sky, and new foliage on the birch trees. And she wears a bright yellow bonnet. Within her is happiness; new hope has been born.

The adventure of the brother and sister in *Six Darn Cows* takes place in the dark forest where they are searching for the cows that have strayed because of the children's carelessness. Leaving the familiar green fields of the farm, the children are very small, standing in the deepening shadows and surrounded by grey tree trunks. However, returning with the cows, they re-enter a world of green colour: the forest is behind them, and on the road ahead they see their mother's flashlight, a beacon leading them back to the security of home. In *Anna's Pet*, the adventures are less exciting, the sharp contrasts less frequent. Blades, however, alternates indoor and outdoor locations as Anna finds and then brings into the house a number of pets that, she learns, cannot survive inside. Appropriately, the last illustration is set outside, as the girl finds a pet that, she now understands, must be kept in a suitable place.

A recurrent illustration in Blades' books is the home, the place of security for the children. Snug in her bed, Mary cuddles her new-found pet; Charlie and his grandparents travel to a distant but warm trapper's cabin; having rescued the salmon, Simon strides confidently towards his house; Pettranella's family builds a log cabin in the lonely Manitoba countryside; the cows returned, the children sit around the kitchen table with their mother and father.

Blades emphasizes the importance of the home in several ways. First, she contrasts it to the wilderness around: through the window of the Fehr home appear the bleak expanses of the winter landscape; Pettranella's small but strongly built cabin is the only building on the vast prairie. In *A Candle for Christmas*, Benjamin's candle shines warmly out into the snow and darkness. Second, Blades uses warm colours in depicting the homes. Often, as in *A Salmon for Simon*, these are seen from the outside, with a warm yellow light shining from the windows; inside, they may be plain, but they are homey, and the families within are grouped together.

Blades' illustrations were less successful in *Jacques the Woodcutter*, a French-Canadian folktale. Here Blades was approaching a different, unfamiliar culture; she had experienced neither the customs nor the landscape. Moreover, she was dealing with adults rather than children. While the illustrations are accurate, they lack spontaneity and warmth.

The adults appear awkward and even grotesque, and the ironic situations seem forced and unnatural.

The watercolour art of Ann Blades has been called simple and primitive, and in a sense it is. An untrained artist, she sets out to capture emotions and situations as clearly as possible. In this simplicity, however, is a purity that enhances the texts of the stories. She understands the changing emotions of her characters and the beauty and power of the landscapes that surround them; she conveys these elements in a manner that has made her one of Canada's foremost illustrators of children's books.

SECONDARY REFERENCES: *BIC* 2 (Dec. 79): 32–33; *CANR* 13; *CCL* 39/40: 21–32; *Profiles;* *QQ* 51 (Oct. 85): 10–11; *SATA* 16; *TCCW* 1; *TCCW* 2.

## Bodsworth, Fred (1918–          )

A dedicated naturalist who has led bird-watching tours to many parts of the world, Charles Frederick Bodsworth was born in Port Burwell, Ontario. He worked for newspapers in St. Thomas and Toronto before becoming a writer and editor with *Maclean's*. Since 1955 he has been a freelance writer, producing both novels and articles dealing with nature. He was presented with the Rothman's Merit Award for Literature in 1974.

Although not specifically intended for children, Bodsworth's first novel, *Last of the Curlews* (1954), has been popular as a high-school text. In this moving tale of the extinction of the Eskimo curlew, Bodsworth almost completely escapes what he calls "the nature writer's sin of anthropomorphism" by insisting that his central character, a lone male searching for a mate, operates primarily from instinct. The novel's structure is at once simple and powerful, alternating fiction and non-fiction chapters. The fiction chapters trace the life of the curlew from one mating season until the next, shortly after the wanton killing of his mate. The alternating nonfiction chapters are excerpts from historical sources. They make note of the former abundance of the curlew and, by recording people's abuse of reason in their wholesale slaughter of it, form an effective contrast to the fictional tale celebrating animal instinct.

Bodsworth has said that the major theme in all of his work is that "man is an inescapable part of all nature." *Last of the Curlews*, one of the finest animal stories ever written in Canada, is a moving, intelligent plea that people recognize their place in nature and their responsibilities to it.

SECONDARY REFERENCES: *SATA* 27; *CANR* 3.

## Bradford, Karleen (1936–          )

Karleen Bradford believes that young people who can read at an adult level do not necessarily want to read books about adult experiences:

"For that reason I write for them — in an adult manner, but about *them*, about the problems and complexities that face *them*." Her primary themes are the development of secure relationships within families, and an understanding of ancestry.

Born in Toronto, Bradford moved with her parents to Argentina when she was nine. She returned to Canada to attend the University of Toronto, graduating with a BA in 1959. Married to a Canadian foreign service officer, she has lived in South America, the Philippines, the United States, England, and Germany.

Bradford approaches adolescent experiences most directly in her two contemporary problem novels, *Wrong Again, Robbie* (1983; originally published as *A Year for Growing*, 1977), and *I Wish There Were Unicorns* (1983). In the former, Robbie, a conservationist, and his grandfather, an avid hunter and fisher, gradually come to understand each other's views, and thus to accept each other. In the latter, Rachel Larrimer, wounded by her parents' recent divorce, gradually develops sympathy for her mother and an acceptance of the new life the family must lead. Both novels resort to contrived dramatic events to force a resolution to problems, but in their earlier sections both succeed in portraying children at odds with their families and the world.

Bradford has said, "I've always been fascinated with the idea of going back into time and doing something to change history." She has used this idea in three novels, each using the device of a modern child resembling someone in a former time, thus symbolically exploring the concept of identity. In *The Other Elizabeth* (1982), Elizabeth goes back to 1813 during the war with the United States, and saves the life of one of her ancestors, thus ensuring her own existence in the future. In the more complicated *The Stone in the Meadow* (1984), Jennifer goes back to Druid England, where her experiences cause the Victorian relative who accompanies her to become an historian. In *The Haunting at Cliff House* (1985), events recorded in a diary by Bronwen, a nineteenth-century Welsh girl, parallel those experienced by Alison, who opposes her widower father's relationship with an attractive woman. By becoming sensitive to the pain of others, she undoes the tragedy of the past and willingly mends her strained relationships in the present.

The focus in Bradford's historical novel *The Nine Days Queen* (1986) is on the way Lady Jane Grey becomes victim of her own family's thirst for power.

Bradford's novels suffer from conventional plotting and, in the first two time-travel stories, from weakly delineated motivation. However, they do succeed in portraying the tense emotions of troubled adolescents. SECONDARY REFERENCES: *SATA* 48; *QQ* 51 (Aug. 85): 29–30.

# Buchan, Bryan (1945–          )

Born in Aberdeen, Scotland, Bryan Buchan grew up in Canada, receiving a BA from the University of Toronto. Since 1968 he has taught in

Richmond Hill, Ontario. He has written three novels for children and a children's Christmas musical, "Only a Baby." "All my writing has been done with a specific audience in mind," he has said, "and the children with whom I have worked often are reflected in the composite characters in my novels."

Buchan's first novel, *The Forgotten World of Uloc* (1970), recounts the relationship between Doug and Uloc, the small creature who is the guardian of the polluted pond by which Doug is playing. On a camping trip in Northern Ontario, Doug courageously helps Uloc defeat the evil spirit Satika. *Copper Sunrise* (1972) is set on the East Coast of Canada in early colonial times. Jamie, a young immigrant, hears terrifying rumours about the "savages"; but he befriends a Native boy who, he discovers, is "so unlike the savages of the village stories." In *The Dragon Children* (1975), a contemporary mystery, John, while wandering in the woods, meets Steve, a strange boy who urges him to stop a confidence-man from fleecing elderly people. Along with his cousin Cathy, and little brother Scott, John spends much of the novel chasing the wrong suspect. Finally they capture the criminal and befriend Mrs. Winch, an elderly neighbour thought by many children to be a witch. Steve turns out to be the long-dead son of Mrs. Winch; he has returned from the spirit world to find people who will assist his mother.

Buchan's three novels deal with ordinary children who are called on to face extraordinary experiences, whether they be forces of supernatural evil, dangers in colonial times, or modern-day criminals. Although the major characters do not undergo extensive development in the course of their adventures, they do learn the importance of trust and responsibility. *Copper Sunrise* is the most successful of the books, presenting no easy answers, but honestly facing some of the unpleasant truths of our country's past.

SECONDARY REFERENCES: *CA* 107; *SATA* 36.

# Burnford, Sheila (1918–1984)

Born in Scotland and educated in Edinburgh, Yorkshire, and Germany, Burnford came to Canada with her husband and children in 1948. They settled in Port Arthur, Ontario, where she began her career by writing scripts for a local puppetry group and sketches about Canadian life for British periodicals. Always fascinated by the ways animals communicated with each other, she used her observations of the relationships between three family pets to create her first book, *The Incredible Journey* (1961).

The novel traces the progress of two dogs and a cat, who undertake a dangerous journey across the rugged Northern Ontario wilderness to the home of their masters. Along the way, they endure every conceivable test of their friendship and determination. The animals have unique, well-defined personalities. Luath, the young Labrador retriever who leads them, is wise and benevolent; Bodger, the dim-eyed old bull terrier, is fun-loving and eager for a fight in spite of his infirmities; Tao, the Siamese cat, appears aloofly self-centred at the beginning, but is just as altruistic as the others. Most critics have complained of the obvious anthropomorphism and sentimentality in the novel, but its simplicity and fast pace made it an immediate commercial success. Winner of the CACL Award, it has been translated into at least twenty-five languages and made into a full-length Walt Disney film.

Burnford published a second book accessible to children, *Mr. Noah and the Second Flood* (1973), a cautionary tale in which a descendant of the original Noah prepares for a flood brought on by people's interference with the planet's ecology. Occasionally humourous in its portrayal of James Noah and his wife as pastoral innocents, the book grows progressively more caustic: in the end, Noah decides that people are so much at fault that he refuses passage on the ark to his own sons and their wives.

SECONDARY REFERENCES: *SATA* 3 & 38; *Profiles; TCCW* 2; *CLR* 2; *CA* 112.

# $C$ ampbell, Maria (1940–       )

"I have brothers and sisters, all over the country. I no longer need my blanket to survive." In the closing lines of her autobiography, *Half-breed* (1973), Métis author Maria Campbell states that she has achieved self-knowledge, an awareness of who she is and where she belongs. This awareness summarizes not only her own life but also the theme of her books for children.

Born in Park Valley, Saskatchewan, Maria Campbell enjoyed a happy childhood in a close-knit family. Her mother read to her from the English classics and her great-grandmother, her *cheechum*, told her stories about the old Native beliefs and ways. With the death of her mother and her father's lapse into despair, she was left with the responsibility of raising her brothers and sisters. To escape increasing pressures and unhappiness, she married while a teenager and later travelled to Vancouver, where she lived frenetically as a member of the subculture for several years. Only when she moved to Alberta and became a member of several women's and Native activist groups did she achieve a sense of purpose and direction. Since then she has written three children's books, *People of the Buffalo* (1975), *Little Badger and the Fire Spirit* (1977), and *Riel's People* (1978). She has written several school broadcast scripts, has served as Writer in Residence at the University of Alberta (1979–1980), and remains active in a number of Native organizations.

For Campbell, part of the goal of writing has been to inform her readers, Native and non-Native, of the proud cultural heritage of her people. Perhaps the most important part of that heritage was the Métis' and Plains Indians' strong sense of personal and cultural identity. As she notes at the conclusion of *People of the Buffalo*, writing of the renaissance of old beliefs and customs, "The most important weapon of all [is] to know who you are and where you come from." In *People of the Buffalo*, this involves not only appreciating the way of life in the physical world — all aspects of which are carefully detailed in the book — but also understanding and sympathizing with the deep spirituality of the people. The circle, the symbol of unity and harmony of all created things, dominated their lives, from tipi design and placement to weapons. The coming of the white people led to violence, drunkenness, and a loss of harmony and unity.

The conclusion of *Riel's People* also emphasizes a people's self-awareness: "History calls them a defeated people, but the Métis do not feel defeated, and that is what is important.... They know who they are: 'Katip aim soot chic' — the people who own themselves." Although the advance of farming and urbanization into the prairies destroyed their traditional lifestyle, they still cling to the family as the centre of strength.

Campbell's major work for children, *Little Badger and the Fire Spirit*, is a literary folktale describing the acquisition of fire by the Native people of the Prairies. Although the people have good lives, they suffer in the winter because they lack fire. Badger, who is blind, journeys to the cavern of the Fire Spirit, receives fire for his people, and is rewarded by the gift of sight. The tale is set within a contemporary framework. Visiting her grandparents on the shores of Alberta's Lac LaBiche, Ahsinee asks her grandfather to tell her a story from the old days.

Although Maria Campbell created the story, she drew consciously on the traditional wisdom and tales she had learned both from her *cheechum*, her great-grandmother, and from other old people. Underlying the narrative is the belief that all living things have a purpose: "That purpose was to serve and help each other." Badger has not acted alone in his journey; moreover he has made new friends: mountain goat, mountain lion, grizzly bear, and rattlesnake, not to mention the Fire Spirit. He has helped to restore harmony and friendship between all beings. Badger's journey has also been one of self-discovery and fulfillment. His new eyesight symbolizes his understanding of friendship and the necessity of co-operation between all beings.

The story's framework reinforces the narrative's meaning. Just as Little Badger must journey into unknown realms to achieve wisdom and fulfillment, Ahsinee must leave the familiar town of Lac LaBiche to visit her grandparents, people who live close to the old ways and remember the old traditions. She is aware of her need to learn the old ways as she asks her grandfather a question about the origin of fire, hoping he will tell a traditional tale. When she returns to the town at the end of the summer, not only will she remember this and other stories told by her grandfather, but she will also possess some of the old wisdom and will, therefore, be surer of who she is and where she belongs. She will have a sense of her Native heritage.

SECONDARY REFERENCES: *CA* 102; *CCL* 31–32: 15–22; *Profiles 2*.

# *Clark, Catherine Anthony (1892–1977)*

Generally recognized as the first writer of fantasy to make substantial use of Canadian materials, Catherine Anthony Clark was born Catherine Smith in London, England, and came to Canada in 1914. After her marriage, she spent a number of years on a ranch in the West Kootenay region of British Columbia, where she gained a particularly sharp understanding of the rugged mountain landscape that is the setting for her six fantasies and one historical novel. She died in Victoria, British Columbia.

Although there are some variations in details, Clark's fantasies are essentially similar: they follow a pattern based on the circular journey of a pair of children who, except in the first book, *The Golden Pine Cone* (1950), feel somewhat alienated. These children, a boy of either ten or eleven and a slightly younger girl, set out from home and soon find that they have crossed over from the Outer World of mundane life into a special, magical world. Here they discover that they are important: the people in the magic realm depend on them to undertake a quest that will lead to restoration of the moral order. Unable to return to the Outer World before completing the quest, the children display courage, compassion, and generosity. Successful, they become certain of their own worth and capable of appreciating others.

Although the pattern of each novel is clear enough, Clark tends to complicate matters by putting her characters through an almost bewildering variety of incidents. Even the quests tend to multiply as a novel progresses. In *The Golden Pine Cone*, Bren and Lucy begin with the idea of returning a golden pine cone necessary for Tekontha, the good ruler of the magic realm, to hold power. Along the way they become involved in a quest to restore the heart of an Indian maiden, and a quest to earn the freedom of their dog. All of the quests are thematically united because they display the power of love, but they also seem more the product of extemporizing than careful plotting. In *The Sun Horse* (1951), winner of the CACL Award, an additional quest is less successfully blended into the main story. A boy and girl search for both the girl's lost father and a magical golden stallion. Suddenly they have to undertake another quest, for the Love Magnet, a metal plate that will destroy the Thunderbird.

*The One-Winged Dragon* (1955) is particularly shaky in its multiplication of quests because Clark unsuccessfully tries to combine Chinese and Pacific Coast Indian strands. Thus, the two children set out in search of an old Chinese farmer's luck stone, which, in turn, leads them to a quest for his missing daughter, which, along the way, involves them in a quest for a whale that is destroying the Indians' fishery. Similar plotting complexities are evident in Clark's other fantasies, *The Silver Man* (1958), *The Diamond Feather; or, The Door in the Mountain: A Magic Tale for Children* (1962), and *The Hunter and the Medicine Man* (1966).

In addition to the numerous episodes, Clark's fantasies are also characterized by a unique, sometimes jarring mixture of both mythic and folkloric elements. Clark creates grandeur through mythic devices: her novels are populated with Indian princesses, warriors, and medicine men who embody basic moral attributes. The children who enter the magic realm also take on new heroic identities, a point stressed in *The Sun Horse, The One-Winged Dragon*, and *The Silver Man* by the fact that they earn new Indian names. Furthermore, familiar characters of the pioneer past — miners and settlers — take on dignity and significance as helpers. Sometimes these characters become effective symbols. In *The Sun Horse*, for example, Old Beard, a miner who refuses to move from his mine, symbolizes the futility of the life dedicated to materialistic pursuit. All of these elements give universality and a timeless dignity to adventures set against a Canadian background.

Clark's use of folkloric elements works to lighten the tone of moral grandeur, often through comedy. She begins her first two books with variations on "once upon a time," introducing a variety of talking animals, many of whom have significant roles as helper figures. Some of these, such as the Head Canada Goose in *The Golden Pine Cone* and the Rock Puck in *The Diamond Feather*, are memorable and original. Unfortunately folkloric creatures, like the comical Rock Puck, the bats in *The Sun Horse*, Foxy and Mammoth in *The Silver Man*, and the beavers in *The Hunter and the Medicine Man*, distract from the seriousness of the mythic elements, making the whole somewhat cartoonish.

Clark also wrote an historical adventure novel, *The Man with the Yellow Eyes* (1963).

In spite of their limitations, Clark's books are generally readable and point to the ways in which Canadian settings and materials can be used in fantasy.

SECONDARY REFERENCES: *TCCW* 2; *CL* 1: 39–45; *CL* 78: 32–42; *CCL* 15/16: 15–30; *CCL* 21: 8–16.

# Clark, Joan (1934–          )

"Anyone who writes down to children is simply wasting time. You have to write up, not down." At the end of her entry in *Canada Writes!*, Joan Clark mentions this quotation by E.B. White as one of her favourites. In a sense it explains both the merits and the limitations of her own books for children. Unafraid of tackling serious and complex ideas in a sophisticated way, Clark has created some challenging works. Although interesting in conception, these works are often puzzling in execution, however, faltering both aesthetically and intellectually.

Born in Liverpool, Nova Scotia, Clark graduated from Acadia University and worked as a teacher in the Maritimes and in Alberta. She took up writing after the birth of her first child.

Clark's children's books show a preoccupation with symbolism, parallel stories, and the theme of identity. Her first book, *Girl of the Rockies* (1968), draws a parallel between the amusing story of a bear cub's growth into an unpredictable yearling and the development of the girl who has kept it as a pet. However, the connection of the story of Heather's development to that of the bear's growth to maturity is, at best, tenuous. Similar attempts at symbolism are evident in two picture books for which she provided the text. *Thomasina and the Trout Tree* (1971), illustrated by Ingeborg Hiscox, tries to show, through a girl's search for the mysterious Trout Tree, that art is everywhere. *The Leopard and the Lily* (1984), illustrated by Velma Foster, parallels the story of a caged black leopard who dreams of a lily and the story of a girl with gossamer wings who presents him with it. Its symbols are, however, vague and enigmatic.

*The Hand of Robin Squires* (1977), a first-person fictional explanation for the mysterious "Money Pit" on Oak Island, Nova Scotia, suggests that the young hero is telling the tale in order to begin a new life.

However, the real theme of the book — identity — is realized in the story of Auctadin, a Micmac whose powers of observation and intelligence have caused him to rebel against tribal traditions and taboos. His tale of rebellion and conformity is not an effective parallel to Robin's tale of victimization by his cruel piratical uncle. Furthermore, it forces Clark to violate point of view, shifting to the third person in three chapters. Although it contains several sharply drawn, exciting scenes, the novel is further weakened by stereotyped minor characters and a strained conclusion.

Far more ambitious in concept than her earlier novels are *Wild Man of the Woods* (1985) and *The Moons of Madeleine* (1987), books related by plot and theme. Both are highly symbolic works that attempt to incorporate symbolic fantasy into an adolescent problem novel in order to explore the theme of identity. The former book is the less successful because it does not convincingly integrate the two approaches. The story of Stephen Gibson, a boy terrified of bullies and fascinated by Native masks, seeks to show the interrelationship of a mythic and mundane world. Stephen dons a Native mask to confront his tormentors and becomes an evil creature who lusts for power over them. When the mask is knocked off and he falls into the lake, he is symbolically reborn, saved from his darker self.

Stephen's symbolic transformations are intriguing, but his too-rapid acceptance of himself when he sees a postcard showing a white Grecian temple with columns, "like gods and goddesses holding back the dark," not only violates the Native symbolism throughout, but also strains credibility. Indeed, the literal story is so contrived that it undermines the symbolism. Thus, Clark fails to explain why a Kwakiutl carver lives in a plains teepee in eastern British Columbia and hangs his masks on trees. Most significantly, she fails to convince us that bullies would be frightened of boys wearing Native masks, no matter how internally transformed those boys feel. The ending, in which the bullies unite in friendship with their former victim, is intended to extend the theme into an anti-war one, but the bullies' change of heart is improbable and the thematic reach too extensive to gain acceptance.

*The Moons of Madeleine*, however, is nearly completely successful in exploring female identity. The mythic echoes this time are Greek. Mad, short for Madeleine, is a loner spending time in Calgary with her cousin Selena, a rebellious teenager whose very appearance upsets the staid visitor. Mad enters a parallel moon world, where she discovers that she has a quest to prevent the return to Chaos by entering the cave of First Woman and proving that she still lives. Mad succeeds; the quest takes her to "the womb of the universe," and to hints about the continuity of the female principle, immortality through memory of others, and acceptance of differences.

The success of *The Moons of Madeleine* is attributable to its blending of the mundane and the fantastic. Throughout most of the novel, Clark allows the possibility that the quest has taken place in a dream. She carefully sets up parellels, especially the echoes between the actions of Selena and of the rebellious moon goddess Aneles (Selena backwards), to connect the two stories. The dialogue and actions of the characters in the realistic sections are, unlike those in the previous novel, believable and consistent.

*The Moons of Madeleine* is so successful in uniting problem novel and symbolic quest fantasy that it lingers teasingly in the mind, a book whose full import requires, and whose skilful prose invites, rereadings. In this novel Clark has avoided most of the plotting deficiencies and the puzzling ambiguity that weakened earlier works. Here she has indeed managed "to write up, not down" to children.

SECONDARY REFERENCES: *Profiles 2; Canada Writes!*

# Cleaver, Elizabeth (1939–1985)

By the time of her death, Elizabeth Cleaver had illustrated thirteen books. Although this is not many over seventeen years, the excellence of her distinctive books established her as Canada's leading illustrator of children's books, and won her numerous awards; she was elected to the Royal Canadian Academy of Arts in 1974. She also achieved recognition abroad, most notably when she was named to the Hans Christian Andersen International Award Honours List in 1972. She continues to be honoured through the Elizabeth Mrazik-Cleaver Canadian Picture Book Award and the Elizabeth Cleaver Memorial Lecture series, held every second year at Vanier College, Montreal.

Born Elizabeth Ann Mrazik, Cleaver received most of her education in Montreal. During the 1950s, however, she accompanied her parents to Hungary. For three years she studied at Sarospatak where, she would fondly recall many times later, Amos Comenius produced *Orbis Pictus*, the first picture book for use in schools. Upon returning to Canada, she studied art at Sir George Williams University, at the School of Art and Design of the Montreal Museum of Fine Arts, at L'Ecole des Beaux Arts, Montreal, and at Concordia University, which awarded her an MFA in 1980.

After undergoing surgery for cancer, Cleaver quit her job at a Toronto advertising agency to work full time as an illustrator. She had immediate success and recognition. Her coloured and black-and-white pictures for *The Wind Has Wings* (1968), her first published work, won her an Award of Merit from the New York Illustrators Society, and in 1971 she received the very first Howard-Gibbon Medal. A revised version, *The New Wind Has Wings*, appeared in 1984.

After completing her initial commission, Cleaver pursued her own interests in later work: "I love fairy tales, myths and legends; they are my 'inner world,' the world I love and want to re-create." Her re-creations fall into several well-defined categories. First were the legends of North American Indians. She was, in fact, a pioneer in the development of the picture-book presentation of Canadian native tales. Such tales had fascinated her since childhood, when she would go on family outings to a reservation near Montreal. Working with William Toye, her editor, Cleaver illustrated four native legends: *How Summer Came to Canada* (1969); *The Mountain Goats of Temlaham* (1969); *The Loon's Necklace* (1977), winner of the Howard-Gibbon Medal and IODE Book Award; and *The Fire Stealer* (1979). She also produced black-and-white linocuts for *Canadian Wonder Tales* (1974), a one-volume collection of Cyrus MacMillan's retelling of Native tales and other Canadian stories, and shadow puppets for an Inuit tale, *The Enchanted Caribou* (1985).

A second interest, the folklore of French Canada, where she spent most of her life, found expression in illustrations for Mary Alice Downie's *The Witch of the North* (1975). Her third interest, the tales and legends of Hungary, country of her family's origin, led to *The Miraculous Hind* (1973). Developed first as a National Film Board filmstrip (1971), this book won the CACL Award.

In addition to her interest in folk and fairy tales, Cleaver also had a deep love for two other art forms, both of which are associated with tales of wonder. Her love of ballet and stage design led to *Petrouchka* (1980), a retelling of Stravinsky's ballet; that book won the Canada Council Prize for illustration. She was at work on *The Wooden Prince*, based on a Bartok ballet, at the time of her death. Part of her joy in doing such work was in translating an experience that depended upon a complex interaction of music and movement: "A ballet has many ways to express character and plot.... With a book you have only a two-dimensional world, but there is a lot happening in that tiny universe."

The other art form that attracted her was puppetry, especially shadow puppetry. When she was a child, her father had entertained her by casting hand-shadows of animals on the walls. With the assistance of Canada Council grants, Cleaver travelled in 1971 to Europe, Iran, and Turkey to study shadow puppetry and in 1972 to Baker Lake, Northwest Territories, to work with Inuit children in adapting their tales for presentation with shadow puppets. Because "shadows are mysteries," Cleaver felt that shadow puppetry was especially suited to the kind of fairy tale and mythic material that most attracted her: "It can be the most poetic form of puppetry since it is ideal for presenting dreams, visions and transformation scenes." Cleaver herself designed shadow puppets based on Inuit tales for a Christmas performance at Montreal's Centaur Theatre in 1971 and for her last published book, *The Enchanted Caribou*.

Cleaver's childhood heavily influenced the characteristic techniques of her work. Her happiest childhood hours were those in which she was left alone with cut-out books, to be "transposed to another world." "Cut-out books are associated in my mind with play and happiness." She still enjoyed cutting paper as an adult — the foundation of the collages she assembled to "create feelings and moods in a contemporary way."

Cleaver began an illustration only after long contemplation of a text, and often, after considerable research into its meaning and the visual elements necessary to picture it accurately. For example, before beginning *The Mountain Goats of Temlaham*, she obtained a Canada Council travel grant to visit British Columbia, where she was able to see the mountain setting and view Tsimshian artifacts in museums. She continued the research in museums and libraries in Toronto, Montreal, and Ottawa. The actual preparation of a picture began with pencil drawings, which she transferred onto linoleum blocks. She would also prepare textured paper (monoprints) upon which she printed the blocks and which she used for her backgrounds. She would then cut and tear the elements of her collage, manipulating them to find pleasing arrangements: "It is not planned completely, but is in part discovered and revealed." Cleaver's materials and methods encouraged creativity: "I can exploit the accidental." Thus, for example, she used the white edges of torn monoprints to form snow caps in *How Summer Came to Canada, The Mountain Goats of Temlaham*, and *The Loon's Necklace*.

Cleaver was always experimenting. She used such things as leaves, grass, pine needles, bark, and lace to give her two-dimensional pictures a three-dimensional quality, and to form a contrast between the sharply delineated natural object and her own stylized linocuts. In *The Miraculous Hind*, she even cut out letters for the text because "children should feel and see that there is beauty in the sound and look of words." Cleaver readily admitted that some would see her process as creative play, but she added that "one has to use the mind, the hands, the eyes and the heart to create a picture."

The most striking feature of Cleaver's collages is their use of colour. In *How Summer Came to Canada* and *The Mountain Goats of Temlaham*, she uses brightly coloured strips of paper arranged in layers to establish stylized settings and, thus, to suggest a mythic world. In the former, she also uses blues and purples to convey the chill of winter, and shocking reds, oranges, and greens to suggest the fertility, vibrancy, and joy of summer. In the latter, colour conveys mood. The book begins with bright, light colours to depict the world before people violated the sanctity of life by abusing the mountain goats. The central portions use darker colours. These are appropriate to both the smoky lodge and the violence of the retribution the goats exact. When peace is restored, the bright colours return.

Less obvious, but just as powerful, is Cleaver's use of symbolism. For Cleaver, who termed herself "an amateur Jungian," a major attraction of a story was "the verbal or visual images, the symbols, in it." In particular, she was concerned with the motif of transformation, using pictures to intensify or extend the meaning of the text.

Such symbolism is apparent in *How Summer Came to Canada*, where the coming of vegetation and the cycle of the seasons indicate the theme: "life and death and change." Cleaver intensifies this symbolic pattern with pictorial symbolism. Thus, when Glooscap dreams and defeats the power of the giant Winter, Cleaver portrays him with a tree sprouting by the side of his head, an illustration she has interpreted as

"a use of the tree as a symbol of imaginative thought." In *The Moun-*
*tain Goats of Temlaham*, in which goats transform themselves into
humans in order to exact retribution from people who do not respect
the sacred bond of life, Cleaver uses the placement and colouring of
totem poles symbolically. In the beginning, the totem pole separating
the villagers from the goats is orange, the initial colour of the sky and
the villagers. To attack the goats, the villagers move to the right past
this totem, symbolically moving beyond human law and restrictions.
Later, on their way to the lodge of the strangers, they again move beyond their totem, but it is now green, the colour of the natural world of
the goats, thereby suggesting that they have entered a territory where
the goats and their laws reign. After the boy is saved, he appears
between two totems. Behind him, an orange and green totem, suggestive of the blending of village life and natural life, separates him from
the world of goats. The totem he approaches, tree-coloured like the one
that saved him, suggests that the village will now have a protective
ceremonial spirit.

Cleaver also develops symbols in other ways. In *The Loon's Necklace*,
she uses the composition of two facing pictures. The circular design of
the pictures illustrating the loon's healing of the blind man is highly
suggestive of a cyclic process. As Cleaver pointed out, in fact, the tale
has a rich meaning: "Symbolically, he [the man] attains inner vision
and becomes whole as he is cleansed by the deep water, symbol of puri-
fication, regeneration and birth." In *The Fire Stealer*, she uses a device
reminiscent of the transformation sequence in Gerald McDermott's
*Arrow to the Sun* (1974). Like McDermott, she uses four panels resembling the frames of a filmstrip. Her sequence shows Nanabozho
transforming himself into a birch tree and suggests his psychic whole-
ness by having his roots cling strongly to the earth. Finally, the very
technique of shadow puppetry used in *The Enchanted Caribou* was
richly symbolic to Cleaver, who overtly connected it to Jung's theory of
the shadow, claiming that both "attempt to lead man to self-realization
and transformation." Indeed, she interpreted the book in psychological
or spiritual terms, suggesting that this tale of a girl who is transformed into a white caribou when she violates an injunction and then
back into a woman when her lover seeks her out is a symbolic presentation of the theme that girls have to get in touch with their animal
natures before becoming women.

Elizabeth Cleaver loved picture books. She believed that they could
educate children's tastes and stimulate their imaginations. No doubt
this happened in her own life. Her brightly coloured *ABC* (1984) was
her way of giving future generations the same loving start with books
that she had. It, like all of her books, expresses her theory of picture
book art: "The picture acts like a living person with whom I can converse. If the picture can talk back to me, it will also be capable of talking to others." Cleaver's pictures will be talking to Canadians for many
years to come.

SECONDARY REFERENCES: *Junior* 4; *SATA* 23; *Profiles; CA* 97–100; *Ocean*, 195–96; *CCL* 4: 71–79; *CCL* 15/16: 67–79; *CCL* 31/32: 69–79; *QQ* 51 (June 85): 26; *The Lion and the Unicorn* 7/8: 156–70.

## Climo, Lindee (1948–      )

When American-born artist Lindee Climo arrived on Prince Edward Island, she expressed her enthusiasm for the landscape by creating the paintings for *Chester's Barn* (1982), which won the Howard-Gibbon Medal.

Animals and art have long been very important to the Massachusetts-born Climo. When she lived in Los Angeles, she spent much of her free time in the country breeding sheep, many of which won prizes. After studying medical illustration, she travelled widely, and in 1974 moved to Prince Edward Island, where she farmed and painted. She has had several exhibitions of her paintings across Canada, and has written and illustrated a second children's book, *Clyde* (1986). She now lives in Halifax.

*Chester's Barn* is a tribute to a past way of life and of farming. However, the author notes, "here on the Island, more often than in many other places, even a specialized farmer might keep an old barn fixed up and full of all sorts of animals, simply out of appreciation and love for the old ways. Chester has that kind of barn." The text and the twenty-four full-colour illustrations describe a day in the life of the barn. The central figure of the book is Chester, who works busily for his animals, caring for, feeding, and loving them.

While the text explains in detail the habits of the animals and the nature of Chester's work, the illustrations communicate the feelings of life, harmony, and love that permeate the barn. Nearly every picture is filled with activity: animals frolic in the barnyard, a Clydesdale prances proudly into the barn, goats leap across bags of feed, lambs clamber over Chester as he bottle-feeds them, and finally, a newborn calf suckles. Although Chester is only depicted in five of the illustrations, his presence is seen everywhere, in the special structures he has built in the barn, in the bags and bales of food he has distributed, and in the loving look the animals give him as he closes up the barn for the night. Throughout, the brown colours create an impression of warmth and security.

If *Chester's Barn* is a tribute to an old way of life, *Clyde* is a story about how that life is threatened by modern technology. The hero, a Clydesdale, is very upset when, looking out the barn window, he sees a new tractor and fears that he will become useless and unloved. In a dream, Clyde assumes a number of fantastic shapes that he hopes will restore his self-esteem and make him valuable to his master. If he had wheels instead of back legs, he could supplant the tractor; if he had cheetah legs on the front, he could work faster than the machine; if he had wings he could feel brave. However, each of his transformations is unsatisfactory; he wakes up to discover that Farmer still loves him and that he has a new role, taking the local children for rides.

The ten full-colour illustrations not only depict Clyde's transformations, but also reveal his foolishness. The wheels and wings and the variety of legs he sprouts make him look ridiculous. In the last illustration he has resumed his horse form, an indication of his rejection of his fantasies, but more important, he is not alone. For the first time in the illustrations, Clyde is surrounded by people, five loving children who take him for a walk.

Climo's books deal with themes common to children's books: a nostalgia for a simpler, happier way of life in the country, and the use of fantasy as an escape from inner fears. In *Chester's Barn* she has realistically presented a place where the old ways still exist; in *Clyde* she has humorously depicted the resolution of inner fears — fears that most younger readers will recognize.

## Clutesi, George (1904–1988)

Like many of his people, George Clutesi, the most famous Native reteller of Indian legends, grew up at a time when white society was attempting to suppress awareness of and belief in traditional customs. Born in Port Alberni, British Columbia, Clutesi had heard the old stories from his father, but worked as a fisherman and as a pile-driver in a world dominated by Europeans. It was not until the 1940s, when he severely injured his back while working, that Clutesi had time to reconsider his heritage. Since then he has been active as an artist, folklorist, writer, and lecturer, dedicated to helping his own people and sympathetic whites discover a proud heritage that had been almost destroyed. His two books, *Son of Raven, Son of Deer: Tales of the Tseshaht People* (1967), a collection of legends, and *Potlatch* (1969), the account of the great winter ceremonies, provide a vivid record of a proud past.

Clutesi's "Introduction" to *Son of Raven, Son of Deer* is an important statement of the nature and significance of traditional tales. Clutesi emphasizes that "tales were used widely to teach the young the many wonders of nature; the importance of all living things, no matter how small and insignificant; and particularly to acquaint [them] with the closeness of man to all animal [and] bird life and the creatures of the sea." The tales gave the young a feeling of deep respect for creation. Moreover, the tales were parables illustrating good and bad behaviour. An awareness of these stories is vital for Native children, he emphasizes, for the European tales they generally read in school present an alien system of values. "This could be part of the reason so many of the Indian population of Canada are in a state of bewilderment today."

The central figures of the twelve stories in the collection are Ah-tush-mit, Son of Deer, and Ko-ishin-mit, Son of Raven. In the opening story, perhaps the best story in the book, Ah-tush-mit steals fire from the dreaded Wolf people. Ah-tush-mit is a classic unlikely hero, succeeding only after the bravest, strongest, fastest, and wisest men of the village have failed. However, in later stories he is not so heroic, and his naiveté and weakness for flattery lead him into dangerous situations. The Ko-ishin-mit stories present the well-known Raven character in his most foolish moments. Three of the stories are built around the "bungling host" motif found in folktales around the world. Always the glutton, Raven inveigles free meals from a variety of animals, and then, bound by the laws of hospitality, he is forced to invite them to his home. But when he uses their methods of procuring and preparing food, he fails miserably, often injuring himself in the process.

As a consequence of their actions, both Son of Raven and Son of Deer acquire physical features now common to their species. For example, deer have black smudge marks at the backs of their knees because Ah-tush-mit carried the fire back to the people in bands attached to his knees; ravens are black today because Ko-ishin-mit burned himself using someone else's way of cooking food. Listening to the stories, young audiences learn such lessons as "Children should not always believe other people" and "It is not good to copy other people." These short stories are told in a lively, entertaining style suitable for children in the early elementary grades.

*Potlatch* is a longer, more complex and detailed work. Clutesi gives a full account of the preparations, songs, dances, and other ceremonies of the twenty-eight days of a great winter festival. What emerges is a sense of the physical and psychological quality of the festival and an awareness of the communal bonds strengthened by the gathering. The book is most appropriate for high-school readers.

Clutesi is a pioneer among post-World War II Native authors, being one of the first to make the traditions of his people accessible to both Native and non-Native readers.

SECONDARY REFERENCES: *Heritage Canada* 3 (Spring 77): 35; *The Beaver* 292 (Spring 62): 4–10.

# Connor, Ralph (pseudonym of Charles William Gordon, 1860–1937)

Under the pen name of Ralph Connor, Rev. Charles William Gordon began turning his experiences as a Presbyterian missionary in Banff, Alberta, into fiction that mixed local colour, sentimentality, and the piety of muscular Christianity. Such novels as *The Sky Pilot* (1899) became Canada's first international bestsellers.

Born in Glengarry County, Canada West, Gordon was educated at the University of Toronto and Knox College. Ordained in 1890, he undertook the missionary work that provided him with the raw material for his fiction. After four years, Gordon became a pastor in Winnipeg, where he began writing as part of a fund-raising effort.

Two of Gordon's books were widely read by children although not specifically written for them. *The Man from Glengarry* (1901) uses authentic pictures of backwoods life as a backdrop to a melodramatic, sentimental tale of Ranald MacDonald, who rejects the lure of sin and becomes a force for civilizing and Christianizing the wilderness. *Glengarry School Days* (1902), the better of his books suitable for children, is a loosely interconnected series of sketches that focus on life in and around the school. The book traces the social history of the school through the tenure of four teachers, including a "gurl" whose soft ways evoke the contempt of almost all the students. The sketches are connected by the major character, Hughie Murray, who learns not to steal, proves his manhood by shooting a bear, and gains control over his emotions, thus fitting himself for life as a minister. In *Glengarry School Days*, the sentimentality and piety do not completely overwhelm the local colour, and the book is still suitable for high-school students interested in a glimpse of pioneer life.

SECONDARY REFERENCES: Keith Wilson, *Charles William Gordon* (1981); *OCCL*.

# Craig, John (1921–1982)

Born in Peterborough, Ontario, John Craig spent his childhood and teenage years enjoying two activities that appear frequently in his books for children and young adults: playing team sports in winter and spring, and vacationing in the summers on a lake in central Ontario. After serving in the Canadian Navy during World War II, he completed high school, and earned a BA at the University of Manitoba and an MA at the University of Toronto. From 1953 to 1969 he worked as an executive for a marketing research firm, and in his spare time began writing. He wrote over two dozen books, four specifically for children: *The Long Return* (1959), *No Word for Good-bye* (1969), *Zach* (1972), and *The Wormburners* (1975). Several of his adult books, especially *The Clearing* (1975), *The Last Canoe* (1979), and *Chappie and Me* (1979), are also suitable for teenage readers.

Craig's novels could be described under a number of headings: adventure stories, sports novels, captivity narratives, mysteries, modern problem novels, and summer vacation stories. However, one category encompasses them all: the *bildungsroman* — the development of a young person, usually male, who grows in understanding of himself, other people, and his role in the world. As Zach remarks, "How can a man know what to believe in unless he first knows what he is?" For Zach, last member of the Agawa tribe, this involves a long journey across the Canadian and American Prairies searching for clues about his ancestors. In *The Long Return*, Thad Cameron, captured by Ojibway warriors, learns to understand and respect his captors before he returns home a mature and confident young man. Joe Giffen, narrator of *Chappie and Me*, barnstorming during the Depression with a Black baseball team, initially thinks "the world I found myself part of was completely foreign to me...." By the end of the summer, he is accepted by the group and understands the other players as individuals.

The most important lessons Craig's young heroes learn are the need to understand others and the need to work with a group. The runners in *The Wormburners*, a group of poor and racially mixed inner city kids, earn their way to the national cross country championships by co-operating. Zach leaves his home alone but returns with four other people — a disillusioned Black athlete, a runaway teenage boy, a rich hippie girl, and a middle-aged man who has left a successful business life — all determined that they will beat the odds as a group. Playing with the All Stars, a diverse group united by their love of baseball and bitterness about the prejudice they face, Joe Giffen learns to understand true teamwork.

Craig's two best books dealing with the theme of maturation portray the relationship between a white teenager and Native people. In *The Long Return*, Thad realizes that if he is going to escape he must learn the skills of his captors; in learning these he develops love and loyalty for his Ojibway "mother and father."

*No Word for Good-bye*, Craig's most acclaimed novel, focuses on Ken Warren, a fifteen-year-old spending the summer with his parents at their lake cabin. Early in July he meets Paul Onaman, an Ojibway teenager with whom he develops a close friendship, learning the Ojibway ways of fishing from him. More importantly, he learns about the dignity and hardships of the Ojibways' lives. Ken hopes to overcome the injustices suffered by Paul and his family. On one level he is successful, solving the mystery of a series of break-ins that the prejudiced campers have blamed on the Indians. On another, Ken fails. A large land development corporation claims the Indians' camp, and when he returns to the lake at Thanksgiving for a visit with Paul, he discovers that the Indians have left for the North. He cannot help them, and he learns the painful truth that there is no word for "good-bye."

At times Craig falls into the clichés typical of the genres he uses. In *The Wormburners*, the underdog team wins against seemingly impossible odds. Both *The Long Return* and *No Word for Good-bye* make use of the staples of boys' adventure stories: cliffhanging chapter endings, overdeveloped mysteries, and stereotyped "bad guys." However, he writes sensitively, sympathetically, and knowledgeably about the traditions and hardships of Native peoples. They are courageous when dealing with an insensitive and exploitative white bureaucracy, and, although no easy solutions to their plight are possible, they combat despair and injustice with dignity and fortitude.

Craig is best when presenting his young heroes as they grow to maturity in a natural setting. Thad Cameron must respond not only to his captors but to the harsh, magnificent landscape. Ken Warren comes to understand that Lake Kinnewabi is more than an idyllic setting for two summer months each year; it is a place where the Ojibway have lived for centuries in dignity and in harmony with nature. He realizes that life offers no easy solutions, that the individual must develop inner integrity and strength in order to live with himself and those around him.

SECONDARY REFERENCES: *CCL* 33: 32–39; *Profiles; SATA* 23; *TCCW* 2.

## Culleton, Beatrice (1949–        )

"It's not meant to be accusatory; it's something for the reader to read and think about." So spoke Beatrice Culleton about her novel *In Search of April Raintree* (1983), one of the few novels about contemporary Canadian Native life written by a Native author. Born in Winnipeg, Culleton grew up in a number of foster homes, as did the title heroine of her novel, experiencing the prejudices directed against her people: "White-skinned people cannot possibly understand what it feels like to be another colour. That fact causes separation." Two of her sisters committed suicide. It was after the death of the second that she decided to create the novel, in part as an outlet for her grief. It was published by Pemmican Publications, a Winnipeg firm of which she is now the manager.

*In Search of April Raintree* is the first-person account of a young Métis woman's long and difficult quest for her personal and cultural identity. Alcoholism and illness cause the breakup of the Raintree family, and April spends her childhood in a series of foster homes. Although some of the foster parents are loving, most are not. In an attempt to find happiness, April denies her Native heritage, which upsets her activist sister, Cheryl. Marriage to a Toronto socialite ends disastrously, and when April returns to Winnipeg she discovers that her sister has fallen victim to prostitution and drugs. Brutally raped by three white men, April is filled with hatred. Only after her sister's suicide and the discovery of her sister's child does April find a focus for her life and a hope for her nephew and her people. While some reviewers were upset by the anger and the harshness in the novel, it has generally been praised for the vivid realism and for the fairness with which it presents social conditions. In 1984, a revised edition was published as *April Raintree*.

*Spirit of the White Bison* (1986), Culleton's second book, is intended for younger readers. The first-person narrative of a buffalo, it recounts the decimation of the herds during the last half of the nineteenth century. "It was not a quiet, accidental extermination," Culleton notes in her "Introduction." "The horror was that the killings were deliberate, planned, military actions. Destroy the livelihood of the Indians and win a war." During his long life, the White Bison sees the arrival of more and more hunters, the building of the railroad, and the disastrous effects of European civilization and disease on the Native people. At the story's conclusion, the bison and his Native friend, Lone Wolf, are buried side by side. Their deaths symbolize the end of a way of life that has been needlessly and foolishly destroyed.

Although Culleton's works do contain anger and sadness because of the wrongs committed against her people and the waste of so many lives, the tone of her two books is optimistic. As she holds her nephew, Henry Liberty, April thinks, "Cheryl had once said, 'All life dies to give new life.' Cheryl had died. But for Henry Lee and me, there would be a tomorrow. And it would be better. I would strive for it." At the conclusion of *Spirit of the White Bison* are the words, "My spirit would return again in the future to walk with those who were gentle but strong." Culleton's works embody the sense of hope, the belief in a renaissance of Native culture that characterizes much contemporary Native writing. SECONDARY REFERENCE: *Canadian Author and Bookman* 61 (Fall 85): 14.

# Cutt, William Towrie (1898–1981)

W. Towrie Cutt did not publish his first book until he was seventy-two. He had wanted to write when he was a child, but his brother warned him that he could not make a living by writing. Instead Cutt, who was born on the island of Sanday in the Orkneys, served in the British Army in France during World War I, briefly studied at the University of Edinburgh, and then came to Canada where, after receiving a certificate from the Normal School at Calgary, he began a long teaching career in Alberta. He received BA, B Ed, and MA degrees from the University of Alberta.

Both of Cutt's historical novels, *On the Trail of Long Tom* (1970) and *Carry My Bones Northwest* (1973), treat the problem of identity experienced by boys with Orkney fathers and Cree mothers. Both also present a moral dilemma as each of the young protagonists tries to understand his "duty" to the land of his birth. In *On the Trail of Long Tom*, Tom Findlater, born in Canada but raised in Orkney, is torn between loyalty to the whites and sympathy for the Natives during the Riel Rebellion. He decides to follow his white heritage, but determines that, once educated himself, he will teach the Natives. Written in opposition to what Cutt perceived as a biased "Ontarian point of view" in previous historical fiction, the novel is notable for its intelligent, balanced presentation of both Native and white positions. Only the somewhat intemperate portrait of Louis Riel as a smooth-talking egocentric mars the objectivity.

Willie Fea makes the opposite decision in *Carry My Bones Northwest*, choosing to live with the Natives, but he, too, finds that his duty includes teaching them Christianity. Much of the novel focuses on Willie's life in Orkney after his parents are massacred by a band of drunken Gros Ventres. The sharp pictures of humble people suffering abuse by authorities and press gangs during the Napoleonic Wars are in keeping with Cutt's belief that the boy heroes in historical fiction should not "go through all sorts of heroics" but should, nevertheless, feel their lives affected by circumstances beyond their control.

Cutt's other novels, *Message from Arkmae* (1972) and *Seven for the Sea* (1972), are fantasies with a didactic purpose: "I wanted to get children interested in sea mammals, seals and porpoises, as I am against seal slaughter and against experiments with porpoise and dolphin." In the former novel, two cousins journey to the cave of the last of the legendary Finmen and receive messages warning that man is destroying the planet. In *Seven for the Sea*, a time-shift fantasy, the boys journey to the time of William IV and find out about their own identity when they discover that their great-great-grandmother had seal blood and returned to the sea when her husband killed a seal pup. This novel is less effective in delivering its ecological message, but is tighter in structure and fleshes out some interesting Orcadian legends.

With his wife, Nancy, Cutt also published *The Hogboon of Hell and Other Strange Orkney Tales* (1979), a collection of retellings of Orcadian legends and of original tales based on folk beliefs.

Although he never achieved the large Canadian readership he desired, Cutt made a small but significant contribution to Canadian children's literature. His historical fiction shows that readable history does not have to be romantic and that children's books can present historical issues in personal terms and without oversimplification.

SECONDARY REFERENCES: *TCCW* 2; *CA* 81–84 & 115; *Profiles 2*.

# De Mille, James (1833–1880)

One of the first Canadian authors to achieve commercial success in the United States, James De Mille was among the most popular writers of his time. Born in Saint John, New Brunswick, and educated at Acadia College and Brown University, which awarded him an MA in 1854, De Mille taught classics at Acadia and then literature at Dalhousie College. He began his prolific publishing career in 1865 with *The Martyr in the Catacombs; A Tale of Ancient Rome*, a work intended to show children something of the development of Christianity.

De Mille achieved his first commercial success by turning to his own observations for material. His travels in Europe provided the basis for the comic sketches in *The Dodge Club; or, Italy in MDCCCLIX* (1869). Like many of his later books, it is packed with incidents that spoof national assumptions and popular conventions of fiction. The characters are racial or national stereotypes. The commercial success of *The Dodge Club* led De Mille to produce a series of sequels intended for children. The Young Dodge Club Series, which includes *Among the Brigands* (1871), *The Seven Hills* (1873), and *The Winged Lion; or, Stories of Venice* (1877), followed the adventures of a group of boys travelling in Europe with a decidedly incompetent adult.

De Mille's most famous work for children depended on experiences closer to home. He based the six books in "The Brethren of the White Cross" series — *The "B.O.W.C.": A Book for Boys* (1869), *The Boys of Grand Pre School* (1870), *Lost in the Fog* (1870), *Fire in the Woods* (1872), *Picked Up Adrift* (1872), *The Treasure of the Seas* (1873) — on his own student days. The books were some of the earliest examples of the school story to appear in North America; they became popular because they were relatively free of the numbing didacticism of the period, and were filled with comical and adventurous episodes set against an authentic maritime background. Solomon, the kind-hearted, bumbling Black servant whom the boys christen "Perpetual Grand Panjandrum," is a stereotype of the period and is offensive today; most of the characters are types used to exploit and to satirize melodramatic adventures.

De Mille's books are dated, but he made an important contribution to the development of Canadian children's literature. At a time when many children's books became bogged down in ethical and religious didacticism, he offered adventure and humour. As a consequence, his B.O.W.C. series showed that, when they gave young readers something they wanted, books based on authentic Canadian settings could succeed, both here and in the United States.

# De Roussan, Jacques (1929–    )

Montreal picture-book author Jacques de Roussan is a person of many talents. Born in Paris, he was twice captured while working with the

French Resistance during World War II. After earning an MA in history from the Sorbonne, he worked in Morocco, and in 1953 moved to Verdun, Quebec, where he began a job in a printing plant. This evolved into a career in journalism. De Roussan established himself as an important French-Canadian art critic, biographer, essayist, and poet. His interest in scientific concepts and abstract painting resulted in the creation of two books: *Au-delà du soleil/Beyond the Sun* (1972), winner of the Howard-Gibbon Medal, and *Si j'étais martien/If I Came from Mars* (1977).

A bilingual picture book, *Beyond the Sun* is at once factual, imaginative, and creative. The story is simple. Peter dreams one night that he is an astronaut and explores the solar system and outer reaches of the universe before returning home. De Roussan presents astronomical information about the heavens through words and illustrations. But more important is the focus on the imagination. Peter is a young boy just beginning to understand his potential for growth and discovery. The silkscreened illustrations are composed mainly of geometrical shapes and have bold primary and secondary colours. They accurately depict space while at the same time giving a feeling of Peter's sense of wonder and discovery.

Peter is also the central character of *If I Came from Mars*. This time he dreams he is the first human being to have been born on the space colony of Mars. Flying his spaceship to Earth, he sees the beauty of the planet from a distance and then views the grandeur of mountains and oceans and, more importantly, the wonder of animals and people. Reluctantly, he heads back to Mars. The simple, abstract drawings depict the sights Peter sees and suggest the beauty of the planet he has never known. If the implicit message of *Beyond the Sun* is that we grow by exploring the unknown, that of *If I Came from Mars* is that we must never forget the joy of life on our own planet; we must refamiliarize ourselves with a beauty to which we have become insensitive.

Although he is the hero of both books, Peter is not depicted in the illustrations. As a result, the young reader can become Peter, imagining himself as a space explorer. More importantly, he can experience Peter's emotions. Having read the two books, readers not only will have acquired knowledge about space but also will have become more sensitive to their own potential and to the world in which they live. SECONDARY REFERENCE: *Profiles*.

# Downie, Mary Alice (1934–     )

Mary Alice Downie has described herself as an author of "false starts": "[*The Wind Has Wings*] sprang from the ashes of an anthology for four- to six-year-olds...; *Honor Bound* from an eighteenth-century diary owned by a landlady. [*The Witch of the North*] resulted from reading done for an ill-fated sequel to *Honor Bound*." However, from these false starts have come eighteen books that have made Downie a significant creator of historical novels, editor of anthologies, and reteller of French-Canadian legends.

Born in Alton, Illinois, Downie moved with her Canadian parents to Toronto, where she attended school and later earned a BA in English from the University of Toronto. Work on the university newspaper led to work as a magazine writer and editor and, later, publicity director for Oxford University Press. After her marriage and subsequent move to Kingston, Ontario, she discovered there were few suitable books of poetry for children in the middle elementary grades. Although her first anthology was refused by the publishers, she and her co-compiler Barbara Robertson persevered, and the result, *The Wind Has Wings: Poems from Canada*, lavishly illustrated with Elizabeth Cleaver's collages, was published in 1968. It became a Canadian classic. A revised edition, *The New Wind Has Wings*, appeared in 1984. The first edition, which won the Howard-Gibbon Medal, includes a large number of poets published before 1945, and therefore presents a considerable challenge to younger readers or listeners. Nonetheless, it is a significant landmark in Canadian children's literature — the first publication of a major anthology for children consisting entirely of Canadian poetry. The second edition has more contemporary material, but it too makes demands of readers.

When told that her proposed edition of an eighteenth-century diary was unsuitable for publication, Downie used it as the basis for her first historical novel, *Honor Bound* (1970), written in collaboration with her husband John. It is the story of the Averys, a Loyalist family that flees from Philadelphia to the eastern end of Lake Ontario to create a new life on a wilderness homestead. As she prepares to leave her lovely home, the mother laments, "Canada! ...that's a wilderness. There's nothing up there but Indians and wild beasts!" However, the courage of the family, their loyalty to each other, and the new and generous friends they meet give them a fulfilling life. The focal character of the novel is young Miles, a hot-headed boy who dreams of the glorious life of a soldier. In his new environment he acquires maturity and a sense of honour, even though it means warning a notorious thief of impending capture. Although the novel does not delve deeply into character and has a relatively slight plot, it gives a strong sense of the life of the immigrant family in its new environment.

Downie's other historical stories, *Scared Sarah* (1974), *The King's Loon* (1979), *The Last Ship* (1980), and *A Proper Acadian* (1981), are, like *Honor Bound*, carefully researched works that provide a feeling for the daily lives of pioneers. Of these, *The King's Loon*, in which the young hero, André, comes to appreciate the foster home from which he ran away, and *A Proper Acadian* (co-authored by George Rawlyk), in which a Bostonian staying with relatives in Nova Scotia bravely casts his lot with the persecuted Acadians, are the strongest, with the main characters facing and resolving conflicts central to their lives.

In *The Magical Adventures of Pierre* (1974), *The Witch of the North* (1975), and *The Wicked Fairy-Wife* (1983), Downie adapts two types of French-Canadian legends: the involved story of a questing young man who, after passing many tests, earns the hand of a beautiful princess, and the tale of people who test their wits against the devil and usually lose. *The Magical Adventures* and *The Wicked Fairy-Wife* are of the former type, and the majority of the stories in *The Witch of the North* are of the latter. In *The Witch*, Downie uses the device of a grandmother telling a group of wondering children stories that supposedly happened to her deceased husband or to other people she knew. The devil, always anxious for souls, is the major actor, enticing unwitting but often overconfident people away from the security of home and church. There is an excellent mixture of humour and terror in the stories.

Downie's other works for children are *Dragon on Parade* (1974); *Seeds & Weeds: a Book of Country Crafts*, with Jillian Hulme Gilliland (1980); *Jenny Greenteeth* (1981; rev. ed. 1984); *Stones and Cones*, with Jillian Hulme Gilliland (1984); *Alison's Ghosts*, with John Downie; and *The Window of Dreams: New Canadian Writing for Children* (1986), an anthology edited with Elizabeth Greene and Mary Alice Thompson.

Although no single book by Downie has assumed the status of a classic, her works taken as a group have considerable significance. She has shown that the lives of relatively ordinary Canadian children living in earlier periods can be both interesting and entertaining. Her adaptations of French-Canadian folktales are among the best available in English. And she has made young Canadians more fully aware of the rich tradition of Canadian poetry available to them.

SECONDARY REFERENCES: *Profiles 2; SATA 13; TCCW 1; TCCW 2.*

# Doyle, Brian (1935–        )

Brian Doyle writes about the problems of adolescence, but he is not a topical novelist: he examines what he calls "the classic concerns, the ones with the capital letters." Although this sounds dauntingly serious, Doyle is actually a comic novelist whose work reflects his vision of life: "Laughter and tears are very close together. I can't do one without the other. When I work on a serious question, a mirror of humour always presents itself."

Doyle's serio-comic art fuses the influences of his father and mother. Born in Ottawa, Doyle had what he calls "an anecdotal upbringing." His father, "a musician of the language," spun tales endlessly and gave him a lasting love for the sound of words. His mother gave him respect for books and for the way poetry uses language for serious purposes.

Doyle did not set out to write for children. After receiving a degree in journalism from Carleton University, he worked for the Toronto *Telegram*, but resigned when he noticed a man on the subway skip past an article with his byline. Wanting "something that would last longer," he went back to Carleton for a BA in English and became a high-school teacher, eventually becoming Chairman of English at Glebe Collegiate in Ottawa, the school he had attended as a boy. He began writing specifically for children when neighbourhood children expressed interest in the story he was developing from notes he and his daughter had compiled about a family trip. After a number of revisions, the notes became *Hey, Dad!* (1978), the first of four novels.

Doyle's novels fall into two groups. *Hey, Dad!* and its sequel, *You Can Pick Me Up at Peggy's Cove* (1979), were inspired by his relationship with his children, Megan and Ryan, whose names he used for the central characters. The second pair of novels, *Up to Low* (1982), winner of the CACL Award, and *Angel Square* (1984), were inspired by Doyle's memories of his own childhood and of the stories his father told.

All of the novels are first-person narratives. Doyle says that when writing he merges with the persona of the narrator, feeling the way the narrator would in any given situation: "My stories may begin as autobiography, but I become so absorbed in the character that it takes over and the story develops a life of its own." The innocence and acute sensitivity of the first-person narrator permits expressions of irony and sympathy, an appropriate mixture of emotions in the presentation of the funny and painful development of maturity that occurs in each novel. And first-person narration allows a fresh and colloquial exploration of the major "capital letter" themes of death, love, and reconciliation. This literary device thus generates both humour and serious interest.

In many ways, *Hey, Dad!* sets a pattern for Doyle's novels. Through a basically realistic description of a family's troubled vacation trip from Ottawa to the West Coast, it presents a symbolic journey to maturation. Thirteen-year-old Megan does not want to go: she begins by irrationally hating her father and even attempts to run away from him, but gradually learns to love him deeply.

A powerful motif stressing the inevitability of death and the transience of human life and relationships runs throughout the novel. Most of the episodes develop the idea in some way. An early episode is painfully funny: a terminally ill boy whom Megan meets at a picnic site assures her that she must be dying because that is the only reason families undertake such trips. A later one is dramatic: Megan catches sight of a dying man at the hot springs and thinks that it is her father. Another one is seriously philosophic: Megan, thinking about the Athabaska River and trying to understand human time and geologic time, realizes the brevity of her parents' lifespans.

Although episodic, as such a novel based on a journey must be, and somewhat contrived, *Hey, Dad!* is engaging because its episodes effectively and humourously develop character. The scene in which the wise-cracking father playfully mocks a group of adolescents at a swimming pool, while Megan watches in embarrassment, is a masterstroke. An amusing incident in itself, it is also moving: the father wins the friendship of all the young people except his daughter, who longs for a father like all other fathers. It is also painful: we sense the embarrass-

ment of an acutely sensitive teenager whose father is completely ignorant of his daughter's feelings.

*You Can Pick Me Up at Peggy's Cove*, which has been made into a film,
is more conventionally plotted and less humorous, although it does
have some fine passages satirizing tourists. It shows the consequences
of a father leaving his family. Deeply hurt, Ryan, Megan's brother, is
sent to Peggy's Cove. The majority of the characters he encounters
there and many of the episodes show in some way either the pain of
loss or the power of love. Ryan shows his immaturity by befriending
Eddie, a petty thief, and by writing a letter to his father telling of his
part in thefts. At the same time, Ryan evinces unselfish companion-
ship when he takes up fishing with Eddie, even going so far as to pre-
tend to be his son when tourists come around. Unfortunately, the novel
has a highly contrived ending in which Ryan proves his maturity
through physical action. When Eddie is attacked by a shark, Ryan has
presence of mind enough to radio for help, something his companion,
the mentally deficient Wingding, cannot do. This is not meaningfully
connected to his reconciliation with his father. His father comes for
him shortly after the rescue, but he has not yet received Ryan's letter,
indicating that he comes purely out of love.

The ideas about love and reconciliation that Doyle develops in his
first two novels receive their finest expression in *Up to Low*. Episodic,
filled with even more memorable eccentrics than the first two books,
based on an unrealistic plot, highly symbolic in its conclusion, this tall
tale is a children's version of a cross between Mark Twain and William
Faulkner. Structurally, it depends upon two journeys. In the first,
Frank, an alcoholic, drives Tommy and his father to their summer
cabin in his new 1950 Buick, which he gradually turns into a wreck.
Stopping at every hotel along the way, the men become progressively
inebriated and talk about rumours of the impending death of Mean
Hughie, something most of the men won't accept because "He's too
mean to die."

The second journey begins at the cabin after Tommy has re-estab-
lished his childhood friendship with Mean Hughie's daughter, Baby
Bridget, who lost part of her arm in an accident caused by her father's
carelessness. Tommy takes her by boat to Mean Hughie, who, lying in
a coffin, confesses sorrow for his treatment of Bridget, thus healing her
heart. No longer too mean for death, he then dies. Tommy places the
coffin across the boat to form a cross, a symbolically appropriate act
that suggests the redemption of Hughie, his daughter, and, because of
his own mature compassion, Tommy. This new maturity expresses itself in the novel's final section. Now able to see Bridget as a woman instead of the mutilated victim of her father's carelessness, Tommy asks
to kiss her. The novel that begins with talk of the death of Tommy's
mother and includes the death of Bridget's father thus concludes with
the comic affirmation of the power of love and the joy of life.

*Angel Square*, which Doyle jokingly calls a "prequel," is set four years before the events of *Up to Low*. Neither as rich as *Up to Low* nor as profoundly concerned with issues of love and death, *Angel Square* presents a comic world entirely different from those in his other novels. Tommy lives in a world of Catholics, Jews, and Protestants, all of whom fight each other every day in the inappropriately named Angel Square. Able to be friends with members of all groups "because I'm not anything," Tommy joins in the daily battles, constantly changing sides. These battles form the comic motif of racial and religious prejudice, the darker side of which is presented by the beating of a Jewish father by a hooded man.

Alongside the theme of tolerance, Doyle presents a comic theme about the development of identity. Tommy, unable to fit into any religious group, tries to be something: he takes on the role of Lamont Cranston, the Shadow. After a number of false starts, he actually exposes the identity of the hooded man. The novel ends triumphantly on a note of wish fulfillment: for at least a while, the rival groups cooperate, and the boy who thought he was nothing gains the romantic identity of a hero, and the love of a girl.

Doyle's books suffer in places from contrivance, a straining after comic or thematic effectiveness, and sometimes from anecdotal looseness. They have the merit, however, of deft characterization, humour, and the presentation of important themes in language that is effective without being artificially poetic or literary. Alternately amusing and moving, his novels demand rereadings.
SECONDARY REFERENCE: *QQ* 48 (Dec. 82): 27.

# *Duncan, Frances (1942–    )*

"I am primarily interested in individuals and how they cope with situations, external crises, and crises of their own making ...," Frances "Sandy" Duncan has said. This interest is a natural extension of her background, education, and professional work. Born in Vancouver, Duncan experienced the pain of parental loss when her father died just as she was entering adolescence. Her mother, a social worker, moved to Toronto and then Regina. After receiving BA and MA degrees from the University of British Columbia, Duncan worked for nine years as a child psychologist, gaining firsthand knowledge of the way children think about things and respond to personal problems. Although this understanding is especially evident in her two adolescent problem novels, *Kap-Sung Ferris* (1977) and *Finding Home* (1982), it adds tension to her historical novel, *Cariboo Runaway* (1976), and depth to her whimsical fantasy, *The Toothpaste Genie* (1981).

Duncan's first work for children, *Cariboo Runaway*, is set during the Cariboo gold rush of the 1860s. The story of a sister and brother who set off from Victoria in search of their missing prospector father, its perilous adventures test the children's physical and emotional resources while providing vivid, well-researched portraits of gold rush society. When they find their father at Barkerville, the children establish their identity as members of a family that can win out over the dangers of a "hard country."

Duncan has a special interest in "Canadian identity, but within the framework of individual identity...." This theme unifies *Kap-Sung Ferris*, an exploration of the anxieties of three adolescent girls who eventually find their identities both as individuals and as Canadians. Barbara Kim Ferris, an adopted Korean, learns to accept herself and Canada after coming to terms with racial prejudice and with the facts of her adoption. Bhindu, an Asian Ugandan driven from her country for looking different, learns to love Canada as a land of possibilities. Mish, the narrator, who had once felt inordinately ungainly, accepts herself, establishes a new relationship with her mother, from whom she had grown distant, and feels the stirrings of patriotism while watching her friends develop love for Canada. Although it does not lack gripping and meaningful events, *Kap-Sung Ferris* is primarily a novel of character that succeeds in presenting plausible portraits of adolescents seeking to know themselves and their parents.

An even more complex and intense investigation of characters coping with internal and external pressure is *Finding Home*. Presented in chapters that alternate the point of view of fifteen-year-old Rondo, whose parents have been killed in an auto accident, and thirty-five-year-old Margery Grey, the best friend of Rondo's mother, the novel is a tense exploration of how grief, impotent rage, and alienation affect relationships. Only when Margery engages in a frank exchange of ideas and feelings with Rondo, who has ran away from the Grey household to commit suicide, do the two come to an understanding that allows them both to cope with their losses and find where they belong.

Duncan's most popular book, *The Toothpaste Genie*, appeals to younger audiences. A highly amusing tale, it focuses on Amanda, who finds a wish-giving apprentice genie in a tube of toothpaste. Because the genie is a practical joker who constantly makes her wishes go awry, Amanda learns that magic is not always the best way of handling life's problems. Many of these wishes, such as her desire to be always neat, humorously explore Amanda's search for a satisfying identity. Gradually Amanda becomes less self-centred; she helps the genie earn his rank as a Master Genie and accepts the fact that her own wishes for a horse and a baby sister will have to come through the ordinary "magic" of life.

Duncan is an intelligent, often witty writer. Occasionally she resorts to episodes that are a bit too schematic or conventional in order to demonstrate the clash of ideas. For the most part, however, her own assessment of her writing is accurate: "Characters control the story, the action, and the plot." Duncan's characters are vivid and convincing as they endure a variety of internal and external crises.

SECONDARY REFERENCES: *CANR* 17; *Profiles 2*.

# *E* ngel, Marian (1933–1985)

Marian Engel, winner of the Governor General's Award for her contro-versial adult novel *Bear* (1976), said of writing children's books, "I know very well that I'm piggy-backing on my adult reputation." Like Margaret Atwood, Pierre Berton, and Mordecai Richler, she produced children's works first for her own children: "It's a direct way of connect-ing our kids with our career." Her twins inspired the basic situations and helped her to invent episodes and dialogue for her three published children's works.

Born in Toronto, Engel began her professional writing career by selling stories to *Seventeen* magazine while still a teenager herself. After receiving a BA from McMaster University and an MA from McGill University, she lived briefly in France, England, and Cyprus. In 1982 she was appointed an Officer of the Order of Canada.

All of Engel's children's stories treat the family of Rufus and Geral-dine Shingle. *Adventure at Moon Bay Towers* (1974), a dream fantasy about city children who have a farcical "adventure" in a cottage with towers, has some funny moments, but Engel herself said that it "got somewhat fouled up by a disagreement between its editor and me about what a children's story was." In *My Name Is Not Odessa Yarker* (1977), a tale of sibling rivalry that deftly mixes realism and fantasy, Geraldine comically struggles to maintain her identity after Rufus changes her name. "The Three Christmases," published in *Weekend Magazine* (25 Dec. 1976), is a social problem story about parents separating at Christmas. Written because "the parents of almost every-body in that school were splitting up that year," it was, said Engel, "my attempt at a Judy Blume kind of thing."

Engel's pieces are short because, she said, "children's novels are best written by people who do that all the time. I haven't got so many gears that I can switch into that one." She did not make a major contribution to children's literature, but the entertaining fantasy in *My Name Is Not Odessa Yarker* makes it a small comical gem.

SECONDARY REFERENCES: *Profiles 2; The World of Children's Books* 3 (Spring 78): 10–14.

# *Etherington, Frank (1945–    )*

Born in Luton, Bedfordshire, England, Frank Etherington studied journalism before emigrating to Canada in 1967. He began his news-paper career in Toronto, then moved to Kitchener, where he won a number of awards for his articles. His four children's books reveal the journalist's eye for amusing anecdotes and concern for timely issues.

Etherington's three picture books are gently amusing treatments of childhood problems. *The Spaghetti Word Race* (1981; illustrated by Gina Calleja) deals with a child's confusion of imagination and reality.

Jacob, believing that he has seen spaghetti-like words moving along the telephone wires, tries to outrace the words he speaks into the telephone. His repeated failures almost convince him that he has mistaken birds on the wires for words; the ending is unnecessarily ambiguous. *Those Words* (1982; illustrated by Gina Calleja) treats the problem of children who seek attention by swearing. Whenever Jeopy uses "those words," he upsets people and causes mishaps. The didactic intent of the book is apparent in the behaviour of his parents, who cure him by ignoring him whenever he swears. The closing episode, in which the father swears after spilling milk, amusingly shows how adults promote the very language they want their children to avoid. *When I Grow Up Bigger Than Five* (1986; illustrated by Suzane Langlois) is an anecdotal tale about the problem of deciding on a future career. Jacob changes his ambition each time he has a new experience. Again, the didactic intent is clear: Jacob's father tells him that he can be more than one thing during his life, and two adults indicate that their present occupations are not what they dreamed about when they were children.

*The General* (1983), a brief prose work for children in grades three to six, differs from Etherington's other works by investigating serious social issues. Through the fictionalized biography of the general, Frank Groff, an eccentric old man whom the Kitchener authorities tried to remove from his voluntary position as a school crossing guard, it probes the treatment of the old and of those who dare to be different. Moving without being sentimental, the story advocates tolerance. More importantly, it celebrates individuality by showing the amusing victory of the general over a hide-bound bureaucracy. The book is completed by newspaper clippings that establish the factual basis of the story and carry it forward to the general's death.

Etherington's weakness as a writer is his reliance on anecdotes instead of fully developed plots. As a result, his stories are sometimes too open-ended to be thematically satisfying. His strength is his ability to make issues amusing and comprehensible to children without ever being condescending. Although he is always didactic, he is more entertainer than preacher.

# *F reeman, Bill (1938–    )*

"I wanted Canadian children to explore their historical roots, to come to know Canada of the 1870s. This was largely still the traditional time — before modern uniformity. It was a diverse country, but economic factors shaped ordinary people's lives, although in different ways in different places." Bill Freeman was discussing the six novels that make up his "Adventures in Canadian History" series and was describing his basic focus: an economic perspective and a concern for the common people.

Although *Shantymen of Cache Lake*, the first novel of the series, was not published until 1975, Bill Freeman's life to that time could be called a preparation for its writing. Born in London, Ontario, he acquired a love of history from his mother, a teacher, and an interest in left-wing politics from his father. He was an avid reader, devouring countless adventure novels. During the 1960s, Freeman vagabonded around Canada and England, working at a variety of jobs, as do his young protagonists, John and Meg Bains. He earned a BA from Acadia University, and an MA and PhD from McMaster University, specializing in Canadian economic history and the history of the workers of Canada. He taught for several years at Vanier College, Montreal, and now lives on Toronto Island, where he writes full time.

Two years of research and countless hours of writing and revision preceded the publication of *Shantymen of Cache Lake*, winner of the first Canada Council Award for Children's Literature. There have been five sequels: *The Last Voyage of the Scotian* (1976), *First Spring on the Grand Banks* (1978), *Trouble at Lachine Mill* (1983), *Harbour Thieves* (1985), and *Danger on the Tracks* (1987). *Cedric and the North End Kids* (1978) is set in modern-day Hamilton and deals with the difficulties faced by a boy newly arrived from Jamaica. *Their Town: the Mafia, the Media, and the Party Machine* (1979) is an adult study of city politics. In 1984, Freeman received the Vicky Metcalf Award for his contribution to Canadian children's literature.

The six "Adventure" novels follow similar patterns. Meg Bains is a young teenager who must leave home to find work to help her widowed mother. She is accompanied in the first three books by her older brother, John, and in the last two by her younger brother, Jamie. At a lumber camp, on a square-rigged ship, on a fishing boat, in a Montreal clothing factory, on the streets of Toronto, and in the western Ontario "frontier," they experience the dangers that provide the plot for each book and meet the characters whose motivations illuminate the themes. Working for very low wages, the two children learn that a few rich and relatively uncaring wealthy men control the destinies of thousands of poor people. Meg and her brothers develop close bonds with the workers. In fact, they become leaders, inspiring the men to unite in an effort to ameliorate intolerable conditions and to achieve a sense of self-respect. Often, the rich owners of the various operations are ignorant of the miseries of their workers, and they frequently fail to see the evil of their selfish foremen. Only through the agency of the children are they enlightened and the conflicts resolved.

*Shantymen of Cache Lake* reveals the basic format of the stories and Freeman's art at its best. After the suspicious death of their father in a logging accident, Meg and John "already...knew the hardships working people had to undergo." Feisty, independent, and determined not to be ignored because of her sex, Meg decides to join her brother John in looking for work at her father's old camp. John is timorous and frightened when he perceives the ambiguities in the issues they confront. The two children become capable workers and earn the trust of the men. Although the foreman, Hardy, is a stereotypical villain, a bully who finally turns coward, the other characters are convincingly portrayed. Freeman is particulary adept at describing in lively fashion the technical details of logging, and at giving a sense of the grandeur and desolation of the wilderness around the lumber camp.

Although John develops as a character during the next two works, becoming surer of himself and discovering his true vocation as an Atlantic fisherman, Meg remains relatively unchanged. In *Trouble at Lachine Mill* and *Harbour Thieves*, she is somewhat of a mother figure, taking care of her younger brother, and in the latter book she plays a decidedly minor role. Freeman vividly describes the various locales and clearly explains details of sailing, fishing, and factory operation. Characterization and plot, however, become progressively more of a formula. After the second novel, readers expect the young characters to be working in miserable conditions for near starvation wages and to play central roles in management-labour confrontations. The noble adult leader of the workers, the rich owner, and the nasty foreman become stereotypes interchangeable between the novels.

Freeman's "Adventures in Canadian History" novels represent a departure from the usual historical fiction. In each novel he provides valuable insights into the lives of ordinary people, the unsung heroes and heroines of the country, and he gives young readers a chance to experience ways of life long past. In *Shantymen of Cache Lake* he has created a minor Canadian classic, a well-written novel containing memorable characters, exciting action, and significant themes.

SECONDARY REFERENCE: *Profiles 2.*

# Gal, Laszlo (1933–    )

The theatre's loss was a gain to children's literature in the case of Hungarian-born illustrator Laszlo Gal. After he had finished high school in Budapest, Gal entered the prestigious Academy of Dramatic Arts. But after a year, he was told he did not have the talent, and he decided to become an art teacher. When the Hungarian Revolution broke out in 1956, Gal came to Canada and was soon working in the graphics department of the Canadian Broadcasting Corporation in Toronto.

Gal's career as a children's book illustrator began in 1962 when, on a vacation in Italy, he showed his portfolio to publisher Arnoldo Mondadori. His work was well received; over the next four years, he illustrated six books for Mondadori, two of which, *El Cid: Soldier and Hero* (1968) and *Siegfried: the Mighty Warrior* (1968), have been published in English editions.

Gal spent several years in Verona before returning to Canada. In 1970 he illustrated his first Canadian book, William Toye's *Cartier Discovers the St. Lawrence*, winner of the CACL Award. The book, a condensation of one part of Toye's earlier *The St. Lawrence*, draws heavily on Cartier's journals to create a sense of how the European explorers felt as they entered a strange new world. Gal's full-colour illustrations, which depict small human figures against a rugged landscape, contrast the plain dress of the Indians with the costumes of the French, and portray the winter sufferings of the Europeans, are a perfect complement to the text.

Before rejoining the CBC in 1977, Gal worked as a freelance artist, illustrating six picture books: Ronald Melzack's *Raven, Creator of the World* (1970), Selve Mass's *The Moon Painters and Other Estonian Folk Tales* (1971), Nancy Cleaver's *How the Chipmunk Got Its Stripes* (1973), Mariella Bertelli's *The Shirt of the Happy Man* (1977), Marian Engel's *My Name is Not Odessa Yarker* (1977), and Melzack's *Why the Man in the Moon is Happy* (1977). For his artwork in the last three books, he received the IODE Book Award.

Because of the high cost of publishing full-colour picture books, Gal was restricted to using one or occasionally two colours for these books. Within these constraints, however, he has achieved a variety of effects. For example, using only blue and black for *Raven, Creator of the World* and *Why the Man in the Moon is Happy*, he created illustrations that look like Inuit soapstone carvings. The blue suggests the cold of the Arctic, and the design of the drawings communicates the sense of spirit power infusing many of the stories. For the Algonkian legend of the first chipmunk, he used brown inks and brown paper, giving a feeling of the woodland setting of the story. *My Name is Not Odessa Yarker* is set in contemporary Toronto, and Gal's black-and-white illustrations give a sense of modern children's activities and conflicts.

In 1979 Gal returned to full-colour illustrations, providing the paintings for Janet Lunn's adaptation of *The Twelve Dancing Princesses*, a Grimm Brothers' tale. Winner of the Howard-Gibbon Medal, it was the first of five lavishly illustrated adaptations of traditional stories. For his art accompanying Margaret Maloney's retelling of Hans Christian Andersen's *The Little Mermaid* (1983), he received the Canada Council Award for Illustration. He has also illustrated Eva Martin's *Canadian Fairy Tales* (1984), Megan Collins' *The Willow Maiden* (1985), and Robert San Souci's *The Enchanted Tapestry* (1987).

With the resources of full-colour at his disposal, Gal is able to interpret these traditional tales with a wide variety of visual effects. And for each one he has subtly altered his style to complement the theme and tone of the text. The seven watercolour-and-tempera-wash double-spreads accompanying *The Twelve Dancing Princesses* are in the style of the Italian High Renaissance, and create a formal elegance. Set completely apart from the text, they are, as it were, visual islands that the reader is invited to contemplate before continuing with the story.

In *The Little Mermaid*, Gal uses illustrations in a variety of sizes and shapes, incorporating the pictures into the text and making them part of the rhythm of the story. *Canadian Fairy Tales*, like the earlier *Cartier Discovers the St. Lawrence*, gives a strong sense of the rugged landscape against which the twelve stories are enacted. Green and brown watercolours dominate *The Willow Maiden*, complementing the story's use of seasonal cycles in the plot. *The Enchanted Tapestry*, an ancient Chinese legend, imitates the style of Oriental landscape painting and approximates the texture of tapestry.

The volumes for which Gal has created art are not picture books in which the narrative and characterization are incomplete without the pictures. Rather, they are illustrated books; the texts could stand and, indeed, have stood alone. The role of the illustrator is to evoke a sense of place, time, and mood so that the reader can return to the text with a stronger emotional response to it. Carefully researched, meticulously planned, and rigorously executed, Laszlo Gal's paintings have justly earned him the reputation of Canada's foremost illustrator of traditional legends and tales.

SECONDARY REFERENCES: *Profiles 2; SATA 32.*

# Gay, Marie-Louise (1952–    )

Marie-Louise Gay is the only person to have won the two major French-Canadian and two major English-Canadian awards for illustration. She did not originally intend to become an artist: born in Quebec City, she had planned on becoming a teacher. However, after high school she changed her mind and studied at the Montreal Museum of Arts School and San Francisco's Academy of Art College. Returning to Quebec, she worked as a freelance artist and illustrated several books, including three children's books by Bertrand Gauthier (*Hou ilva*, 1976;

*Hébert Loué*, 1980; and *Dou ilvien*, 1981). She also wrote and illustrated several books: *De Zéro à minuit* (1981), a counting book; *La sœur de Robert* (1983), about quarreling siblings; and *Drôle d'école* (1984), a collection of concept books. *La sœur de Robert* won the Alvine-Belisle Prize for the best French-Canadian children's book of the year. *Drôle d'école* won the Canada Council Illustration Prize for a French-Canadian book. In 1984 Gay illustrated her first English-Canadian book, Dennis Lee's *Lizzy's Lion*, for which she received the Canada Council Illustration Prize for an English-Canadian book. *Moonbeam on a Cat's Ear* (1986), which she both wrote and illustrated, won the Howard-Gibbon Medal. *Rainy Day Magic*, also written and illustrated by Gay, appeared in 1987.

Speaking of her work, Gay has stated, "I feel that I'm principally an illustrator who can add words to round out the illustration." She notes that for *Moonbeam on a Cat's Ear* the illustrations are more important than the words: "If you just looked at the pictures, you would understand the whole story without the words." In her illustrations, Gay reinforces the rhythms of the poems, develops characterization, and gives fuller depiction of actions.

The action of *Lizzy's Lion* all takes place in Lizzy's bedroom, where a burglar is confronted by the girl's pet. Gay uses a double-spread for each four-line verse. The opening pen and watercolour illustration shows the friendly clutter of Lizzy's room, the tousle-haired heroine, and only the lion's tail. On the following page the lion is revealed; he is huge, but completely controlled by Lizzy, who casually wraps his tail around her neck. These two illustrations foreshadow the scenes to come. The lion is not seen when the robber enters the room; when the robber faces it, his face reveals shock and fear. Later the clutter of Lizzy's room will be replaced by the torn pieces of the robber's clothing, and Lizzy will have to control the lion as she did at the beginning. Although Lee's verse carries the story along, Gay's exaggerated cartoon-like illustrations emphasize the humour.

Gay's fourteen-line poem for *Moonbeam on a Cat's Ear* gives the barest plot outline. Toby arrives at his sister's bedroom one moonlit night and invites her to come outside. He climbs the apple tree to pull down the moon, which they ride over sea and through sky. At the conclusion, the poet asks the reader, "Was it a dream or did they really try to steal the moon right out of the sky?" By looking at the last two illustrations, we find the answer. At the beginning the cat and mouse who accompany the children were sleeping on Rosie's bed; at the end, they are dozing on the curve of the crescent moon.

Realizing that the events really happened, the reader/viewer can now go back and look carefully at the illustrations as a record of an exciting adventure. The double-spread depicting the children standing at the front door, silhouetted against the moonlit sky, indicates that no ordinary nocturnal stroll awaits them. Bolts of lightning zig-zag across the wallpaper, and the landscape seen outside the door contains no familiar objects; it is as if the two were stepping into an alternate world. Four double-spreads depict the children's changing emotions as they ride the moon. They smile quietly as it bobs across the waves, break into excited smiles as it becomes airborne, and cry out in fear as lightning strikes their craft, forcing them to jump overboard.

*Rainy Day Magic* is also an adventure story; but in this case it appears to be the fantasy of two small children caught in the basement when the lights go out. When Joey and Victor play inside one rainy day, they are warned by their father that they must be quiet. However, the illustrations reveal that they are barely able to control themselves. They race their tricycles around and over the wonderful clutter in their playroom, through the hall, and over the chesterfield. An ashtray crashes, a lamp teeters precariously, pictures tilt on the walls, and the cat flees in terror. Banished to the basement, they create a pyramid of old chairs, on which they stand while dancing and playing musical instruments.

The opening illustrations are not only humorous exaggerations of normal children's play but also symbols of the state of the children. The children are filled with energy that they cannot release because they are confined inside and repressed by adults. In addition, the illustrations contain several objects that will be seen again in the adventure the children experience after they follow a mysterious blue light shining in a corner of the darkened basement. They crawl over the back of an angry-looking tiger, which they mistake for a huge bumblebee, are blown by its sneeze onto a slithery snake, and, reaching the end of its tail, plunge into the ocean, where they are swallowed by a whale. Once again they are in darkness.

Gay ends *Rainy Day Magic* ambiguously. Father asks, "What's that in your hair?" The illustration shows Joey wearing a small purple starfish like the one the children had met on the ocean floor. As in the conclusion of *Moonbeam on a Cat's Ear*, the reality of magic is made a distinct possibility.

The success of Marie-Louise Gay's picture books with both young readers and adults is not difficult to explain. The books are bright, lively, and humorous. Each picture is full of activities and objects that engage the viewer's attention. But equally important, the stories the illustrations tell are accurate reflections of human nature. The fantastic adventures are fun, and the children who experience them react in ways children recognize and, intuitively at least, understand.
SECONDARY REFERENCE: *QQ* 51 (Oct. 85): 6.

# German, Tony (1924–      )

"We're all immigrants, as are my characters. Their stories are fictional, but I try to conjure up some of the adventures, problems and difficulties a young person of the earlier nineteenth century might experience." Tony German's young immigrant heroes live in pre-Confederation

Canada; they respond to the dangers and excitement of the new country and mature as they confront their environment and their own inner doubts and hopes.

Born in Ottawa, German attended school in Toronto and devoured the novels of such late nineteenth-century adventure writers as Rudyard Kipling, Jack London, and Robert Louis Stevenson. After training at Royal Roads Military Academy on Vancouver Island, he joined the Canadian Navy, serving at sea during World War II. He remained with the Navy until 1966. He says that he discovered the romance of Canadian history by reading the journals of Alexander Mackenzie.

For German, the writing of a novel is preceded by a great deal of research: "I must know the times and the settings of a story thoroughly before I can begin developing character and plotting events." *Tom Penny* (1977) and two sequels, *River Race* (1979) and *Tom Penny and the Grand Canal* (1982), are set in the Ottawa Valley during the early nineteenth century. *A Breed Apart* (1985) takes place in the Northwest Territories during fur trading times; as part of his research, German canoed through much of the area.

German has called Tom Penny "an unusual boy, a hero. Young people then had to be tough, resourceful, and determined. It was an active time and sparks flew. We need to look back at our forebears, people like Tom, with pride." At the beginning of *Tom Penny*, Tom's father is murdered just as the family prepares to sail for Canada. As events follow thick and fast in the tradition of the adventure story, Tom requires all the toughness, resourcefulness, and determination he can muster. The ship carrying him and his mother to the New World is wrecked, he is picked up by rum-runners, and when he finally joins his uncle Matthew on the family land, he must contend with the winter weather and the villainous Dirk Black. In *River Race*, Tom and his uncle are on a lumber raft, determined to reach Montreal in time to get the best prices for timber. Along the way Tom is accused of a murder committed by Oliver Sharpe, who seeks to become rich through others' misfortunes. In *Tom Penny and the Grand Canal*, Uncle Matthew and Tom's new father-in-law, Jamie Macpherson, hope to become rich by building a canal to Georgian Bay.

Donald Cameron, the teenage hero of *A Breed Apart*, is half Cree and half Scots. Returning from several years at school in Montreal to the trading fort run by his father, he becomes embroiled in the struggles between the Hudson's Bay and Northwest companies, and is forced to face and to resolve his conflicting thoughts about his double heritage. Along the way, he is also able to expose Harry Whistler, who attempts to manipulate both companies for his own gain.

German's minor characters are generally stereotypes familiar to readers of mystery and adventure stories, and his major characters are not very complex. They emerge as symbols: Tom Penny and Donald Cameron become representatives of the youthful, masculine spirit possessed by thousands of unknown pioneers. One of the strongest elements of these historical adventures is the portrayal of setting. German knows the rugged landscapes of his stories well, and he presents these concretely and convincingly.

SECONDARY REFERENCE: *CA* 97–100.

## Godfrey, Martyn (1949–      )

"There are two kinds of books. First, there are the stories that kids devour. Then there are the ones that get the gold crests — you and I enjoy them; librarians love them; they're super books. But their covers don't fall off because kids don't take them home." Martyn Godfrey, the speaker of these words, acknowledges that he is a commercial writer aiming at the first kind. "I am a first step," he says. "By giving children enjoyable reading, I may be encouraging some of them to take the next step and to read the books with the gold crests."

Godfrey has developed his ideas about children's books through years of observing children in the classroom and in workshops. A native of Birmingham, England, he came to Canada in 1957, graduated from the University of Toronto with a BA in 1973 and a BEd in 1974, and then began teaching elementary school, first in Ontario and then in Alberta, including two years on the Denetha Indian Reserve. He now works as a substitute teacher, devoting most of his time to writing and to speaking engagements.

Godfrey has written in various genres. He began by writing science fiction in response to a challenge from a student. His first novel, *The Vandarian Incident* (1981), is a conventional space adventure complete with evil reptilian aliens. His second, *Alien Wargames* (1984), treats issues of racial prejudice and imperialism by having the reader sympathize with a hunting culture that is mistreated by the humans who colonize its planet. Although it contains considerable violence, episodes suggestive of conditions in such racist outposts as South Africa make this a surprisingly sensitive social novel.

Godfrey's classroom experience has especially equipped him to write his controlled-vocabulary adventures aimed at reluctant readers in junior high. Told in the first person to create what he calls "the instant hook of identification," they keep psychologizing and character development to a minimum. Instead, they focus on physical action in chapters deliberately designed to end with a cliff-hanger. In the most action-packed of them, *Wild Night* (1987), a boy working the night shift at a convenience store must deal with a robbery, an attempted suicide, a birth, and a nearly fatal accident. Other titles are *Spin Out* (1984), *The Beast* (1984), *Fire! Fire!* (1985), *Ice Hawk* (1985), and *Rebel Yell* (1987). *The Last War* (1986), a grim novel about the aftermath of an atomic war, follows basically the same pattern but is designed for slightly more accomplished readers.

Godfrey has also written mainstream fiction for accomplished readers. In *Plan B Is Total Panic* (1986), a multicultural adventure in which a teen discovers his inner resources, the plotting is a bit heavy-handed and implausible, but the novel does successfully develop the character of the introspective protagonist. The other mainstream works are humorous tales designed to attract the audience that reads Gordon Korman's books, but are less dependent on slapstick and generally more polished. *Here She Is, Ms Teeny-Wonderful!* (1984), in which a girl whose talent is jumping garbage cans with her bike seeks the title of Ms Teeny-Wonderful, is his most successful comic tale because the contest provides a focus for conflict. In the sequel, *It Isn't Easy Being Ms Teeny-Wonderful* (1987), Godfrey awkwardly balances questions of growing maturity with an implausible tale of physical heroism. *It Seemed Like A Good Idea at the Time* (1987), a story about the disasters that descend upon a boy when he disguises himself in order to attend an all-girl party, is more of an extended anecdote than a novel. Lacking the freshness of character and situation of the first Teeny-Wonderful book, it is predictable in plot and forced in its humour.

Godfrey's books do contain some of the disadvantages of commercial writing: contrived plots, thinly developed characters, and awkward or inconsequential themes. But Godfrey can be genuinely funny and entertaining, and, as he has shown in the Teeny-Wonderful books, he can create engaging, memorable characters.

SECONDARY REFERENCE: *QQ* 52 (Oct. 86): 18.

## Grey Owl, also Wa-Sha-Quon-Asin, or He-Who-Flies-By-Night (pseudonym of Archibald Stansfeld Belaney, 1888–1938)

Few Canadians have achieved the international popularity of Grey Owl; probably none have been so roundly denounced. Following the publication of his second book, *Pilgrims of the Wild* (1934), the British acclaimed him as the incarnation of the Noble Savage, standing against mechanization and greed to defend the wilderness. After his death, the newspapers that had celebrated this romantic figure denounced him as a fraud, a white who passed himself off as a Native in order to achieve fame and fortune. Because of the scandal, it was many years before his genuine achievements as both conservationist and author were acknowledged.

Born Archibald Stansfeld Belaney in Hastings, England, he dreamed throughout his unhappy childhood of becoming an Indian. In 1906 he came to Canada, quickly passing himself off as the son of a Scots father and an Apache mother. He became a guide and trapper in Northern Ontario, meeting and living among the Ojibway. After serving with the Canadian army in France during World War I, Belaney again took up his life as a trapper. His Iroquois common-law wife, Anahareo (Gertrude Bernard), profoundly changed him by convincing him of the

need for conservation. Grey Owl, as he was now universally known, made his message of respect for and preservation of the wilderness the theme of a number of articles and four very popular books, *The Men of the Last Frontier* (1931), *Pilgrims of the Wild* (1935), *The Adventures of Sajo and Her Beaver People* (1935), and *Tales of an Empty Cabin* (1936). He also acted in and directed two National Film Board films, *The Little People* (1930) and *The Beaver Family* (1931), and produced a third, *The Trail: Winter Men Against the Snow* (1936). The Canadian government gave official support by appointing him warden of a beaver conservation program, first in Riding Mountain National Park, Manitoba, and then in Prince Albert National Park, Saskatchewan.

Grey Owl's only book for children, *The Adventures of Sajo and Her Beaver People*, is based on his own famous experiences with the beavers McGinnis and McGinty. The story of a Native girl, Sajo, whose father presents her with two beaver kittens, it is both a realistic animal story and an urbane maturation tale. The Canadian animal story tradition is evident in the first part, an exposition of beaver habits. The narrator discusses the beaver's living arrangements and defensive strategies and then shows the development of the two kittens, Chikanee (Little Small) and Chillawee (Big Small). Throughout, he stresses their charm and their harmlessness, evoking sympathy for them by strongly portraying their personalities, intelligence, and feelings: "...don't let anyone ever tell you that animals cannot feel despair!"

Although the opening episode, the attack of an otter upon a beaver dam, shows the cruel ways of Nature, the major concern is with a contrast between the cruelty of men who callously exploit animals in zoos and the ideal harmony of Sajo and the beavers. This theme develops after the father is forced to sell one of his children's pets to pay a debt owed to the trading post. At this point the novel becomes a maturation tale, following English conventions typical of the period: it depends upon an obtrusive narrator, uses a physical journey and the resulting changes in setting to develop character, and keeps to a restricted yet significant time scheme.

As a result of hearing a message from her deceased mother, Sajo convinces her brother to help her save her pet. Narrowly avoiding destruction in a forest fire, they travel to the city, where they are able to locate the pet and, after displaying their concern for its well-being, obtain its release from the park's owner. The journey thus shows their love and dedication. Furthermore, it shows that people will display kindness for both humans and animals if they are presented with all the facts of a situation.

The novel effectively uses a compressed time scheme to advance its maturation theme. It begins with the discovery of the stranded beavers in the spring, the symbolic time of new beginnings. It follows the development of both the beavers and Sajo through a long summer and into the fall, the symbolic time of ripeness and maturity. Although it is somewhat dated in technique, *The Adventures of Sajo and Her Beaver*

*People* is important both as a significant step in the development of the animal story and as a novel in its own right. Alive with humour and passionate concern for animals, it is not the work of Archie Belaney, expatriate Englishman: it is the legacy of the symbol he became, the man who spoke for inarticulate nature, Grey Owl.

SECONDARY REFERENCES: *OCCL; OCChL; TCCW* 2; *SATA* 24; *CA* 114; Lovat Dickson, *Wilderness Man: The Strange Story of Grey Owl* (1973); Anahareo, *Devil in Deerskins: My Life with Grey Owl* (1972).

# H aig-Brown, Roderick (1908–1976)

Perhaps no Canadian writer for children has achieved such high excellence in so wide a range of literary genres as did Roderick Haig-Brown. *Starbuck Valley Winter* (1943), the story of a boy growing to manhood while spending a winter trapping on Vancouver Island, won him the first CACL Award. He won the award again for *The Whale People* (1962), a novel about the Nootka Indians. In addition, he wrote a sequel to *Starbuck Valley Winter, Saltwater Summer* (1948); two animal stories, *Silver: The Story of an Atlantic Salmon* (1931) and *Ki-yu: A Story of Panthers* (1934); an historical biography, *Captain of the Discovery: The Story of George Vancouver* (1956); and *The Farthest Shores* (1961) and *Fur and Gold* (1962), historical documentaries about British Columbia. He also wrote eighteen books for adults, most of them on outdoors subjects.

Born in Lansing, Surrey, England, Haig-Brown came to North America when he was seventeen, travelling to the Pacific Northwest, where he worked as a logger, a fisherman, a trapper, and a guide. During the 1930s he moved to Campbell River, British Columbia, where he lived for the rest of his life, serving as a magistrate in the provincial courts. In addition he was an active conservationist, a member of the Canadian Army during World War II, a participant in many government committees and commissions, and chancellor of the University of British Columbia.

When he was a child, Haig-Brown knew he wanted to become a writer. His father, a naturalist and an author, introduced him to the English novelist Thomas Hardy. The works of Earnest Thompson Seton and Sir Charles G.D. Roberts were regular gifts from an aunt living in Canada. When he began his writing career, his deep knowledge of and love for the land, its people, and other living beings were the sources of his inspiration. As it is impossible to consider all of his books for children and young adults, we shall focus on four, each illustrative of his achievements in different genres.

In *Ki-yu*, the panther must engage in frequent combat against other animals and man. The main conflict is between the panther and David Milton, a professional hunter. Haig-Brown sees this as an heroic confrontation between the most noble animal of the area and the most dedicated hunter, a man who respects and understands the adversary he will eventually kill and who has a deep sense of the responsibility attached to his profession. The book's naturalistic portrayal of the panther makes it a significant work in the tradition of the realistic animal story.

In *Starbuck Valley Winter*, the teenage hero, Don Morgan, spends a winter trapping in order to earn money to buy a fishing boat. The book records his struggle and, more importantly, his growth to maturity. He proves his worth in the wilderness and comes to understand Jetson, a renegade old trapper he had viewed with suspicion and hostility. Haig-Brown is very successful in depicting the hero's outdoor activities and inner thoughts.

*The Whale People*, about the precontact Nootka Indians of the West Coast, again centres on the growth to maturity of a young man. There is no doubt that Atlin, son of the great whale chief Nit-gas, will become chief. The question that arises is, "Will he prove worthy of the title he will eventually inherit?" Like his father, Atlin is ambitious and impatient; he wants to rush into the hunt without sufficient preparation. He learns that his training must be according to a ritual that involves spiritual readiness and practical instruction. There is little inner conflict in *The Whale People*. Instead, Haig-Brown presents the logical and ritual steps of the creation of a whale chief. It is, in fact, his ability to present the dignity of this ritual, along with his sensitive and accurate treatment of the West Coast landscape, that gives the book its great beauty.

In his historical writings, especially in *Captain of the Discovery*, Haig-Brown combines factual accuracy with interesting characters and sensitivity to the land. Haig-Brown called Vancouver a "quiet hero," whose greatness was not in one or two spectacular deeds, but in the day-to-day strength he revealed over many years. Friendship was important to Vancouver, as is evident in the descriptions of his relationships with the Spanish explorer Quadra and the Hawaiian king Tamaah-maah. Vancouver also showed respect for the rights of Native peoples, whose ruthless exploitation by other Europeans he strongly opposed.

Some critics have suggested that Haig-Brown's writing is dated, that it is an outgrowth of literary tastes no longer shared by young adult readers. He was influenced by two popular literary forms of the early twentieth century, the realistic animal story and the boys' adventure tale. Within the frameworks of these genres, however, his novels achieved considerable depth and sensitivity. Most evident is his response to the land. "The only real ownership of the land is knowing and feeling it," he once stated. In addition, he displayed a remarkable ability to project himself into characters different from himself, and to understand their lives as they might have seen them. Although Haig-Brown's novels are not as widely read as they were two decades ago, they justly deserve their status as Canadian classics.
SECONDARY REFERENCES: *CCL* 2: 9–22; *CCL* 11: 21–38; *OCCL*.

# *Hall, Pam (1951–    )*

When Pam Hall, an art consultant for the Newfoundland Department of Education, was asked by a friend to illustrate a book of children's poems he had written, she had no idea her first book would win the Howard-Gibbon Medal for illustration. *Down by Jim Long's Stage*

(1976), written by Al Pittman, was about Newfoundland fishes, but the words and pictures quickly became popular with children across Canada. In 1982, Hall illustrated a second book, this time of her own writing, *On the Edge of the Eastern Ocean*.

Born in Kingston, Ontario, Hall grew up in several Ontario and Quebec cities. After receiving her Bachelor of Fine Arts degree from Sir George Williams University in 1972, she taught for a year in a Newfoundland junior high school before accepting a position as an art consultant. In 1978 she earned a Masters in Education at the University of Alberta, and since 1980 has been the Director of Communications for the Government of Newfoundland and Labrador.

Creating the illustrations for *Down by Jim Long's Stage* was, she said, a real challenge: "I started with research, mainly because I wasn't visually familiar with the fish. The publisher allowed me to design the entire book, so I did the graphic layout and decided where the type would be set amidst the illustrations." The result is a mixture of zoological accuracy and humorous personification. Characters like Lucy Lumpfish and Rodney Cod preserve their anatomical peculiarities but also have distinct personalities. This results, in part, from the expressions of the eyes: Rodney looks supercilious, Rosie Rosefish is flirtatious, and Lucy is bewildered.

*On the Edge of the Eastern Ocean* is a long free-verse poem that combines elements of the classic solitary journey of initiation with an ecological warning. A fledgling puffin finds himself alone on the ocean after he has fled from Goth, a black-backed gull. At the Sacred Island of Funk, home of the spirits of the extinct auks, he is given wisdom by the leader/teacher and learns of the dangers living birds face from oil spills. He returns to his own kind and teaches them of the threats to their well-being. Thirteen full-colour illustrations enhance the story, suggesting the emotions and status of the puffin as he moves from vulnerable infant to lost seeker, dedicated student, and finally respected leader of his flock.

Although Pam Hall's literary output is limited to two books, she has established herself as a significant Canadian author-illustrator. The illustrations for *Down by Jim Long's Stage* demonstrate her talents as a creative illustrator and book designer. *On the Edge of the Eastern Ocean* is noteworthy for her ability to use both words and pictures to present a story that is both timely and universal in its implications. SECONDARY REFRENCE: *Profiles 2*.

# *Halvorson, Marilyn (1948–        )*

Marilyn Halvorson is doing for Southern Alberta what Kevin Major has been doing for Newfoundland: combining local colour — life on the ranches, at the rodeos, and in the small-town schools — with the universal problems of adolescents, especially their love-hate relationships with parents. Authentic in her presentations of both settings and teenagers, Halvorson has quickly established herself as one of Canada's most promising writers of juvenile literature.

Born in Olds, Alberta, Halvorson grew up on a ranch near Sundre, Alberta, and was, she says, "a rodeo freak." She attended the University of Calgary and graduated with a degree in education. A confirmed country dweller, she lives with her mother on the family ranch and teaches at the nearby Sundre school, which she once attended.

Like Kevin Major, Halvorson owes much to her observation of her students. "That's where the ideas come from,..." she has said, "the emotions, the problems, and even the vocabulary of the kids come straight from the classroom." She presents life in upheaval — beset by alcohol and drug abuse, school violence, and estrangement of family members — and she concentrates on characters who do not belong to the comfortable urban middle class. Unlike Major, however, Halvorson has shown less stylistic experimentation, keeping to first-person narrative. Nevertheless her narrators, who speak authentic adolescent jargon and show a mixture of wise-cracking cynicism and vulnerability, are memorably alive.

The narrator of Halvorson's first novel, *Cowboys Don't Cry* (1984), winner of the Clarke Irwin/Alberta Culture Writing for Youth Competition, is Shane Morgan, a hot-tempered redhead who blames his alcoholic, rodeo cowboy father for the accident that killed his mother. Ranch and rodeo life provide the two most important events in the novel. In one overtly symbolic scene, Shane comes to understand that his desperate lashing out against circumstances makes him just like his mother's horse, which gets tangled in barbed wire and seriously wounds itself trying to fight free. In the climactic scene, the father saves his son from a charging bull at a rodeo. The father, no longer running away from his responsibilities, and Shane, no longer letting the past fill his present with hatred, lovingly accept each other.

Acceptance and understanding of others is also the primary message of Halvorson's second novel, *Let It Go* (1985), in which Halvorson balances two stories showing the tension between parents and children. The primary story is not that of the narrator, Jared (Red) Cantrell, but of his Métis friend, Lance Ducharme, who was deserted in childhood by his mother, a country and western singer. Lance becomes rebelliously despondent and takes up with a drug pusher when his mother returns with the intention of fighting a custody case. In the end, a symbolic exchange of gifts indicates that, although they will not live together, Lance and his mother do love each other. The plot involving Red Cantrell is less dramatic in its resolution, but it also shows that understanding can begin only when fighting stops. Red feels that his policeman father has been so attached to Red's older, more gifted brother that he has been unable to appreciate Red. The brother has, however, suffered irreparable brain damage from drug experimentation, something the father cannot admit. More devoted to the comatose son than the one still living with him, the dictatorial father ignores and alienates Red. Only when Red shows courage and devotion in helping Lance does the father come to appreciate Red's qualities and to feel proud of him. This story has a quieter, less complete resolution than Lance's, but it illustrates the primary message of Halvorson's books: true love requires the strength to let another be himself.

In *Nobody Said It Would Be Easy* (1987), the sequel to *Let It Go*, Halvorson combines a problem novel and a wilderness survival tale. Lance, the narrator, discovers that he may never regain full use of his injured hand, and thus may never realize his dream of becoming an artist. At the same time, he is involved in an emotionally charged battle with his cousin Kat, a beautiful and wilful girl who accuses him of posturing to make himself look important. When Lance, Red, and Kat must survive in the wilderness after an airplane crash that kills Kat's father, Lance learns that he can establish meaningful relations with his friends and relatives only by sharing his feelings with them. He also discovers that he will regain the use of his hand when he uses it in a desperate attempt to save Kat from drowning. *Nobody Said It Would Be Easy* successfully portrays the painful maturation of Lance, who learns, as he says, "to accept what life gives you, instead of holding out for everything — and ending up with nothing."

Halvorson's plots are sometimes mechanical, but her books have the compensating strength of convincing characterization. She probes her characters to reveal the vulnerability and fears beneath the wisecracking, confident surface they present to the world. She convincingly shows their painful attempts to understand life and to come to grips with their emotions. Although she acknowledges the power of sentiment, Halvorson does not herself descend into sentimentality. She has succeeded in her stated aim of writing books that "show what life is like from the kids' point of view."

SECONDARY REFERENCE: *QQ* 51 (June 85): 15–16.

# *Harris, Christie (1907–        )*

One of the most honoured of Canadian children's writers, Christie Harris did not publish her first book until she was fifty years old. She was not, however, a newcomer either to stories or to writing. Born in Newark, New Jersey, she was the daughter of a farmer who, after moving the family to British Columbia in 1908, developed a wide reputation as a storyteller.

Although she began writing while she was still in high school, reporting news for a rural weekly, Harris did not immediately discover that she possessed the family gift for stories until she began teaching and entertained her students with her own stories. She sold her initial efforts to *The Vancouver Province*. Once she had quit teaching, after her marriage in 1932, she devoted herself to writing, mostly for radio, often creating stories based on family incidents. Over the years she also wrote dramas for both adults and children, women's talks, and hundreds of school broadcasts. It was not until she received a commission to turn one of her school broadcasts into a book, *Cariboo Trail* (1957), however, that she began the career that has led to two CACL Awards, a Canada Council Prize, the Vicky Metcalf Award in 1973, and induction into the Order of Canada in 1981.

Harris has strong beliefs about the significance of story. By removing the "hodge podge" from life, she says, it satisfies a basic human need: "Story puts pattern and order to the world." When it comes to children's literature, she is equally concise and emphatic. Children's literature, she declares, requires "a good story" and "graceful language." Harris has tried to meet these requirements in a variety of children's books — historical fiction, fictionalized biography, contemporary fiction, fantasy, and retellings of Northwest Coast myths and tales. As different in form as they are, all of them reflect her background and her intellectual interests.

Harris's interest in the early days of the Canadian West and her own experiences on a homestead have led to three novels, *Cariboo Trail*, *West with the White Chiefs* (1965), and *Forbidden Frontier* (1968). The first two emphasize the hardships and heroism of ordinary people who crossed the mountains. Both *West with the White Chiefs* and *Forbidden Frontier* develop issues of racism and reputation. In these books Harris does bring to life many historical conditions and hardships, but she fails to make her characters convincing.

Mrs. Harris has jokingly said that she turned to a more personal form of history, fictionalized biographies of three of her children, "because they won't sue or charge Mother." All three are episodic first-person narratives. *You Have To Draw the Line Somewhere* (1964) is a series of nine "sketches" tracing the career of Linsey Ross-Allen from childhood in rural British Columbia to life in New York as a freelance *Vogue* fashion artist. *Confessions of a Toe-Hanger* (1967) is the story of Linsey's sister, Feeny, who feels very ordinary because the rest of her family is so much more talented. *Let X Be Excitement* (1969) traces the development of Ralph Ross-Allen, who finds excitement and meaning in a dual career as an aeronautical engineer and test pilot. *You Have To Draw the Line Somewhere* successfully dispels the glamorous image of the fashion world, but it is dated. The other two have interesting moments, but they depend on too many sketchy episodes to be gripping or convincing.

In 1958, shortly after her first novel was published, Harris moved with her husband to Prince Rupert, where she became fascinated with the remnants of Northwest Coast Native culture. Her research for a series of school broadcasts convinced her that this culture had produced "one of the world's great art styles and...one of its great oral literatures." That research provided the basis for *Once Upon a Totem* (1963), the first of her retellings of this oral literature.

As a reteller of Native stories, Harris has always functioned as a mediator, one who creates a story pattern that reflects both the character of the oral original and the needs of the modern reader. Because Northwest Coast Native tales are "complex and sophisticated," Harris understands that vast differences in outlook make the versions recorded by anthropologists almost incomprehensible to modern readers. Therefore, she builds in a sense of the Native value system so that modern readers will understand motivations. To make these even clearer, she devotes more effort to character portrayal and emotions than the sources do. She also shapes the story by choosing from various versions episodes that are true to Native culture yet comprehensible to modern readers. Her tales are, therefore, more structured and less anecdotal or episodic than the originals. Furthermore, she uses devices of European folklore, such as repetition of key speeches and descriptions, to suggest both the oral nature of the tale and the "fairy tale" world it portrays. Her changes reflect a belief that "always, it's the *story* that's important. The pattern must be satisfying to modern readers while still remaining true to its origins."

As a mediator, Harris's favourite device has been the introduction that draws comparisons between European and Native culture. In *Once Upon a Totem*, she compares the figures on a totem pole to a European knight's coat-of-arms, and explains that Prince Hayis, the hero of an "historical adventure, based firmly on actual happenings,...was as wrongfully deprived of his rights as was Robin Hood living in Sherwood Forest, or as was Richard the Lion-Hearted." In *The Trouble with Princesses* (1980), winner of the Canada Council Prize, Harris insists that the princesses of the new world's "fairy tales," although they dressed differently and lived in different kinds of houses, were "just as important" as those in the old world's tales. Her prefaces to individual tales cite similarities between her characters and the more familiar European ones. Likewise, in *The Trouble with Adventurers* (1982), she pointedly connects Native adventurers to such familiar old world heroes as "Ulysses, Marco Polo, Sinbad the Sailor."

Harris herself has deepened her understanding of the tales and the culture that produced them. In *Once Upon a Totem*, she spoke of the dangers Coastal Natives saw in the forest: "Ignorance and imagination added even more terrors." She also clearly revealed a patronizing outsider's view: "Lacking science, the aborigines found fanciful reasons for the mysteries of nature." Later collections lack all such condescending references.

The change came, according to Harris, when she was doing research for her first book to win the CACL Award, *Raven's Cry* (1966), a fictionalized history of the decline of the mighty Haida nation: "I became so engrossed in that world that I began to think I was tuning in on an old Haida spirit." This led to a new valuation of her material: "The old Indian notions are very much in tune with today, maybe even more in tune with tomorrow." She believes, in fact, "that science is tending to validate this spirituality." Thus, although she tries to make her retellings accessible by showing their similarities to European tales, she also, at least in her public statements, shows how different they are: "While Old World folklore tends to feature the struggle of Good vs. Evil, Light vs. Dark, this is not so in the Northwest Coast legends. In them, there are mighty forces out there in the world, but all have potential for Good OR Evil, depending on what the character does." According to Harris, "that's an ethic today's children can identify with."

Although her attitudes towards her material have changed, Harris has been fairly consistent in the themes she has developed in her retellings. The primary theme is ecological-spiritual, stressing respect for all nature and the need to maintain balance in nature. She announced this theme and stressed its authenticity by describing the purpose of Native tales in the introduction to *Once More Upon a Totem* (1973) and again in *The Trouble with Princesses*: "Many were also a warning. An emotional reminder of what happened to a proud, wealthy people when it forgot to be worthy of its wealth and importance. When it failed to keep the sacred laws of life." This theme finds its earliest expression, however, in the very first tale of *Once Upon a Totem*, "The One-Horned Mountain Goat," in which hunters are destroyed for wantonly violating the old law.

Perhaps the most authentic and artistic presentation of this theme, however, comes in the Mouse Woman trilogy, *Mouse Woman and the Vanished Princesses* (1976), winner of the CACL Award; *Mouse Woman and the Mischief Makers* (1977); and *Mouse Woman and the Muddleheads* (1979). Harris treats Mouse Woman, a *narnauk* or spirit able to appear as either a mouse or the "tiniest of grandmothers," as the "Good Fairy of the Northwest Coast," the helper and protector of erring young people. The major concept Mouse Woman supports is evident in "The Princess and the Bears," from the first book of the series. A princess whose people do not show respect for the bears they kill is kidnapped and married by Prince-of-Bears, who can be either human or bear. From this her people learn the necessity of showing reverence for all life, of giving gifts when they take the gift of life.

In addition to their themes about the balance of nature, Harris's tales are similar in their use of violence. She sees this violence as a natural product of the rugged setting that produced the tales: "If you're going to cope with a ruthless land, you're going to have to have a certain ruthlessness in your culture." She also says that the blood code, which demanded revenge when anyone was killed, represents "Violence cloaked in a sort of beauty of concept." This concept is, of course, the maintenance of equality or balance. Harris insists that we should not deny the reality of death in stories for children, but she is equally insistent that the formulaic distancing of tales protects children. Thus, she opens many Mouse Woman tales with, "It was in the time of very long ago, when things were different."

Although she has achieved her greatest success as a reteller of tales, Harris has also used Native material in other books. In *Raven's Cry*, she combined history and fiction to portray the decline of the Haida nation. Covering more than two hundred years by focusing on several generations of chiefs, all named Edinsa, Harris shows how the once mighty Haida became victims of white ignorance and prejudice and of their own feuding and inability to meet the challenge of white society. The vast span of the book forces Harris to resort to textbook chronicle and does not permit full development of the characters. The scenes dramatized are, however, highly effective and quite emotional. Combined with the choric repetition of key statements, these scenes give the book some qualities of tragedy.

A complex work, *Raven's Cry* has two major themes. The first is the humiliation of a people whose pride was the basis of their culture. The other stresses the art that was the most demonstrable sign of pride. The Haida society succumbs, but Tahayghen, the last Edinsa (named Charlie Edenshaw by the whites), keeps the art alive. He is the artist-hero who replaces the earlier warrior-hero.

Harris's other attempts to incorporate Native material into her work have had limited success. The best of these, *Secret in the Stlalakum Wild* (1972), is also the earliest. Combining problem novel, Native mythology, and fantasy, it shows the moral development of Morann, an unhappy girl whose encounter with *stlalakums*, or spirits, tests her. She passes her most significant test when she decides to remain quiet about a nugget of gold she has found because the undisturbed natural beauty of the wilderness is a treasure far more valuable. Her moral decision thus supports Harris's recurring ecological concerns.

*Sky Man on the Totem Pole?* (1975) and *Mystery at the Edge of Two Worlds* (1978) use Native materials far less significantly. The former tries to combine a science fiction story with a retelling of Native myths to suggest that stories about Sky Man had a logical origin: Earth was visited by men from a dying planet. Unfortunately, the novel makes the Natives appear the gullible victims of space tricksters, not humans finely attuned to a spiritual world. *Mystery at the Edge of Two Worlds* tries to combine several elements, but its mixture of adolescent identity problems, mystery adventure, and Native mysticism fails. Lark Doberly's adventures do not command credence, and her psychological and spiritual awakening is much too indefinite.

Although Harris has written in various genres, her reputation depends on her work as a mediator of Native tales. In these, Christie Harris is without compare. She has brought the legends of the Northwest Coast grippingly alive in a number of books. Her very best, *Mouse Woman and the Vanished Princesses* and *The Trouble with Princesses*, are not merely collections; they are unified by a focus on a character type and by themes. The artistry, wit, and sensitive understanding of human nature evident in them is, however, also present in the less unified collections. Regional in setting, these books are universal in significance.

SECONDARY REFERENCES: *Profiles; CL* 78: 26–30; *CCL* 15/16: 47–56; *CCL* 31/32: 9–11, 53–62; *SATA* 6; *CANR* 6; *CLC* 12; *TCCW* 2; *Canada Writes!*

# Harrison, Ted (1926–        )

"My first impression of the Yukon was one of absolute joy. I had seen the movie *Lost Horizon* with Ronald Coleman when he finally reached Shangri-La. The music breaks out as he gazes out on the scene of this earthly paradise. I felt similar to that. I suddenly had a light — this is the place, this is the place I've been looking for all my life and never knew existed." This joyous initial response to the Yukon has remained with Ted Harrison since he first looked down on Crag Lake in 1968, and has provided the inspiration that has made him Canada's best-known painter of the contemporary North, and the author of three very popular picture books for children. *The Last Horizon* (1980) is an illustrated autobiography.

Born in the coal mining town of Wingate, in northern England, Harrison studied art at Hartlepool College of Art and King's College of the University of Durham. However, the intensely academic basis of his instruction stifled his creativity and, although he taught art in high schools in England, Malaya, and New Zealand, he found that he had lost the love of painting. A study of Maori and other Polynesian art suggested new approaches, but it was not until he reached the Yukon that he developed his distinctive characteristics: flowing lines, vivid, non-naturalistic use of colours, towering mountains, and a clutter of human and animal activity.

An exhibition of Harrison's paintings drew the attention of Montreal publisher May Cutler, and resulted in the publication of *Children of the Yukon* (1977). As the preface notes, "Children in the towns of the Yukon do many things other North American children do.... But they do other things children further south never do, and this is what I have presented." Each of the twenty-one paintings is filled with busy activity. Children build snowmen, tease ravens, create skating "trains" pulled by dogs, and fish through the ice. They cluster around watching the adults in their lives. Of particular interest is Harrison's non-naturalistic use of colour, as in, for example, his depiction of a blue moose. Such colours help to create the fantasy atmosphere that he feels is an important aspect of his vision of the Yukon: "Fantasy is a marvellous escape. And the blue moose and the pink dogs and the coloured suns are the world of fantasy. In *Lord of the Rings*, we disappear into a medieval world, and in my painting I like to think we disappear into a wonderful world of colour and line."

Harrison notes that his second children's book, *A Northern Alphabet* (1982), "is also a puzzle book, a story book, and a games book." Children are invited to look at the illustrations for examples of the objects that begin with the illustrated letter, and are encouraged to use the accompanying short text as the opening sentence for their own stories. For example, the letter "B" includes the caption "Brenda and Betty are being chased by a bear." The illustration includes among other things a

beaver, berries, and boots. The reader can ask why the children found
themselves in this predicament and how they escaped.

Harrison's most recent children's book, an illustrated version of
Robert Service's poem *The Cremation of Sam McGee* (1986), is set in
the days of the Klondike gold rush. His twelve illustrations depict the
narrator's journey to fulfill Sam's dying wish, a magnificent cremation.
The dominant blues and whites early in the book emphasize the frigid
climate that Sam rails against. Warmer colours are gradually introduced, however, until the climactic illustration, in which Sam, re-
splendent in red long-johns and with a smile on his face, reclines on his
back in the red-hot furnace that is his crematorium.

Three themes underlie the illustrations in Harrison's books. The
towering mountains, flaming suns, and icy moons in the background
embody the enduring power of nature. The adults and children at work
and play in the foreground emphasize the vitality of the people who
live in this rugged environment. Between these are two kinds of buildings: abandoned hotels, churches, and outbuildings are reminders of
the long-past glorious days of the gold rush; homes and modern buildings are symbols of the abiding human spirit.

SECONDARY REFERENCES; *CA* 116; *Arts West* 6 (Summer 81):
20–25.

# Hill, Douglas (1935–        )

A resident of Britain, Douglas Arthur Hill has established a reputation as one of the leading writers of juvenile science fiction. Born in
Brandon, Manitoba, he received a BA from the University of Saskatchewan, and after two years of graduate study at the University of Toronto, decided to pursue a freelance writing career in England. He has
written or edited books for adults on a variety of subjects, from Western Canadian history to science fiction. He began writing for children
by collaborating with his wife, Gail Robinson, on the twelve stories in
*Coyote the Trickster: Legends of the North American Indians* (1975). He
followed this with his own retelling of Greek myth in *The Exploits of
Hercules* (1977).

Hill's juvenile science fiction consists of three series; the individual
novels in each series narrate one stage of a story that spans the entire
series. "The Last Legionary Quartet" — *Galactic Warlord* (1979), *Death-
wing over Veynaa* (1980), *Day of the Starwind* (1980), and *Planet of the
Warlord* (1982) — traces the exploits of Keill Randor, last of the
renowned fighters of Moros, who seeks vengeance on the mysterious
Warlord who destroyed his planet. *Young Legionary* (1982) rounds out
this series by telling of earlier adventures of Randor. The Huntsman
Series — *The Huntsman* (1982), *Warriors of the Wasteland* (1983), and
*Alien Citadel* (1984) — tells of Finn Ferral, a man with an almost supernatural understanding of the wilderness, who leads a group of
humans intent on overthrowing the coldly scientific aliens enslaving

Earthmen. The ColSec Series — *Exiles of ColSec* (1984), *The Caves of Klydor* (1984), and *ColSec Rebellion* (1985) — follows the adventures of Cord MaKiy and a band of teenagers exiled to the planet Klydor, who conduct a revolution against Earth's totalitarian regime.

Although each is different in plot and setting, Hill's novels have a number of elements in common. All include battles between the forces of good and evil. The heroes stand for freedom and the rights of the underdog. Portrayed with few complexities, they are somewhat primitive compared to the villains. The villains are all physically repulsive. Callously intellectual, they are insensitive to the rights of others and intent on domination. Their primary weakness stems from their arrogance, the major sin in Hill's universes.

Except for his opposition to totalitarianism, Hill does not deal with ideas in his novels: his focus is consistently on thrilling adventures which, although frequently violent, are not offensively graphic. His books are predictable and his characterization is thin, but Hill is an accomplished prose writer who produces gripping futuristic adventures. SECONDARY REFERENCES: *SATA* 39; *CANR* 4.

## *Hill, Kay (1917–        )*

Kay Hill is a native of Halifax and one of the best-known Atlantic Coast writers for children. She entered the field almost by accident. Hill had been writing radio and television scripts for several years when she received a new type of assignment. "One day," she remembers, "a producer gave me a collection of Indian legends and asked me to create a pilot for a projected series. I did, it was accepted, and I was commissioned to do a thirteen-week series. The next twelve were a lot harder than the first one!" The legends, focusing on the Wabanaki trickster-hero Glooscap, formed the basis of her first book, *Glooscap and His Magic* (1963). Its success led to two more collections: *Badger, the Mischief Maker* (1965) and *More Glooscap Stories* (1970). She has written two biographies on historical figures: *And Tomorrow the Stars* (1968), winner of the CACL Award, is about John Cabot, the sixteenth-century explorer who landed on Canada's east coast; *Joe Howe: The Man Who Was Nova Scotia* (1980) is the life story of the nineteenth-century statesman.

The adaptation of traditional Native stories presented Kay Hill with many challenges. She had to select those that were accessible to and appropriate for younger readers, and then make them both entertaining to her audience and faithful to the original culture. She achieved her goals by including dialogue not found in the originals and by emphasizing those elements of Indian life that would appeal to children: courage and concern for others.

The central character, Glooscap, creator of people and animals, wants all his creatures to respect each other. Although his presence is felt in all of the stories, he plays a minor role in many of them, being content most of the time to allow people and animals to act as much as possible for themselves. The characters are placed in situations in which their inner strengths and weaknesses are tested. Only when the characters have exhausted their inner resources does Glooscap step in to help. However, he is not above having fun with his people while he is working on their behalf, for he is a benevolent trickster.

The title character of the second book of the series, *Badger, the Mischief Maker*, is a trickster who is both fearless and impudent. Perpetually causing trouble, he would have found himself in even more trouble, except for the indulgence of Glooscap, who admires his indomitable spirit. Badger, though, has a saving grace — his devotion to his little brother, whom Glooscap has hidden. Badger's devotion sends him on a long search for his brother. Badger is almost a picaresque figure as he moves from village to village looking for the boy. He must learn, as Glooscap says, "how much better it is to give pleasure than pain."

*More Glooscap Stories* introduces a new theme: the quest of the individual for a sense of identity. This is humorously presented in the opening story, "The Rabbit Makes a Match," in which Ablegumooch discovers that he is engaged to an otter and realizes that he must remain true to his rabbit identity. The theme is more seriously presented in several stories about orphans who, not always through wise means, try to find out who they are.

In writing *And Tommorrow the Stars*, Kay Hill was faced with another difficult problem: the name of John Cabot is famous, but very little is known about him. As a result, she wrote what might be called fictional biography, a blending of a few biographical facts with general historical and geographical knowledge, understanding of human nature, and imagination. "This," she notes in her introduction, "is how it might have been."

A biography of statesman Joseph Howe for young adult readers presented more challenges. How did one create an interesting story where there was little physical action and a lot of politics? "It wasn't like writing a biography about an almost legendary American hero where there are plenty of tales of derring-do. So I fell back on the writer's primary tool, imagination, trying to make my readers understand the inner courage of the man and how he felt about the things which were happening in his time, a time far distant from my readers."

Although Hill frequently refers to her use of imagination, that does not mean her works are not true. She does invent certain details for the sake of the story, but she captures the essence of her subject, whether it be the mythical history of the Wabanaki Indians, the boyhood and adulthood of a sixteenth-century explorer, or the determination of a nineteenth-century statesman. She justly deserves the Vicky Metcalf Award she received in 1971.

SECONDARY REFERENCES: *Profiles; SATA* 4; *TCCW* 2.

# Houston, James (1921–          )

"Shortly after I left the Arctic, I met Margaret McElderry, the well-known children's book editor. I told her about a wonderful Inuit story I'd heard and suggested that it would be a great children's book, if she could find someone to write it. 'Why don't you write it?' she said. So I went home that night, wrote all weekend and the result was the story of Tikta'liktak." This accidental meeting began the writing career of James Houston, three times winner of the CACL Award, 1977 recipient of the Vicky Metcalf Award, and author of thirteen legends and novels for children.

Houston, who was born in Toronto, enjoyed reading adventure stories and writing and illustrating his own tales. He enrolled in classes at the Toronto Art Gallery, where he met Arthur Lismer, a member of the famous Group of Seven. "One day, we were in our class, when down the hall, we heard a drum beating and in a moment, a man entered the room wearing a huge mask. It was Lismer. He'd been in Africa, and I knew from that moment that I, too, wanted to visit distant places like he had and to meet people from primitive societies." Houston did meet people from traditional cultures. During his summers at Lake Simcoe, many Ojibway shared with him some of the old stories and legends. "I grew up to respect these people and I could never lose this now."

After serving in the Toronto Scottish Regiment during World War II, Houston studied art in Canada and Europe before deciding to wander about Northern Canada with his sketchbook. One day he found himself standing by a plane in the Arctic and making a momentous decision. "The pilot told me that a severely injured child had to be flown to a hospital immediately. I'd just arrived and I wanted to see more of this marvelous country and these marvelous people. I decided to stay for a few days and ended up living in the North for twelve years. But at the moment, I wondered what I'd done. There I was with a sleeping bag and some clothes, surrounded by a handful of people with whom I couldn't converse, hundreds of miles from the nearest town."

Between 1948 and 1962, he spent twelve years in the Arctic, nine of them as the first civil administrator of West Baffin Island, living and working with the Inuit, hunting, travelling, and listening to their stories. Perhaps the outstanding event of his life there was explaining printmaking to his Inuit friends and thus helping them to begin the printmaking tradition that has become famous around the world.

Houston left the Arctic because, as he has said, "I had many lives to live and I wanted new experiences." He moved to the United States, where he began a distinguished career as a designer with Steuben Glass, as an author of children's and adult books, and as a filmmaker. He returns frequently to the North and actively assists Native peoples in the production and distribution of their art. Houston divides his time between a home in Connecticut and a cabin in the Queen Charlotte Islands.

Houston's books for children can be divided into three categories: retellings of traditional Inuit legends and myths (*Tikta'liktak* [1965], *The White Archer* [1967], *Akavak* [1968], *Wolf Run* [1971], *Kiviok's Magic Journey* [1973], *Long Claws* [1981], and *The Falcon Bow*

[1986]), West Coast Native legends (*Eagle Mask* [1966] and *Ghost Paddle* [1972]), and four novels set in the contemporary North (*Frozen Fire* [1977], *River Runners* [1980], *Black Diamonds* [1982], and *Ice Swords* [1985]). He has also edited *Songs of the Dream People: Chants and Images from the Indians and Eskimos of North America* (1972).

Houston's Inuit legends involve long, perilous journeys in which the hero (or in *Long Claws*, hero and heroine) must leave the security of home and family and confront the dangers of weather and wild animals. Tikta'liktak, caught on broken ice while hunting for food for his starving family, survives on a barren island before devising the means to return to the mainland and his family. When Kungo, central figure of *The White Archer*, has learned the skills of survival and archery, he travels by himself to the land of little sticks to seek revenge on the Indians who have killed members of his family. Akavak travels through blizzards and over dangerous terrain to take his dying grandfather to the home of his brother. Punik, the hero of *Wolf Run*, wanders into the barren lands in search of food for his starving family. The young brother and sister in *Long Claws* fight off a grizzly bear so that they can bring food from a distant cache back to the village.

At the beginning of his adventure, Tikta'liktak "wished most of all to be a good hunter" like his father. When he is marooned, he must remember the survival skills of his people, and must draw on inner courage to stave off fear and despair. Only by exercising his skills and utilizing his inner strengths can he be reunited with his people. The exciting adventures, vividly portrayed by Houston, give him the opportunity to develop as a person.

*Tikta'liktak* won the CACL Award, as did Houston's third children's book, *The White Archer*, a story about overcoming hatred through reconciliation. After Kungo's family has been massacred by Indians seeking revenge, "a terrible anger started to grow within him." Journeying to the distant island of Tujak, he lives for several years with an old hunter and his wife, who teach him their practical and spiritual wisdom. As Kungo is about to avenge the deaths of his family, he realizes that reconciliation rather than revenge is the best course of action.

Although much of the adventure in these stories takes place away from family and friends, family is a dominant theme. Alone on his island, Tikta'liktak is sustained by his hope of rejoining his family. Panik and the brother and sister of *Long Claws* face dangers so that they can bring food back to their families. Kiviok undertakes his magic journey to rescue his wife and children, who have been enchanted and stolen away by the evil Raven.

During their adventures, the heroes make use of lessons taught by wise old people. Ittok and his wife teach Kungo, the White Archer, practical knowledge and inner wisdom. As he prepares to take his grandfather on the long journey to his brother, Akavak is told by his father, "Listen to his words and learn from him, for that is the way in which all knowledge has come to this family." In *Wolf Run*, the grandmother is the teacher: "She carried ancient knowledge deep inside herself, wisdom that women have always possessed, wisdom that they have carefully handed down to their children and grandchildren since the beginning of mankind."

Houston's stories about the Northwest Coast deal with an entirely different social structure. Rather than small, loosely organized groups of nomadic hunters, the villages of the British Columbia coastline embodied complex social structures and intricate clan genealogies. Whereas Houston's Inuit heroes have only to find their place within their families, his West Coast heroes must learn their roles in a highly political, rigorously defined system. They must develop a full awareness of their family, village, and cultural histories and systems and must carefully and ritualistically prepare themselves for their assigned roles.

This preparation provides the basis of the plot of *Eagle Mask*. Early in the story, Skemsham, whose name means Mountain Eagle, hears a mysterious voice in the night. He is told, "If it were a spirit, he must wait until it revealed itself secretly to him alone." He learns those things he must know in order to understand his eagle spirit and assume his role as a nobleman in his clan. *Ghost Paddle* examines a young son's political role in ending hostilities between neighbouring peoples. Hooits, when told by his father that he will join a group of unarmed people on a peace mission to the enemy village, is unsure of himself: "He loved the idea of peace, but he did not know whether he had the courage." Not only does he prove instrumental in bringing peace, but he falls in love with the chief's daughter, cementing the political union with personal love.

Personal admiration and respect for differing cultures is the dominant theme of Houston's four novels set in modern times. The point of view is that of a white teenager, Matthew Morgan in *Frozen Fire, Black Diamonds*, and *Ice Swords*, and Andrew Stewart in *River Runners* (Houston's third CACL Award winner). Placed in a totally unfamiliar environment, Matthew Morgan comes to understand and love his new home and to develop a deep friendship with a non-white teenager. Matthew has arrived at a remote Arctic settlement with his father, a restless prospector in search of the big strike. He quickly forms a friendship with Kayak, an Inuit, and the two of them, frequently alone in the wilderness, experience a series of fast-paced encounters not unlike those of typical boys' adventure stories. At the conclusion of the third book, Matthew remarks, "This is hard country,...but somehow I feel that I belong here. It has come to seem like home to me." Away from the pressures of the civilized world, he discovers a family and contentment. Andrew Stewart, the son of an international banker, has been sent into Northern Quebec to serve as an apprentice to a fur trading company. At first he is lonely and bewildered, but with the help of his Naskapi friend Pashik, he acquires knowledge and love for the land and its people. Returning to the trading post after a dangerous winter spent inland, he "raised his arms in joy. He felt as though he, too, had become a part of everything upon this earth."

Houston brings to his stories his intimate knowledge of the landscape and people of Canada's North and his love of telling a fast-paced and exciting story. He is at his best in the Inuit survival legends, describing the heroes' physical and psychological adventures in simple, concrete, sharp language. The West Coast legends, while very interesting, do not achieve the clarity or intensity of the Inuit stories, perhaps because the descriptions of such a complex society blur the focus on the main character. The novels are at their best when dealing with the relationship between the young heroes and the land and its animals; they are less convincing when they deal with the intricate relationships between cultures, and they become somewhat forced when they fall into the standard patterns of the adventure story — cliff-hanging chapter endings, eccentric characters, and improbably dangerous situations.

Houston brings to his children's stories a number of underlying assumptions of what a children's book should be. These can best be understood by comparing his children's books with his four adult novels, each of which treats themes and character types found in the children's books. *The White Dawn* (1971) deals with the violence that erupts between an Inuit village and three marooned sailors from a whaling ship; *Ghost Fox* (1977) is the narrative of a young woman captured by the Abanaki Indians during the British-French wars; *Spirit Wrestler* (1979) traces the life of an Inuit shaman; *Eagle Song* (1983) recounts the hostilities between whites and Native peoples along the West Coast. Unlike the stories of Matthew and Andrew, which deal with the development of harmony between cultures, the four adult novels emphasize violent hostilities and the impossibility of reconciliation. Houston is also well aware of the rich and mysterious spirituality of the Inuit, and has convincingly presented this in *Spirit Wrestler.* He has, however, stated that this spirituality is not appropriate for children: "I don't want to deal with religious matters in a superficial way. Religion is a rich, heady subject that requires careful explanation." As a result, Houston's stories about Native peoples, though accurate and sympathetic, focus most on the universal aspects: courage, loyalty, and the development of inner strength and wisdom. His great achievement as a writer for children is his ability to present these universal themes in exciting, fast-paced, and vivid stories.

SECONDARY REFERENCES: *CCL* 20: 3–16; *CCL* 31/32: 30–40; *CLR* 3; *Junior* 5; *Language Arts* 60: 907–913; *OCCL*; *SATA* 13; *TCCW* 2.

# Hudson, Jan (1954–          )

Few first novelists have achieved the critical acclaim accorded Jan Hudson. Her historical novel, *Sweetgrass* (1984), won both the Canada Council Prize and the CACL Award. Hudson was not, however, an overnight success: *Sweetgrass* took her more than five years to write, and it went through at least seventeen drafts. As she often tells young people, "I'm a rewriter, not a writer."

Born in Calgary, she was raised in Edmonton, and spent a year in Oregon, where she was a runner-up in a major high-school writing contest. Intent on having a book published before she was thirty, Hudson decided to write about a young boy because, friends assured her, only boys' adventures were publishable. Gradually, Hudson began listening to the voice inside instead of her friends. Consequently, Sweetgrass became the central character, and the story became more than another formula adventure story. Hudson worked on *Sweetgrass* while obtaining a BA from the University of Calgary and a law degree from the University of Alberta. A draft won second prize in the Alberta Writing for Young People contest.

The major focus throughout *Sweetgrass* is the maturation of the heroine of the title, a Blackfoot growing up in Alberta in 1837. The novel divides into two parts, each with a separate emphasis. In the first part, an historical study of manners, Sweetgrass must learn to accept the limitations her culture imposes on women. She endures life in a time of cultural change brought on by contact with white traders. Blackfoot men, eager for horses, guns, and white trade goods, have abandoned many of the old customs, including monogamy, because additional wives will be able to tan more hides for trading. Drunkenness and smallpox are even more visible signs of the destructive changes brought about by contact with the whites.

The dramatic tension in the first part of the novel comes from the conflict between the rigid restraint placed upon girls and the desire Sweetgrass feels. In love with a young warrior, she must face the fact that "wanting is not right for a young woman." She repeatedly fails to convince her father that not only is she mature enough for marriage but she should also be allowed to choose her own husband. She endures as a test of her maturity the drudgery of pemmican-making and of preparing hides. All the while, she silently envies the freedom granted to her brother and other males.

The second part is a survival story that reveals the power and heroism within Sweetgrass. Heroically resisting the urge to give in to her own desires, Sweetgrass does her duty and saves her family when smallpox strikes them during the winter. She even overcomes a taboo against eating fish because she sees that it will be the only way to save the family. Sweetgrass thus shows that women, although not warriors, can be heroic. Her father recognizes that she is ready for marriage and worthy of the man she loves.

*Sweetgrass* is a remarkable work of anthropological accuracy and of feminist realism. As a study of Native manners, it provides a clear, accurate picture of Blackfoot life. To ensure accuracy, Hudson not only thoroughly researched the book, as her bibliography suggests, but she also sent the manuscript to several Blackfoot people for comment. As a sensitive exploration of female identity, the novel dramatizes the

pressures females have always felt to conform to strict codes of conduct, but it also shows the heroic grandeur of those who selflessly devote themselves to saving others. Brilliantly, Hudson uses both Native expressions and colloquial diction for this first-person narrative. Consequently, Sweetgrass seems neither a Hollywood Indian nor the kid next door. One could quibble with the romanticism of leaving Sweetgrass as the only person with a face unmarked by the smallpox, but that is a minor point. Although simple in form, *Sweetgrass* is gripping fiction that compels us to think about both the limitations society imposes on females and our views of indigenous peoples.
SECONDARY REFERENCE: *Emergency Librarian* 12 (Sept.–Oct. 84): 46–47.

## Hughes, Monica (1925–        )

"I chose juvenile writing purely by chance — except I don't really believe in 'chance,'" Monica Hughes says. The chance event she speaks of was her reading of a library book about writing for the juvenile market. Inspired to try, she soon became one of Canada's foremost writers for children, winning the Canada Council Prize twice and receiving the Vicky Metcalf Award in 1981.

Born in Liverpool, England, Monica Hughes spent her earliest years in Egypt, where her father, Edward Ince, was Chair of Mathematics at the University of Cairo. The family returned to England when she was seven. Her school in London was richly stimulating, especially because frequent outings to the British Museum gave her a deep feeling for the development of civilization, a concern in many of her novels. Later the family moved to Edinburgh, and Hughes, enrolled in a school concerned only with the passing of examinations, found solace and stimulation in constant reading.

Hughes served in the Women's Royal Naval Service from 1943 to 1945, worked as a dress designer in London, England, and spent two years working in Rhodesia (now Zimbabwe). She came to Canada in 1952, intending to make her way across the country and eventually to reach Australia. Hughes held a variety of jobs before she married in 1957, the year she became a Canadian citizen. After moving to Edmonton and raising her four children, she turned to writing as a creative outlet. She did not publish her first book, *Gold-Fever Trail: A Klondike Adventure*, until 1974, but since then has been a prolific writer, averaging nearly two novels a year.

Hughes has frequently traced the influence of her own childhood reading. From E. Nesbit she acquired a love of magic and the idea of alternative worlds. Combined with her reading of James Jean's *The Mysterious Universe*, this gave her what she calls "the magical universe," a "sense of the marvellous magic of space." From Charles Dickens she acquired a sense of the power of language, a delight in idiosyncratic characters, and, possibly, some of her concern for treating social matters in fiction. From Jules Verne and nineteenth-century adventure novelists like Anthony Hope, R. M. Ballantyne, Richard Blackmore, and Robert Louis Stevenson, she received "the adventure and the making real." The influence of writers of swashbuckling adventures is particularly evident in such early books as *Crisis on Conshelf Ten* (1975), in which she sometimes resorts to mechanical plot devices. Later works show less concern for adventure and more for meaningful action, significant settings, and convincing motivations.

Although she has published historical, adventure, and contemporary novels, Hughes considers herself primarily a writer of science fiction, which she sometimes calls speculative fiction because of its tendency to be based on the question "What if?" Many of her own stories do depend on such speculation. Thus, *Crisis on Conshelf Ten* and *Earthdark* (1977) treat the possibility of colonies, undersea and on the moon respectively, being exploited by Earth corporations, just as multinational corporations exploit underdeveloped countries. *The Tomorrow City* (1978) and *Devil on My Back* (1984) explore computer-dominated societies. *Beyond the Dark River* (1979) speculates about the survivors of a nuclear war. Even when her stories are not so obviously based on projections of scientific possibilities, however, Hughes still considers herself a science fiction writer because all of her worlds follow the principles of Newtonian physics. In her most revealing comment, though, she claims for science fiction both the moral concerns and the external wonders of traditional stories: "Speculative fiction is the mythology of today.... It is good versus evil."

The major evil in Hughes' modern myths is limited knowledge, especially scientific knowledge that fails to value human feelings, individual freedom, and even life itself. In *The Tomorrow City*, the visible villain is a giant computer that establishes totalitarian rule of the city. The hidden villain is the deification of science and logic. The heroine, Carol Henderson, matures when she recognizes that compassion and freedom are essential to humanity and therefore tries to destroy the computer. *Devil on My Back* takes a similar stand. In a rigidly caste-structured futuristic society dedicated to preserving knowledge, the leaders are weighed down by computer paks that feed in information directly through sockets in their necks. Lord Tomi Bentt discovers that no possible future benefit justifies enslaving people, and that true humanity demands both compassion and freedom for all citizens.

The computer is not the only villain, however. In *The Dream Catcher* (1986), the sequel to *Devil on My Back*, Hughes reverses the situation, showing the evils of even benevolent conformity. Ruth, the psychokinetic heroine, initially humiliated when she is unable to fit into a telepathic society that values group identification above individuality, is able to free Lord Tomi's city only because of her individuality. Even more limiting than conformity is ethnocentrism, the group's refusal to respect ideas and values outside of its own. In *Beyond the Dark River*, a brilliant novel set in the period after a nuclear war, the surviving

Hutterites again face destruction because, sure that their ways are the only valid ones, they refuse to have contact with the world.

The treatment of knowledge is at its most complex and extensive in the *Isis* trilogy. The first volume, *The Keeper of the Isis Light* (1980), Hughes' most original and probably her finest novel, explores the individual's knowledge of self and others. Earth-settler Mark London refuses to accept the humanity of Olwen Pendennis, a girl surgically altered by her robot Guardian into a lizard-like being able to withstand the radiation and thin atmosphere of her planet. Literally and morally, he falls when he sees her for the first time without a mask, symbol of the social facade all people erect. For her part, Olwen displays maturity and self-acceptance by refusing the chance for an operation that would make her look like the settlers again. She also displays spiritual heroism by isolating herself, even though she now knows the pain of loneliness, the emotion that makes her human and distinguishes her from Guardian. *The Guardian of Isis* (1981), winner of the Canada Council Prize, shows the dangers of blind faith. Mark turns violently against science, which he blames for altering Olwen and humiliating him. The leader of the colony, he governs by superstition (Olwen is spoken of as "the Ugly One," death), refusing to admit new ideas and constraining women to a subservient position. Only an iconoclastic boy, who violates the colony's purposeless taboos and enlists the aid of Olwen and Guardian, is able to save it from certain destruction. In the final volume, *The Isis Pedlar* (1982), naiveté, combined with greed, is the villain. A confidence man from a more sophisticated society gets the Isis settlers to value gemstones more than the land, nearly destroying the settlement.

In addition to their focus on evil, the majority of Hughes' science fiction novels display another characteristic of traditional literature, the use of the journey as an organizing device. In all cases, the journeyer is young, and the journey both tests identity and leads to maturity.

As a modern mythologist, Hughes is also careful to provide a large number of female heroes who discover an identity separate from that imposed by society. Although she knows that she risks charges of sexism in defining separate male and female qualities, Hughes says that "feminine qualities are the nurturing qualities as opposed to making, wisdom as opposed to intelligence, caring and intuiting as opposed perhaps to finding out and thinking." She often identifies the feminine with the indigenous peoples, who have a deep commitment to the land, and the masculine with technocrats, who see the universe as man-centred and the land as something challenging them, something to change and dominate.

Both of these ideas are apparent in *Ring-Rise, Ring-Set* (1982), a runner-up for the British *Guardian* prize. Liza Munroe, living in a rigidly structured society that emphasizes women's inferiority, seeks adventure in the polar world outside her domed city. She must be rescued by the indigenous people, the Ekoes, who show her familial love, individual worth, and a connection to nature that she has never before experienced. Symbolically reborn, she becomes a nurturer and a healer of the dying tundra.

The heroic journeys of other novels are also symbolic. Both *Devil on My Back* and *Sandwriter*, in fact, use the same death and rebirth symbolism. In the former, Lord Tomi leaves his domed city when he falls through a garbage chute that plunges him into a river. He returns, significantly, nine months later, hoping to work within the city for the well-being of those outside. The dominating technocrat is, then, reborn as a nurturer. In *Sandwriter*, Antia's journey from her rich home to the caves at the heart of the desert continent also provides a symbolic rebirth and acceptance of new values. She learns her own insignificance in the universe and comes to love the land, both signs of her spiritual development. In *Beckoning Lights* (1982), Julia Christie climbs up a mountain and enters a narrow cave in spite of her fear of the dark in order to save aliens who require a fungus growing inside. In the *Isis* books, journeys beyond the settlers' valley and visits to a cave also permit rebirth, but the symbolism is not as overt.

The mythic journeys do not always depend on rebirth imagery. Sometimes the growth of personal or cultural awareness receives emphasis. In *The Tomorrow City*, Caroline Henderson journeys when she climbs inside a building (climbing up is always a significant and positive action in Hughes' novels) and destroys the computer that has taken complete control of people's lives. In *Beyond the Dark River*, a Native girl and a Hutterite boy, who understand neither themselves nor the culture of the other, journey to the destroyed city (obviously Edmonton) to search at the university for books that will explain a mysterious illness killing the Hutterite children. The Hutterite learns that his people, who have shut out the world, have not developed immunities to protect them from diseases. His companion learns that she cannot selfishly avoid her destiny as the one who is to serve the needs of others: she must fulfill her place in the pattern.

Hughes has done some notable work outside of science fiction, combining realistic description and a symbolic resolution of significant problems. As its title suggests, *My Name is Paula Popowich!* (1983) is about a search for identity. Paula Herman, raised without any real knowledge of her father or her Ukrainian ancestry, eventually discovers her own identity, symbolized by a half-German and half-Ukrainian Easter egg she paints at the end of the novel. In *The Ghost Dance Caper* (1978), Tom Lightfoot, confused because he is part Native and part white, steals a medicine bundle from the provincial museum in order to partake in the ghostdance ceremony and thus to discover his spirit or identity.

A Native's ceremonial search for his spirit also forms the symbolic core of *Logjam* (1987), a novel in which the separate journeys of two adolescents converge, providing them with an understanding of themselves and their choices in life. Isaac Moneyfeathers, a Native escaping from prison, rescues from a canoeing accident Lenora Ridz, a troubled white girl. Both are transformed. Lenora, symbolically reborn after nearly drowning, accepts her foster father and her new life. Isaac, who finds his spirit by heroically slaying a bear attacking Lenora, comes to terms with his past and finds new hope for his future.

*Hunter in the Dark* (1982), the most celebrated of Hughes' problem novels and winner of the Canada Council Prize, is one of two novels (the other is *Sandwriter*) in which Hughes feels she has come "closest to finding a true pattern." A story of maturation and identity, it focuses on Mike Rankin, a teenager who discovers that he has leukemia. Desperate for a trophy head, his symbol of manhood, Mike sneaks off to the woods alone. As he is about to kill a prize buck, however, Hughes makes her symbolism overt. Mike recognizes that the game tag he is to clip to the buck's ear and the hospital tag he wears around his wrist are both symbols of victimization. His refusal to kill the deer affirms life. Knowing that he cannot run from death, he comes to terms with the dark — the death that had terrified him — and with his own situation and identity. Although a victim of his disease, Mike, through his journey, is a hero because he takes conscious charge of his feelings and of his life.

Hughes' other novels are *The Treasure of the Long Sault* (1982), an early adventure published only after she had established her reputation, and *Blaine's Way* (1986), a symbolic social history based on her husband's life.

As might be expected of such a prolific author, Hughes has produced work of uneven quality. Especially in her early novels, she relies on mechanical plot devices and highly artificial dialogue. Even in such later works as *Blaine's Way*, she is sometimes too insistent and repetitious in developing symbols. At her best, however, she creates gripping situations to explore both the psychological and social implications of a variety of serious themes. Uncompromisingly honest, she demonstrates that intelligent children's books can also be exciting ones.

SECONDARY REFERENCES: *CA* 77–80; *SATA* 15; *CLR* 9; *Profiles 2*; *CCL* 17: 20–26; *CCL* 26: 6–25; *CCL* 44: 6–18; *BIC* 12 (Dec. 83): 33, 35; *Quarry Magazine* (Winter 85): 65–68.

# Hunter, Bernice Thurman (1922–      )

Like thousands of teenage Canadian girls, Toronto-born author Bernice Hunter devoured the novels of L. M. Montgomery. Unlike nearly all of them, she had the opportunity to have tea with the creator of Anne Shirley, and she received encouragement from Montgomery to continue her own writing. However, although she had written stories for her siblings and for her own children, it was not until she became a grandparent that her first novel was published. *That Scatterbrain Booky* (1981) was based on her experiences growing up in

Toronto during the Depression; it won the IODE Book Award. She has written four other children's novels: *With Love From Booky* (1983), *A Place for Margaret* (1984), *As Ever, Booky* (1985), and *Margaret in the Middle* (1986).

For Booky, as her mother affectionately calls her, life in 1932 is not easy. Her father is frequently out of work, her mother is expecting another baby, and the family moves frequently because it is unable to pay the rent. Christmas is bleak: they have no Christmas tree, they rely on charity for presents and food, and Mother and Father are fighting. However, although *That Scatterbrain Booky* unflinchingly portrays the unhappy aspects of the heroine's life, the tone is generally joyous. Through Booky's eyes we experience more of the happy than of the unhappy times. Hunter successfully evokes the sights and sounds of a large city as it would have been perceived by a ten-year-old girl.

*With Love from Booky* focuses more directly on Booky's growing pains. Mr. Jackson, her teacher, encourages her writing. She feels shame when her father rummages for coal at the dump, suffers the indignities of babysitting for a rich couple, and is kissed for the first time at a mixed party. At the end of the novel her grandfather dies and she feels guilty that she has not visited him more often. At the beginning of *As Ever, Booky*, the heroine is in high school and is encouraged by L. M. Montgomery to continue her writing; although she receives several rejection slips for her stories, she does win a newspaper prize for her essay, "The Bravest Man I Know is a Woman." The novel closes with an epilogue describing her adult life.

While the Booky stories are not developed around any major conflicts and do not contain significant character growth, they are very successful in their evocation of a girl's response to the world around her. The vignettes that comprise them not only give readers an idea of what it was like to live in the 1930s, but also capture the reactions of a character who, though she experienced the events fifty years ago, is universal in her emotional responses.

*A Place for Margaret* and *Margaret in the Middle* are set in the 1920s. The title heroine, sent to her aunt and uncle's farm to recover from tuberculosis, comes to love her relatives as a second family, and reveals her affinity for animals, especially the horse Starr. She realizes that she wants to become a veterinarian, helps to discover a treasure of one hundred dollars, breaks her leg rescuing a kitten from a tree, and generally grows in self-confidence. Not so lively as the Booky series, *A Place for Margaret* and *Margaret in the Middle* strongly evoke farm life as it was sixty years ago.

While Bernice Thurman Hunter's books do not deal with sensational adventures or shattering conflicts, they are very successful presentations of times now past and of the timeless emotions of growing up.

# *I* *taliano, Carlo (1920–      )*

When Montreal-born artist Carlo Italiano was a boy, he used to sit at his window watching and sketching the many sleighs that passed by during the winter. He lived, he later remarked, in the "sleigh center of the world." After study at l'Ecole des Beaux Arts and the University of Montreal, Italiano worked in an ad agency, for Montreal newspapers, and as a freelance artist. After *Weekend Magazine* published a series of his paintings of old sleighs, Montreal publisher May Cutler suggested he publish a book on the subject.

The result was *Sleighs of My Childhood* (1974; retitled *Sleighs: The Gentle Transportation*), winner of the Howard-Gibbon Medal. Based on his childhood sketches and memories, as well as careful research, the twenty-three full-colour paintings of such vehicles as the chip wagon, the milk sleigh, the brewery sleigh, and the fire-steamer sleigh are vivid reminders of a method of transportation as well as a way of life now past. The bilingual text accompanying each illustration not only outlines the uses of the various sleighs, but also captures both the boy's wonder and the adult's nostalgia. Pen and ink sketches show a variety of small sleighs with children pushing, pulling, or riding them. Young readers of the book will receive both an education about Montreal life earlier in the century and a feeling for what it was like to be a child then.
SECONDARY REFERENCE: *Profiles 2.*

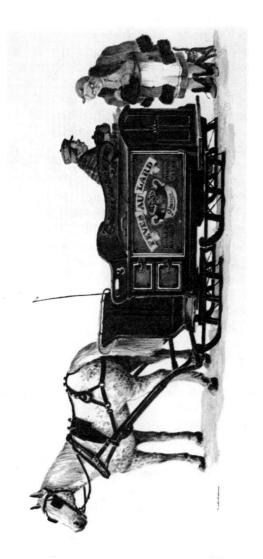

Italiano, Carlo. SLEIGHS OF MY CHILDHOOD / LES TRAÎNEAUX DE MON ENFANCE. Tr. by René Chicoine. Montreal: Tundra, 1974. Reprinted with permission from Tundra Books Inc.

# *J* ohnston, Basil H. (1929–        )

"I write for Native people and I do not write for children," says Basil Johnston, an ethnologist at the Royal Ontario Museum in Toronto. Although the stories in his books can be enjoyed by children, they were not written to be read to or by them. Instead, they are for adults to read, ponder, and then retell in their own words.

Born on the Cape Crocker Ojibway Reservation, Johnston did not speak English until he went to school, but he did listen to dozens of Ojibway legends told by his grandmother. After graduating from Loyola University, Montreal, in 1954, and taking teacher training, he taught for several years before joining the Museum staff in 1968. Since the publication of his first book, *Ojibway Heritage* (1976), he has sought to resensitize his people to traditions many have abandoned and even more have never learned.

*Ojibway Ceremonies* (1982), companion volume to *Ojibway Heritage*, is an introduction to the rituals that a traditional Ojibway would have experienced during the various stages of his life. *Moose Meat & Wild Rice* (1978) is a humorous collection of stories set on a modern reservation and is intended for adults. Three books contain tales suitable for children: *How the Birds Got Their Colours* (1978; illustrated by Del Ashkewe); *Tales the Elders Told: Ojibway Legends* (1981; illustrated by Shirley Cheechoo); and *By Canoe & Moccasin: Some Native Place Names of the Great Lakes* (1986; illustrated by David Beyer).

The stories contain a great deal of humour, humour that is not always apparent to non-Native readers and that can probably best be understood by Ojibway people who can speak their own language. *How the Birds Got Their Colours* contains parallel English and Ojibway texts, and explains how Papeekawiss, the great dancer, gave each bird its present distinctive markings. Because they waited until the last, vainly attempting to get the best colours, Eagle is now bald and Crow, black. Their foolishness is used not only to explain their physical characteristics, but also to teach a lesson to the attentive listener.

The central figure of several stories in *Tales the Elders Told* is Nanabush, the Ojibway trickster hero, who, Johnston has noted, "symbolizes mankind and womankind in all their aspirations and accomplishments, or in all their foibles and misadventures. He resides in every man, every woman." Thus the importance of keeping the stories alive is not just to preserve records of a mythic past: in marvelling at his accomplishments or laughing at his misadventures, listeners are applauding or scorning their own better or worse selves.

*By Canoe & Moccasin* traces the journeys of Nanabush from Ontario through Michigan, Wisconsin, Minnesota, and Manitoba. The purpose of the book is to explain the origins of the many Ojibway place names contemporary travellers encounter, and also to reveal to them the original names that have often been superseded by European ones. In addition, by hearing of the exploits associated with various locations, the audiences learn more about the character of Nanabush and, by extension, themselves.

*Daebwae* is an Ojibway word frequently applied to storytellers. Loosely translated, the word is intended as a compliment and means, "What he has said is right and correct as far as he knows." The word *daebwae* can certainly be applied to Basil Johnston, for in his writings he has tried to come as close as possible to his heritage and to transmit that heritage to his people.

SECONDARY REFERENCE: *QQ* 49 (May 83): 16.

# atz, Welwyn (1948–    )

A great distance separates the cold, precise rationality of mathematics from the intense, emotional power of mythology and legend. However, mathematics teacher Welwyn Katz of London, Ontario, travelled the distance in the early 1980s when she began a career as a writer of fantasy. An avid reader of fiction as a child, and as an adult a careful student of mythology, particularly that of Celtic Britain, she published her first children's book in 1982.

*The Prophesy of Tau Ridoo* is the story of five brothers and sisters who, during their summer vacation on a farm, search a dark cupboard for lost toys and enter into a strange universe. The story, showing the influence of the fantasies of Edith Nesbit and C. S. Lewis, and bearing some resemblance to Pierre Berton's *The Secret World of Og*, anticipates many of the themes of Katz' later work. In it, ordinary children are confronted by conflicting forces of light and dark, and, although often unsure of themselves, are instrumental in the defeat of evil powers.

Both *Witchery Hill* (1984) and *Sun God, Moon Witch* (1986) focus on a North American child spending a summer vacation in Britain. In the former, Mike Lewis, an insecure fourteen-year-old, travels with his highly successful author father to Guernsey. There, with his new friend Lisa, he uncovers a witch's coven. Mike learns to stand on his own, while Lisa must face the truth about her stepmother's wicked nature. Although the two children are safe at the story's conclusion, the ending is not happy. Mike realizes that he will never have a close relationship with his father; Lisa's father and stepmother are dead, killed as a result of the forces unleashed partly because of the stepmother's evil.

In *Sun God, Moon Witch*, Hawthorn McCall is sent to western England to stay with her aunt while her domineering father and his new bride honeymoon in Europe. When the local industrialist threatens to destroy Awen-Un, the prehistoric stone circle, Hawthorn is drawn into a power struggle between ancient forces of good and evil. Told by a mysterious White Lady that she must work to save the powers embodied in the stones, Hawthorn protests, "I'm just a kid!" However, she conquers her inner uncertainties and, with the assistance of her cousin Patrick, courageously prevents the disaster that threatens the area.

The setting of *False Face* (1987) is Katz's home town of London, Ontario. Living unhappily with her selfish mother and sister, young teenager Laney McIntyre discovers an Iroquois False Face mask in the marsh near her home. However, when her mother takes it from her, the evil powers of the mask are released, infecting her mother. With her Native friend, Tom Walsh, Laney struggles against her transformed mother, seeking to contain the dangerous forces of the mask. In the end, not only is she successful, but she has gained a sense of her own self-worth and an unhappy recognition of her mother's inherent inadequacies. Solidly based on Katz' careful research into Native spiritual beliefs, the novel is more disciplined and controlled than the author's earlier works, and is an extremely powerful portrait of intense family conflicts.

Although they are in the tradition of such high fantasy novelists as J. R. R. Tolkien, C. S. Lewis, and Susan Cooper, Katz' works are strong original creations. In addition to presenting, as those novelists do, the cosmic clashes of good and evil, she uses her mythological materials as symbols to delineate the intense struggles of young people on the verge of adulthood. Although the novels end with the heroes and heroines safe, they are painfully honest in their resolutions. The characters have gained in self-respect and self-confidence, but they have also acquired an unhappy knowledge of the inadequacies of their parents and have realized that they can never hope for happy, fulfilling relationships with them.

# *Korman, Gordon (1963– )*

When he was in the seventh grade, Gordon Korman became carried away with an English assignment. The project turned into *This Can't Be Happening at McDonald Hall!* (1978), his first novel, published when he was only fourteen. In order to prove to himself and to others that publication of the book was not a "fluke," Korman had already completed another by the time the first was in print. The Montreal-born writer, who had moved with his parents to Thornhill, Ontario, when he was seven, had thus established a pattern for himself. He continued to write a new book every summer during school vacation, so that he had five in print when he graduated from high school in 1981. In that year he was presented with the Canadian Authors Association Air Canada Award for authors under the age of 35. Now a resident of New York City, Korman, who graduated from the Dramatic Writing Program of New York University in 1985, is intent on a career as a script writer, but he has continued writing books. His twelve novels published to date have, in fact, established him as one of the more popular of Canadian children's writers.

Korman's novels follow a formula. They are set in a place, usually a school or camp, in which the restrictions of authority force boys to use their ingenuity to overcome adults. These boys tend to be intellectually superior to others or to have extraordinary powers in manipulating others. They also have a complete disregard for the rulings of adults. Secondary characters tend to be either eccentrics passionately devoted to one subject, or people identifiable by a single dominant trait. The action of the novels is a series of slapstick episodes in which disasters, often physically destructive, accumulate until order is restored in a happy ending. Korman's comedy depends upon a combination of these slapstick situations and repetition of both incidents and stock phrases.

Designed to entertain, Korman's books avoid deep themes or messages: "I wouldn't be able to deal with serious themes and I don't want to deal with them."

Korman's formula is most evident in the four Bruno and Boots books — *This Can't Be Happening at McDonald Hall!*, *Go Jump in the Pool!* (1979), *Beware the Fish!* (1980), and *The War with Mr. Wizzle* (1982) — which are set in a boys' boarding school outside Toronto. The protagonists, Bruno Walton and Melvin "Boots" O'Neal, who are practical jokers, constantly break the school's rules, although usually for a good reason. In *Go Jump in the Pool!*, for example, the two launch a series of elaborate schemes to raise money for a pool so that parents will not be tempted to enrol their sons in a school with better facilities. The comedy depends upon the absurdity of the fund-raising efforts, the repeated arguments between the headmaster and Miss Scrimmage, who is head mistress of an adjacent girls' school, and the accidents that befall Miss Scrimmage.

Korman has said of his books, "I tend to write about stages which I've just been through." Thus, although he has shown little variation in his techniques, his books do touch on settings or subjects of interest at various times to adolescents. *Who Is Bugs Potter?* (1980) and its sequel, *Bugs Potter Live at Nickaninny* (1983), are farcical presentations of the youthful obsession with rock and roll and the adult distaste for it. *Our Man Weston* (1982) shows the desire of every adolescent to have his summer job become something exciting. A kind of Hardy Boys farce, the novel is the story of twins, one of whom tries to be a detective. He causes numerous disasters, but he does stop a plot to steal a secret airplane.

Although most of the violations of adult regulations in Korman's books are for good purposes, those in two novels are more ambiguous. Both concern summer camps, which Korman himself disliked. In *I Want To Go Home!* (1981), Rudy Miller, a genius and a gifted athlete, is determined to escape from camp, where fun is regulated by the "clones," the counsellors. In so far as it has a theme, the book suggests that children find their meaning, their identities, and considerable joy in opposing the conformity that adults demand. A similar idea seems to be behind *No Coins, Please* (1984), the first of Korman's books with an American setting. Here, however, the focus is on the teenage counsellors who must somehow keep in check Artie Geller, a precocious financial wizard who is part of a group making a camping tour across the United States. The point seems to be that Artie simply wants to show that he can outsmart adult society. What is disconcerting here, however, is that he, even more than Rudy Miller and Bugs Potter, is so self-absorbed that he can spare no thought for others or their feelings.

Korman's last three books, all set in American schools, do not contain as much slapstick. They suggest themes commonly presented in American problem novels, but they do not develop them fully. In *Don't Care High* (1985), two boys attending the notoriously apathetic Don

Carey High in New York get the students to exhibit exceptional school spirit when they promote a strange, inarticulate eccentric as student leader. Somehow, this helps one of the two, Paul Abrams, adjust to his move from Saskatoon to New York. Even weaker in connecting the problem story and comedy is *Son of Interflux* (1986), an attempt to treat a variety of adolescent concerns, including parent-child and boy-girl relationships, and pollution by powerful corporations. Simon Irving, whose father wants him to become a businessman with Interflux, a notorious polluter, insists on becoming an artist. He leads the opposition to Interflux's plans to destroy a green belt separating the school from the factory. Korman initially raises issues of pollution and corporate manipulation of the law, but he does not develop them. In *A Semester in the Life of a Garbage Bag* (1987), Raymond Jardine, a boy who believes that winning a trip to a Greek island will bring luck into his disaster-filled life, upsets the staid existence of Sean Delancey, his partner in an English poetry project, when he convinces Delancey's grandfather to play the role of a deceased and insignificant Canadian poet. The novel combines a decidedly light approach to such problems as low self-esteem, conformity, the generation gap, and attitudes towards the elderly — none of which receives a satisfying resolution — with slapstick satire mocking technology and the bureaucratic deceptions that permit expensive technological failures to continue receiving government funding.

Korman's books are predictable. Deliberately unrealistic, they depend on repetitious and exaggerated slapstick humour of the type found in *Archie* comic books. The characters are caricatures who never develop significant individuality and complexity. For all of their conflict, the plots are devoid of significantly developed themes. Nevertheless, Korman's books are undeniably popular, reluctant readers finding his early books especially appealing. Many of his readers are delighted with these stories of children successfully opposing adult authority. Perhaps Korman's greatest contribution is in providing fast-paced amusement for children, showing them that reading can be fun.

SECONDARY REFERENCES: *CA* 112; *SATA* 41; *BIC* (Dec. 80): 20; *Profiles* 2; *CCL* 38: 54–65.

# Kurelek, William (1922 — 1977)

"I have found in Canada that...Canadian artists are far in advance of Canadian writers. For every important quality Canadian writer that you could name, I could probably name you ten artists of comparable stature. And this being so, I have found it easier in Canada to produce quality children's books starting with the artists rather than with writers. I asked William Kurelek to do his prairie childhood, and his book came out of that, and I asked him to do the nativity because I knew it was something that interested him. Then he added the text." This is how May Cutler, publisher of Tundra Books, described the genesis of the children's books of one of Canada's best-known painters of the 1970s, William Kurelek. The books — *A Prairie Boy's Winter* (1973), *Lumberjack* (1974), *A Prairie Boy's Summer* (1975), and *A Northern Nativity* (1976) — embody Kurelek's vision of Canadian life.

Born near Whitford, Alberta, the first son of immigrant farmers, he spent his school years on a farm near Winnipeg. Awkward, shy, and quiet, he was made miserable because of his father's harsh attitude towards him and because of his inability to fit into the social groups at school. Early in his life Kurelek decided he would become an artist, a choice that would later displease his father, who felt that his sons should better themselves by educating themselves for such professions as medicine or law.

After a brief stay at the Ontario College of Art, Kurelek attended the University of Manitoba, where he received a BA in Fine Arts. He worked summers as a lumberjack in Northern Ontario and Quebec, travelled to Mexico, and from 1952 to 1959 lived in England, where he was hospitalized for treatment of intense depression. At that time he converted to Roman Catholicism. Returning to Canada, he became associated with the Avrom Isaacs Gallery of Toronto and began a career that saw him produce over two thousand paintings before his death. Exhibitions across Canada and publications of collections of his paintings brought him Canada-wide renown in the late 1960s and early 1970s. Both of the *Prairie Boy* books won the CACL Award and were published in six foreign languages. In addition to the four books noted above, Tundra also published *Fox Mykyta* (1978), Ivan Franko's Ukrainian classic retelling of the Reynard the Fox stories, for which Kurelek supplied seventy-two sketches, and *They Sought a New World* (1985), a collection of Kurelek paintings depicting the immigrant experience. He died in Toronto, a victim of cancer.

Kurelek categorized his paintings as either "nostalgic-pastoral" or "religious commentary." In the former group were recollections of his childhood on the Prairies. The latter embodied his intense conviction that modern people, living in a technological, materialistic world, had forgotten the messages of Christianity and were bringing about their own destruction. Although the religious spirit is present in his children's books, the nostalgic-pastoral tone is dominant.

The dedications of *A Prairie Boy's Winter* and *A Prairie Boy's Summer* reflect the dual aspects of Kurelek's work. The former bears the inscription, "For everyone who ever spent a winter on the prairies — and for all the others who wonder what it was like." The dedication to the latter book is more complex: "With love for my sister, Nancy, who more than anyone else shared with me the surprise and wonder of prairie seasons as a child — who has added to that surprise and wonder a sense of awe and love for the Creator of those wonders. Many call it the living whole — ultimate cause — nature. We two call it: God." Unlike many picture books in which the illustrations are merely a gloss on the text, the paintings for these two volumes are the reasons for the books; the text is an addition. Both contain twenty chapters, each with a full page painting of a prairie activity accompanied by three or four paragraphs discussing it. The theme of *A Prairie Boy's Winter* is the relationship between people and the land. From October to May, the horizon, snow, and cold dominate. As the accounts of the blizzard indicate, winter can be a dangerous, life-threatening time. Yet, working and playing together, living with rather than in opposition to the land, the people thrive. The book opens with the autumn departure of the crows and concludes with their return in the spring. In between are such events and activities as the first snowfall, the making of the rink, skiing behind the hayrack, and skating on the bog ditch.

The hero is the artist as a young boy, and he is somewhat like Charlie Brown, on the fringes of his society. He has been made the goaltender in hockey because of his poor skating, and often he is on the edge of the action, at best a reluctant participant. One of his greatest joys is skating for miles along the bog ditch, "because it appealed to his exploring instinct."

*A Prairie Boy's Summer* follows the life of young William from his school activities in early June, through the summer, to his September return to school. William is still inept at school sports: children laugh at his awkward attempts at high jumping, and during softball games he is relegated to the distant outfield. Much of his summer involves doing chores, but even these allow him plenty of time to daydream. The book ends with the arrival of threshing time, signalling the beginning of autumn. As he admires straw stacks rising in the distance, William engages in the one activity at which he really excels — archery. "It seemed to the boys that they were conquering the awesomeness of the prairie expanses at last. The arrow went clear out of the school yard into the pasture on the other side of the highway." Obviously, they have not conquered the Prairie, for the illustration reveals the always present but distant horizon and, between it and the boys, the golden, rich, enduring land.

Comparing the contents of these two books with Kurelek's record of his childhood in his autobiography *Someone With Me*, one is immediately struck by the fact that the picture books emphasize the happy times; the autobiography stresses many unhappy ones. Perhaps Kurelek felt that, writing for children, he must tone down the extreme unhappiness, making the central character, William, merely a typical outsider, not unlike those loners frequently found in children's books.

*Lumberjack* deals with the time Kurelek went to work as a logger in Northern Ontario to earn money to pay for art school. He also had a deeper motive: "I did it to prove to my father (and myself) that I could make it on my own.... What I felt I was really working for all that summer was my independence, my manhood." In the book, Kurelek again captures a way of life now past. His "Epilogue" specifically captures the pastoral note. After talking about the harvesting machine that has wrought a mechanical revolution in the lumbering industry, he muses, "Was our old way, for all its hardships, more romantic, more humane, more socially satisfying? I leave the answers to others. I only know I am glad to have been a part of that good life before it passed into history." The pictures capture the beauty of the old life of lumber camps: times in the cookhouse and bunkhouse, the joys of swimming in icy lakes after a sauna, and the demanding but satisfying work in the bush. The book also traces the further growth of William's character. Still a loner, he is determined to stick out his time in the bush and gains a great deal of self-confidence. "I was shy and timid," he writes, "but from the first I found myself drawn into the hearty camaraderie that prevailed." Interestingly, more of the pictures in this volume deal with people interacting, working in the bush, chatting together in the evenings.

A *Northern Nativity*, considered by many critics to be Kurelek's finest children's book, presents a hypothesis: what would have happened had Christ been born in twentieth-century Canada. Kurelek's sense of the Canadian landscape is evident in the depictions of twenty Canadian scenes as the settings of this hypothetical birth. They include an igloo shelter in the Northwest Territories, a bush camp in New Brunswick, and the riverbank near the Parliament Buildings in Ottawa. In each, the bleakness of the landscape mirrors the loneliness of the Holy Family and provides a contrast to the warmth of their love for each other. The illustrations are of two types. When the Holy Family is rejected, mother, father, and child are isolated and usually ignored by people busily pursuing materialistic concerns. When they are given charity, they are with others, generally inside poor but warm and cozy homes.

Kurelek's almost mystical feeling is captured not only in the depictions of Joseph, Mary, and Jesus, but also by the presence of William in many of the paintings. He looks yearningly at the family, with love and devotion and with a feeling of sorrow for their predicament. He also has intimations that he, too, will reject them during his period of atheism. His sorrow is well founded, for the theme of the book is that the Nativity would not be well received by large numbers of twentieth-century Canadians. This is dramatically depicted in the final illustration, where young William dreams that he is chasing a Mennonite carriage that contains the fleeing Holy Family. They tell him: "We will return one day — when *you* are ready to receive Us with undivided love."

Some critics have maintained that Kurelek's books should not be considered children's literature, that their nostalgic look at a vanished childhood represents an adult point of view and that their social-religious themes are beyond children's interest and understanding. The majority of critics, however, consider his works Canadian classics. Kurelek's detailed presentations of work and play in a harsh and demanding landscape introduce children to a way of life now past. In pictures and words Kurelek represents the joy, loneliness, and humour experienced by the central character. And the religious and social

Kurelek, William. A NORTHERN NATIVITY. Montreal: Tundra, 1976.
Reprinted with permission from Tundra Books Inc.

themes are certainly not too sophisticated for children in the upper elementary and junior high grades. Each of Kurelek's children's books is a unique and moving work; and each is also very Canadian in its presentation of a harsh and difficult life lived in the presence of a dominating and demanding landscape.

SECONDARY REFERENCES: *CCL* 39/40: 8–20; *CL* 6: 141–49; *CLR* 2; *Junior* 4; *SATA* 8.

# Kushner, Donn (1929 —          )

Donn Kushner is a person of many talents. The Louisiana-born microbiologist has been teaching at the University of Ottawa since 1965 and is the author of over one hundred articles on his subject. He is also a musician who enjoys playing the violin and viola with loving friends in Canada and abroad. And he is an accomplished storyteller who has used his considerable talents to produce two moving short novels for children and young adults, *The Violin-Maker's Gift* (1980), winner of the CACL Award, and *Uncle Jacob's Ghost Story* (1985).

Set in the French Pyrenees in the early nineteenth century, *The Violin-Maker's Gift* is the story of Gaspard l'Innocent, a hardworking but ungifted violin-maker, and Matthias, a stolid tollman. Both of their lives are changed after Gaspard gives the tollman a small bird he has rescued from a ledge on the village church. When the bird proves to be magical — it can talk and tell the future — and Matthias sets out to make his fortune, Gaspard realizes that he must provide the bird with a gift: freedom. Stealing it from the tollman, he allows it to join its own kind. The bird, in gratitude, gives him the secret of making violins that can sing with a human voice.

In the manner of traditional folktales, *The Violin-Maker's Gift* mixes the ordinary and the fabulous. Marvellous events occur in the lives of undistinguished individuals, who are then tested. Gaspard's violins have been a mirror of his character: they are "as carefully made as ever — and as undistinguished." Modest, peaceful, and respected, he rescues the bird as a simple act of kindness. But when he perceives its marvellous powers and realizes how its exploitation by Matthias is killing it, he unselfishly gives it freedom. He is truly worthy of the gift he receives in return. Although Matthias later becomes a prosperous innkeeper, he has changed little as a result of his contact with the bird. He is as selfish as the people who pay money to hear it predict their own futures. The recipient of a wonderful gift, he has given nothing in return.

*Uncle Jacob's Ghost Story* combines Kushner's interests in science, music, and storytelling: The title hero is a rationalist, looking for natural causes for all occurrences; two of the ghosts of the story are street musicians; and a young boy to whom Jacob's story is told realizes that he has the responsibility of keeping the story alive.

After Jacob's closest friends, Simon and Esther, are killed in a typhoid epidemic, Jacob leaves his Polish village to seek a new life in the

United States. Jacob's demand for natural proof for everything is test-ed when he meets the street players, who closely resemble his dead friends. Only gradually does he accept the fact that they are the ghosts of these friends.

Jacob's story is enclosed in a framework. Paul, a young boy of the 1980s, learns about his great uncle as he sits in his grandfather's nurs-ing home, listening to the old man and his crony, Mr. Eisbein, recall events of Jacob's life and discuss rumours they have heard about him. As he listens, Paul's attitude fluctuates between skepticism and belief. However, he realizes that in hearing the story he has assumed an obli-gation: "Someday, only I will know it, and it must be told." When Paul becomes a scientist (a microbiologist, like the author), the story fades from his mind. Only after the ghosts of Jacob, Simon, and Esther ap-pear before him as he walks through Central Park does he remember his unfulfilled responsibility.

Kushner is here dealing with a sophisticated theme: the importance of story as a record of human realities of the past. More than mere en-tertainment, story is a vital element of human life and must be given continued existence.

Although Kushner is an able creator of character, he is essentially a thematic writer. Gaspard, the violin-maker, Matthias, the tollman, and Jacob, are vividly portrayed, but their importance is to reveal the messages of the stories. The two novels require sensitive, careful read-ers, but these readers will find the reading of this fiction extremely rewarding.

SECONDARY REFERENCE: *CA* 113.

# *L*aurence, Margaret (1926–1987)

The winner of the Governor General's Award for two of her adult novels, *A Jest of God* (1966) and *The Diviners* (1974), Margaret Laurence was Canada's leading novelist for over a decade. Her Manawaka books, based on a small prairie town much like Neepawa, Manitoba, where she was born and raised, gained her international recognition. After graduation from United College (now the University of Winnipeg), she and her husband lived in England, Somaliland, and Ghana before returning to Canada. After her divorce, Laurence lived in England for five years before returning permanently to Canada. She was named a Companion of the Order of Canada in 1971.

Laurence's four children's books are distinctly different from each other and from her adult work, although her first, *Jason's Quest* (1970), is thematically connected to the Manawaka books. As in *The Stone Angel* (1964) and *The Diviners*, the past exerts an oppressive hold on the characters in this animal fantasy. Jason the mole lives in Molanium, a city governed by the contradictory motto "Hasten Slowly." Accompanied by an owl and two cats with their own quests, he sets out to find a cure for the invisible sickness destroying Molanium. After a number of adventures, including a battle with rats running a protection racket, all of the animals succeed, Jason becoming the new leader of the moles for discovering that the illness is boredom. Although Laurence makes it clear that resistance to change is destructive, the new life of the moles, patterned after night club life in modern London, seems every bit as shallow as the old way. Obviously inspired by *The Wind in the Willows* (1908), another story of a mole who leaves his home to seek a better life, *Jason's Quest* lacks both its engaging characters and thematic richness.

Laurence's other children's works are far more successful. *Six Darn Cows* (1979), illustrated by Ann Blades, is remarkably rich for a book written with a limited vocabulary for beginning readers. The story of two farm children tired of having to tend the family's "darn cows," it develops the themes of the irony of wishes, the power of duty, the need for co-operation on a farm, and the love of family. Jen and Tod Bean, having wished the cows would get lost, must accept responsibility when the cows wander away through a gate the children left open.

*The Olden Days Coat* (1979), illustrated by Muriel Wood, is Laurence's best work for children. Like Philippa Pearce's *Tom's Midnight Garden* (1958), it is a time-shift fantasy in which a child discovers the child within an older person. Sal, bored and miserable with having to spend Christmas at Grandma's house, is transported back in time when she puts on an old-fashioned coat. Aided by a blue jay, she helps a girl recover a beautiful box lost in the snow. Returned to her own time, Sal discovers that the girl was her Grandma when Grandma gives her the same box as a present. With its subtle use of the symbolic blue jay and its simple plot, *The Olden Days Coat* is an elegant statement of the continuity of time.

The published version of Laurence's last children's book, *The Christmas Birthday Story* (1980), illustrated by Helen Lucas, is a rewriting of a story she wrote when her own children were young. It is a simple retelling of the birth of Christ that stresses the parental love of Mary and Joseph.

Laurence's reputation depends on her achievement as an adult writer. Nevertheless, she has made a mark as a children's writer; *The Olden Days Coat*, which was released in a film version in 1980, is a popular work likely to endure in Canada as a minor seasonal classic. SECONDARY REFERENCE: *OCCL*.

# Lee, Dennis (1939–          )

If you had asked somebody twenty years ago to give you the name of a famous Canadian children's poet, chances are you would not have received an answer. And with good reason — there just was not that much children's poetry, good or bad, being produced in Canada. Today, if you asked the same question, thousands of Canadian children and a growing number of adults would probably come up with the same answer: Dennis Lee, the author of two of the best-selling Canadian children's books of all times: *Alligator Pie* (1974) and *Nicholas Knock and Other People* (1974).

Born in Toronto, Lee had his first poem published in *Wee Wisdom* magazine when he was four. After receiving a BA (1962) and MA (1964) in English Literature from the University of Toronto, he taught for eight years at York University and the University of Toronto, helped found the publishing firm The House of Anansi Press, and wrote several volumes of poetry, one of which, *Civil Elegies and Other Poems* (1972), won the Governor General's Award for Poetry.

Lee's career as a poet for children began in the 1960s when he started reading Mother Goose rhymes to his two young daughters. "It was completely unpremeditated," he later recalled. "I just started making rhymes for my kids. Rhythms would knock around in my head and I'd start finding words for them." Many of these were gathered together in *Wiggle to the Laundromat* (1970). Later ones, with several of the early poems, were gathered together in the companion volumes *Alligator Pie* and *Nicholas Knock*. *Alligator Pie* won the CACL Award. A third collection, *Garbage Delight* (1977), received the same award. *Jelly Belly* appeared in 1983. Two illustrated versions of single poems have also appeared: *The Ordinary Bath* (1979) and *Lizzy's Lion* (1984). In 1986 Lee won the Vicky Metcalf Award for "a body of work inspirational to Canadian youth."

*Alligator Pie* and *Nicholas Knock* are complementary books. *Alligator Pie* embodies the poet's belief that nursery rhymes linguistically contain the elements of play that are also found in the physical games and body language of young children. *Nicholas Knock* involves the older child's awareness of the conflicts between the inner liberating impulses and the social constraints he feels.

Lee contends that nursery rhymes "reflect a sense of community, a sense of a stable world, of an at homeness. In their play with words, sound, rhythm, and imagery, they parallel the child's sense of play." While he admired and enjoyed the traditional nursery rhymes, as did his children, he realized that "they were no longer on home ground.... Shouldn't the child also discover the imagination playing on things she lived with every day? Not abolishing Mother Goose, but letting her take up residence among hockey sticks and high-rises too."

The thirty-seven poems that make up *Alligator Pie* celebrate the play of the young child, the joys of his or her liberated imagination, and at the same time the securities of the familiar world. The title poem, which opens the collection, is in a sense the child's request or demand to be allowed the freedom of the imagination. She is willing to give away familiar, everyday things, but not her alligator pie, stew, or soup, for she worries that without them she may die, may droop, and may be unable to cope.

There follow a number of short, chanting poems that mix the familiar with the marvellous: mailmen, ice cream, rattlesnakes, and an elephant who sits on the speaker. In "Billy Batter" and "Ookpik," however, a serious tone is added. In the former, the child is worried at the loss of his parents and relieved at their return; in the latter, the title character becomes a symbol of imaginative freedom, dancing on Niagara Falls and whistling on walls. Security is the theme of "The Special Person" and "Like a Giant in a Towel," whereas the liberty of the child is highlighted in "Flying Out of Holes." "Tricking" deals with a child's imagined sense of superiority over his father who, in actuality, has tricked the youngster into eating dinner. Foolish adults are laughed at in "Higgledy Piggledy" and "Nicholas Grouch." In "The Friends," the narrator explains how he incurs much trouble for the sake of his imaginary companion. The volume closes with a sense of security in "Windshield Wipers," the musings of a sleepy child being driven home late at night.

*Nicholas Knock and Other People* has a much different tone from *Alligator Pie*. Lee has noted that underlying *Nicholas Knock* is the question: "Can we sustain play, joy, or any of the deeper and more vibrant modes of being which tantalize us?" The answer is, at best, a very qualified yes. More often than not repression and restriction impede movement towards fulfillment. The vibrant aspects of life are symbolized by Ookpik who in the opening poem, "Ookpik and the Animals," acts as a liberator, releasing a number of animals from the zoo. In the penultimate poem, the speaker addresses his plea to Ookpik:

Ookpik
   Ookpik

By your
  Grace,
Help us
  Live in
Our own
  Space.

Unlike *Alligator Pie*, which began with a plea and then went on to celebrate life and play, *Nicholas Knock* concludes with a plea, an indication, perhaps, of lack of fulfilment. Indeed, the final poems of the two volumes reinforce the contrast. "Windshield Wipers" concludes *Alligator Pie* with a sense of sleepy contentment. On the other hand, "You Too Lie Down," including as it does the phrase, "you too can sleep at last," emphasizes the need for rather than the joy of rest.

Although friendship is the theme of many poems, including "With My Foot in My Mouth," "The Cat and the Wizard," and "The Question," the strongest poems in the collection deal with the failure of individuals to achieve full relationships with unusual creatures, who represent what Lee has called the "emissaries of larger life." Mr. Hoobody, who helps children release their repressions, disappears when a young child deliberately searches for him. In "The Thing," three boys lead a tormented Ancient Mariner-like existence after they have refused to acknowledge the strange creature who, they later realize, had wanted friendship and the right "to be."

In the title poem, Nicholas Knock had a mind with "funny edges," a quality that apparently enabled him to make contact with the Silver Honkabeest, a creature symbolizing imaginative power and integrity. However, the adults deny that such a being can exist and send Nicholas to psychologists and finally to the Supreme Court, where he is sentenced to death by beheading for his firm insistence on the reality of the honkabeest. Nicholas escapes. Although he remains faithful to his vision, he no longer sees the honkabeest, and wanders on Bloor Street searching for it. He is at once an admirable and pathetic person. Not surprisingly, here and in other poems, adults are the repressive figures. They seem, like the adults who fear sunshine in Richler's *Jacob Two-Two Meets the Hooded Fang*, frightened of children's visionary powers and intent on making sure that these powers do not survive.

Lee's third collection, *Garbage Delight*, contains many echoes of earlier poems. There are short chants, tongue twisters, and poems containing Canadian place names. However, the focus and tone are different from those of *Alligator Pie* and *Nicholas Knock*. Lee remarked: "After finishing the first two books, I didn't know if I'd write any more children's poems. But two years ago, things started again as I began making poems for my five year old son. I wanted wild and wooly hijinks poems; but I also wanted to capture the inward, musing voice of the younger child. When I gathered the poems together I found I could move back and forth between the two types."

"Between" would be a good word to describe the tone of the book, and this tone is embodied in the opening piece, "Being Five," which the poem's speaker concludes:

> I've thought about it in my mind —
> Being Five, I mean —
> And why I like it best of all
> Is cause it's In Between.

On the one side are solitary, quiet moments. In "Half Way Dressed," the child complains of the difficulty of getting a sweater on; in "The Moon," he gazes out of his window and wonders about other children who are also looking at the moon at the same time. "The Coming of Teddy Bears" is a record of his jumbled thoughts as he falls asleep in bed. The collection concludes with "The Secret Song," which, he tells his audience, is as "secret and special / As anything."

On the other side are his active moments, when the child remembers a visit to Stanley Park in Vancouver, where he enjoyed a strawberry soda, or to the Summerhill Fair, where he met a special girl. "The Last Cry of the Damp Fly" details his observations of a fly in his soup; "The Worm" is a portrait of an unusual pet; in "Smelly Fred," he envisions the heroic climbing of a little bug only to discover that the creature has fallen off his shoe.

*Garbage Delight* also contains a gallery of memorable characters, the most important of which are the narrator's three stuffed animals, McGonigle, Bigfoot, and Hannah V. Varoom. They are introduced in "The Animals," in which the speaker indicates his position as an authority figure: "All of them are friends of mine / So none of them are scared." In "McGonigle's Tail," the narrator tries a variety of methods to re-attach the title character's tail, which, he notes, was lost because of its foolishness. Yet the animals provide him with a sense of security. "Bigfoot" celebrates the heroism of the title character — when the boy plays scary games, his friend is always ready to protect him from dangers. The narrator is not always kind to his friends, and in "The Operation" his solicitude for Hanna, who has lost stuffing from a rip in her head, is a result of his guilt — he has mishandled her.

As in earlier volumes, there are several silly and exaggerated characters. "Suzy Grew a Moustache" recounts the foolish ways in which two girls try to rid themselves of facial hair. In "Inspector Dogbone Gets His Man," a famous detective commits himself to jail because he has allowed a fugitive to escape by devouring himself. "I Eat Kids, Yum, Yum!" depicts a girl who is not frightened by the approach of a cannibalistic monster. "Bloody Bill" avoids being pressured into a fight with a bully by recounting his spectacular victory over a ferocious pirate.

*Jelly Belly* is the least successful of Lee's four collections. Only seventeen of the seventy-five poems are over ten lines — the rest are short chants. While length is not the test of a good poem, most of Lee's best pieces have been much longer, tracing mood and developing character and theme. In this book, the short poems emphasize rhyme and rhythm without capturing as successfully as in the earlier works the element of play and the sense of the child's view of the world. In addition, the grouping of several poems on one page, often up to six on a double spread, tends to overwhelm the reader rather than create a cumulative effect. There are chants, action rhymes, counting rhymes, tongue twisters, and lullabies. And there are short portraits of characters: garbage men, paper boys, children and parents, from the real world; Jelly Belly, lazy Liza Briggs, and Mrs. McGee who lives in a tree, to name a few, from an imaginary one.

*Lizzy's Lion* is a single poem illustrated by Marie-Louise Gay. Set in a girl's bedroom, it tells of the fate of a night-time robber who is devoured by Lizzy's pet lion. The initial situation, as in the case of many of Lee's poems, is exaggerated and ridiculous: a pet lion is under the complete domination of a girl, who controls it by calling out its very ordinary name: Lion. When the robber confidently enters through the window, he brings candy with him to tame the lion, but because he does not know its name, he is devoured. The reasons for the poem's popularity are easy to spot: its humourous situation; the control exhibited by the girl; the exaggerated justice dealt to the robber; and, most important, the skill of Lee's verse. The quatrains move rapidly, carrying the reader quickly from event to event, and there is plenty of alliteration, exaggerated sounds to parallel the exaggerated events. Gay's illustrations, which expand on the text, earned her the Canada Council Prize for illustration.

Lee's poems for children have achieved the status of classics in just over a decade. As successive groups of Canadian children move through the various age levels, they respond to the different poems. The reasons for the success of the poems are many. As he set out to do, Lee has created contemporary *and* Canadian nursery rhymes: short poems capturing the strong rhymes and rhythms that children love and using these to depict familiar characters, situations, and settings. In his longer poems, Lee exhibits his mastery of a number of complex rhythm patterns and stanza forms, which he skilfully employs to communicate a variety of tones. He has also created a gallery of characters that reflects the growing sensibilities of children and that treats these sensibilities with understanding and respect.

SECONDARY REFERENCES: *CCL* 4: 28–58; *CCL* 12: 26–34; *CCL* 25: 4–17; *CCL* 33: 15–21, 22–31; *CLR* 3; *OCCL*; *Profiles; SATA* 14; *TCCW* 1; *TCCW* 2.

# *Little, Jean (1932–        )*

"What I am trying to say through my books is that there is humanity in other kids and in parents; and that all these people are real. And then I am trying to share with them some of my own feelings of excitement about living. That living is a Yes thing rather than a No thing."

In her children's novels, Jean Little celebrates this joyous optimism. In coping with physical handicaps, emotional strains, and social pressures, her young characters grow in understanding and appreciation of themselves, their families, and their friends.

Shortly after her birth in Formosa, Jean Little was discovered to have severely limited vision. When she returned to Canada, she studied in special education classes before she attended high school and the University of Toronto, where she received a BA in English. At the Institute for Special Education in Salt Lake City, she trained to become a special education teacher, and then began teaching in Guelph, Ontario. She has also taught at Florida State University and the University of Guelph. However, in recent years she has combined the profession of a full-time writer with travel in twenty-nine countries, including a two-year stay in Japan, where she studied the language. Now almost completely blind, she composes her works with the aid of a Synthetic Audio Microcomputer.

As a young child, Little discovered the joys of writing fiction: "I lived in a world in which I was constantly making up stories. I wrote my first book in grade five, filling a whole scribbler.... The first real pull to write came from the fact that I found that I could escape through writing just as well as by reading." Assisted by a very encouraging father, she had her work first published when she was seventeen years old — two poems in *Saturday Night*. However, it was not until she heard American children's writer Virginia Sorensen speak that she decided to write her own children's novel. *Mine for Keeps* (1961), the story of a girl with cerebral palsy, was written for the children she taught.

Since then, Little has written twelve novels: *Home from Far* (1965), *Spring Begins in March* (1966), *Take Wing* (1968), *One to Grow On* (1969), *Look Through My Window* (1970), *Kate* (1972), *From Anna* (1972), *Stand in the Wind* (1975), *Listen for the Singing* (1977), *Mama's Going to Buy You a Mockingbird* (1984), *Lost and Found* (1985), and *Different Dragons* (1986). Little has also published two volumes of poetry, *When the Pie Was Opened* (1968) and *Hey World, Here I Am!* (1986). She was awarded the Canada Council Prize for writing for *Listen for the Singing* and *Mama's Going to Buy You a Mockingbird*. In 1974, she received the Vicky Metcalf Award. Her novels have been translated into many languages including braille.

Most of the novels are set in Guelph, called Riverside, and Toronto. They deal with boys and girls who must find their place among family and friends, cope with physical handicaps, and face the traumas occasioned by household moves, adults, prejudice, and death. Several of the novels can loosely be called sequels. *Spring Begins in March* deals with Meg, younger sister of the heroine of *Mine for Keeps*; the Soldens are the central figures in *From Anna* and *Listen for the Singing*; the title heroine of *Kate* is the best friend of Emily, the central character of *Look Through My Window*.

"Often a book starts with a problem that interests me," Jean Little has said. Although the problems of Sal Copeland in *Mine for Keeps* and Anna Solden in *Listen for the Singing* are physical, they also symbolize the emotional problems faced by many children. Thus, Sal's father tells her: "The real you, the you that matters, has nothing to do with crutches." Like many of Jean Little's characters, "she was shutting herself behind a high wall." Upset at leaving the security of a residential school, Sal worries about adjusting to her family and an ordinary school. Visually impaired, Anna faces a similar problem: her family does not seem to understand her difficulties, as she moves with them from Germany to Canada and enters a new school. For others, the problems are solely emotional. In *Spring Begins in March*, Sal's sister Meg is unhappy about being the youngest in the family. In *One to Grow On*, Jane must learn to tell the truth if she is to earn the trust of her family. In *Look Through My Window*, Emily, a solitary child, must establish friendships with peers. Jeremy, hero of *Mama's Going to Buy You a Mockingbird*, hides behind his sorrow and anger over the death of his father. Ben Tucker, in *Different Dragons*, must overcome his fear of dogs. What his father tells him is true of Little's other characters: "Everyone has to fight a dragon some time.... You have different dragons to fight."

In order to mature, these boys and girls must move from behind the walls they have built and must face their dragons. To dramatize this movement, Little often has her characters change residences, as in *Mine for Keeps, Look Through My Window, From Anna, Lost and Found*, and *Mama's Going to Buy You a Mockingbird*. Sally Copeland is frightened as she looks out the window of the airplane that is taking her back to her family: "It meant leaving the life you were used to and beginning a new one full of unfamiliar places and people." For Anna Solden, the move is even more traumatic, as her father decides that the family must leave strife-torn Germany for a new home in Canada: "Overnight, Anna's sometimes happy, often unhappy, but always familiar world turned upside down." At the beginning of *Lost and Found*, Lucy Bell feels lost. It is Saturday of Labour Day weekend, and the family has moved to a new town; however, as the weekend progresses, Lucy makes new friends and acquires a sense of belonging. In *Different Dragons*, Ben makes a temporary move to his aunt's home, where he faces his fears.

Of course, the greatest moves are internal; the central characters must achieve new relationships with themselves, their families, and their friends. Early in *Kate*, the title heroine says to herself, "I think I've been moving toward a new place." She arrives at this new place by coming to a fuller understanding of her father and the long-standing quarrels he has had with his own father. Anna Solden grows in sympathy towards her brother as she becomes aware of the tensions he feels when preparing to fight in the Canadian armed forces against his homeland, Germany. In *Look Through My Window*, Emily Blair's mother explains that her daughter understands prejudice because she has qualities that others lack; she considers the point of view of her friends: "It's not obvious to everyone. It's only obvious to you because you've looked through Kate's window."

Achieving an understanding of others is not always easy for Little's characters; they are often so wrapped up in their own problems that they fail to appreciate those who would be their friends. Because of her unhappiness at having moved, Lucy Bell, in *Lost and Found*, often feels angry towards her neighbour Nan. Grieving over his father's death, Jeremy Talbot, in *Mama's Going to Buy You a Mockingbird*, does not want to associate with Tess, thinking angrily to himself: "Who'd want to be friends with a girl, anyway, especially a weird, snooty girl like that?"

Critics of Jean Little's works have emphasized the often overt moralizing of her books and the forced resolutions to many of the conflicts. Others remark that her characters are too nice; seldom is there real malice, only misunderstanding. However, the most significant criticism is that her books are only bibliotherapeutic exercises; that is, in showing the characters overcoming major problems, they appear to indicate that readers can also find similar solutions. While there is some truth to these criticisms, many are overstated.

On the other hand, Little has been praised for her realistic portrayal of character, particularly in depicting tensions within families and between close friends. Undoubtedly these are her strongest gifts as a writer, as can be seen by looking more closely at two of her novels, *Listen for the Singing* and *Mama's Going to Buy You a Mockingbird*.

*Listen for the Singing* is organized around a series of tensions. Anna worries about her ability to cope at a new high school, away from the friends who had been with her at the special education school. As World War II breaks out, the family feels torn in their loyalties between their German homeland and their adopted country. Their anxieties increase when they learn that Aunt Tania has been taken away by the German secret police and when Rudi leaves his university studies to enlist. Although Anna soon makes new friends, she is aware of prejudice both at school and in the neighbourhood, where the family's grocery business falls off. The crisis occurs when Rudi is blinded in a maritime accident and Mrs. Solden goes into a state of depression. However, the family survives courageously because of its love and because, in the midst of calamity and disaster, its members have continued to "listen for the singing," have continued to find love and joy in their relationships.

*Mama's Going to Buy You a Mockingbird* centres on Jeremy Talbot's difficult struggle to accept the death of his father. During summer vacation at the family's lake cottage, Jeremy feels anger when he thinks he is being kept away from his father. However, he does spend special moments with his father before the latter's death, when they watch an owl perched in a tree, and when his father asks him to take care of Tess Medford, a lonely student he had taught.

The statue of an owl, the father's last gift to his son, becomes one of the major symbols in the novel. At first, Jeremy is very protective of it, for it represents the special relationship he felt with his father; but by the end of the novel, he is able to give it to his mother as a Christmas gift. He is, as well, able to share his memories with other people and to let go of the anger that has been a large part of his life since his father's death.

Tess Medford is the person most responsible for helping Jeremy to accept his father's death. At first, Jeremy is hesitant to establish a friendship, fearing peer group ostracism. However, he begins to understand Tess's sensitivity, loyalty, and courage, and learns about her unhappy background: she was the unwanted child of an unwed teenage mother. Learning about Tess helps him to overcome the selfishness that has characterized his life since his father's death.

Although *Mama's Going to Buy You a Mockingbird* deals with a common theme of contemporary children's literature — the death of a parent — it achieves levels of excellence not often found in such books. Perhaps the most tightly structured of Little's novels, it clearly presents Jeremy's struggles. Little is also extremely successful in introducing and developing symbols. Finally, in this novel Little makes the best use of one of her favourite devices, literary allusion. In her earlier books, references to the works of other writers had often seemed forced and contrived. In *Mama's Going to Buy You a Mockingbird*, reading such works as Kipling's *Kim*, Dennis Lee's "Prayer to Ookpik," and Katharine Paterson's *The Great Gilly Hopkins* helps Jeremy to understand the reality of his father's death, the continuing life of the family, and the troubled background of Tess Medford.

As a writer of stories about children with physical handicaps, Jean Little is a pioneer, presenting her characters honestly and unsentimentally. As a writer of the modern family story, she has created a number of novels of considerable excellence. Most important, her presentation of the difficult problems children and adolescents must all face as they grow and mature has earned her a major position in the history of Canadian children's literature.

SECONDARY REFERENCES: *CA* 21–24; *CCL* 36: 6–22; *CLR* 4; *Junior* 4; *OCCL*; *Profiles*; *SATA* 2; *TCCW* 1; *TCCW* 2.

# Lunn, Janet (1928–      )

"I honestly believe," says Janet Lunn, 1981 winner of the Vicky Metcalf Award, "that writing stories is magic. It either comes to you or it doesn't." Although she has written nonfiction for adults, she finds "the excitement of pure magic" compels her to write children's fiction. Children's books also afford her a direct way of expressing ideas: "I don't like subtleties; I like to get to the bone, to the marrow."

Born in Dallas, Texas, Lunn grew up in Vermont, New York, and New Jersey. She attended Queen's University, Kingston, where she met her husband and began both her writing career and her involvement with children's literature by reviewing children's books for the newspaper. After moving to Toronto in 1955, Lunn began to establish a significant reputation in the children's book industry as a reviewer, a consultant for school readers, and a children's book editor. Her first book, *The County* (1967), written with her husband, was a Centennial Project history of Prince Edward County, Ontario.

The concern with the past evident in *The County* has also carried over to Lunn's children's books, forming one of their major threads. It is most evident in *Larger than Life* (1979), ten stories of such Canadian heroes as Madeleine de Verchères, Alexander Mackenzie, Crowfoot, and John A. Macdonald. Lunn wrote the book because, having herself grown up with such American heroes as George Washington, she became "quite irked that there were no heroes here" for her Canadian children. Extensively researched to ensure authenticity, the book is anecdotal history, recreations of how characters responded under special circumstances. Lunn, who became a citizen in 1963, acknowledges that the book does not generally treat acts of overt grandeur like those celebrated in the stories of American history she grew up with: "I now feel because I've become a Canadian in more than just a slip of paper that maybe that isn't our way."

A concern for the past and tradition is also apparent in *The Twelve Dancing Princesses* (1979; illustrated by Laszlo Gal), winner of the IODE Award. She studied a number of versions of the tale, but for the text she finally took that by the Brothers Grimm and a French version and "sifted them through myself." Although severely criticised by some reviewers for departing from the German version, Lunn places herself in a living tradition of storytelling by insisting that "Every generation brings fairy tales up to date."

Lunn's most creative use of research and her most significant presentation of her concern for the past have come, however, in her novels. For her first, *Double Spell* (1968) — more appropriately titled *Twin Spell* in its U.S. edition — she did considerable research in the Royal Ontario Museum to give authenticity to her story of twins beset by an unshriven ghost, whose guilt terrifyingly pulls them back into Toronto's past. Only by forgiving the ghost do the twins dispel its malignancy and come to some understanding of their own family's history.

Even more impressive in showing the continuing force of the past on the present, however, is *The Root Cellar* (1981), winner of the CACL Award. This time-shift fantasy explores issues of adolescent and national identity by following the adventures of Rose Larkin, an American orphan living with Canadian relatives, who enters an abondoned root cellar and is transported into the nineteenth century. Disguised as a boy, she sets off to find Will Morrisay, a Canadian who has run off to fight on the Union side in the American Civil War. Because the magic of the fantasy is confined to events in the twentieth century, the scenes of the past are as realistic as those in any historical novel, and Lunn uses them to paint a horrifying vision of the Civil War and its aftermath. Many of the soldiers sent off as heroes return to face scorn; many, including the mutilated, are forced to steal because they can find no work. When Rose finds Will and he tells of his grim experiences, Lunn creates a powerful anti-war statement, revealing herself to be, as she says, "quite a violent pacifist."

Like *The Twelve Dancing Princesses, The Root Cellar* shows Lunn's sense of belonging to a tradition of storytelling that she can update for her purposes. She has said that one of her favourite childhood books was Frances Hodgson Burnett's *The Secret Garden* (1910). In *The Root Cellar*, Lunn overtly refers to it, and she makes characters and situations parallel Burnett's. Will Morrisay, like Burnett's Dickon Sowerby, plays a flute and tries to talk to birds with it. To Rose he thus suggests the simplicity and harmony of nineteenth-century life. Will is also like Colin Craven because he is temporarily "sick" with delusions and must be cured by a girl who has transformed her own character. In this novel the secret garden is internal; Rose, as her name suggests, blooms into love. Lunn also uses parallels to one of the twentieth century's most successful time fantasies, Philippa Pearce's *Tom's Midnight Garden* (1958). Like Tom, Rose makes a number of journeys into the past, never ageing, although those she meets continue to get older. Like Tom, she at first wants to remain in the world of the past. In both books, a storm that destroys a tree marks a significant turning point in events.

*Shadow in Hawthorn Bay* (1986), an historical novel that won both the Canada Council Prize and the CACL Award, has a simpler plot than *The Root Cellar*, but it explores similar questions of personal and national identity. Furthermore, like all of Lunn's work, it mixes a number of elements. This book combines a comparative study of manners and beliefs in the old and new worlds, a gothic romance with an unusual wilderness setting, and a gripping psychological investigation. Mairi Urquhart, a young Scots girl possessing "second sight," travels to Canada in 1815 after she hears within her a call for help from her beloved cousin Duncan Cameron, who had emigrated four years earlier. Instead of bringing happiness, however, Mairi's journey tests her when she discovers that Duncan is dead. Mairi comes to understand and value the customs of the settlers among whom she lives. Her burdensome gift of second sight, however, alienates her from the community, which does not share Mairi's beliefs in fairies and the spirit world. Furthermore, she fears the land, believing that evil resides in its dark woods.

Lunn has said of Catharine Parr Traill's observation that the Irish and Scots left their superstitions behind when they settled in Canada, "She was right; myths don't travel well." That observation forms the basis for Mairi's development. When she is in Scotland, Mairi is alert to the world of spirits and conscious of myth. In Canada, she must accept a more mundane reality. Once she realizes that it was not the fairies but Luke Anderson who helped her, and once she understands that Duncan, who continues to call her, has committed suicide and now wants to bind her to him in death, she shakes off the hold of the old world and its beliefs. In a richly symbolic scene, both Mairi and her homestead are transformed. No longer haunted by the black despair of the old world, symbolized by the corpse of Duncan, the transformed Mairi accepts her new land for the first time by walking into the woods she had always feared. She also accepts her own personal destiny, which she had strenuously denied, when she agrees to be Luke's wife.

In addition to the concern for the past, Lunn's novels display strong moral concerns, especially in their use of images of redemption or restoration. *Double Spell* treats the healing power of forgiveness: the twins are free from psychological terror when they forgive the guilty ghost. In *The Root Cellar*, which began as a Christmas story, Lunn uses the Christmas dinner that appears from the past, she says, as "an allegory" to convey the "sense of redemption." Rose's experiences in nineteenth-century Canada and the United States teach her that she belongs to the twentieth century, to Canada, and to her new family. Having pretended to be a boy for many of her adventures, she now accepts herself. The dinner from the past is a tangible sign of traditional values — it quite literally nourishes family life. Rose determines to restore the old house in which her adoptive family lives, thus ensuring a perpetuation of those loving values. The climax of *Shadow in Hawthorn Bay* is thematically like that in *Double Spell*. Mairi wades naked into the black water of the bay but realizes in time that Duncan was a black, despairing man who only wanted to bind her to him. She demonstrates the redemptive power of love when she attempts to forgive him, setting his spirit at peace and freeing herself from the hold of the land of her birth.

A magic strangeness is evident in Lunn's most significant works. It permits her to combine a detailed presentation of the mundane world of ordinary social relationships and a symbolic presentation of the inner world of her heroines. Particularly concerned with the way the past influences the present, Lunn has created novels that focus not on magnificent historical deeds but on the moral and psychological heroism that enables individuals to achieve their identities. Her books are thus successful in using the personal identity crisis of adolescent girls to explore the way in which alienated individuals come to accept themselves and their country. Lunn has said that she realizes that her focus on girls has made her a girls' novelist. Perhaps her books do appeal more to girls than boys, but they are not narrowly feminist. The questions of identity her heroines face are universal.

Lunn's books have become progressively more sophisticated and challenging. "Unless you make demands on your readers," she says, "then you have nothing to share. I think a quick easy story is cast aside as easily as eating marshmallows; there's no nourishment in it." None of Lunn's work, even the relatively simple *Larger than Life*, is likely to be cast aside easily. In *The Root Cellar* and *Shadow in Hawthorn Bay*

she has created novels that will nourish young imaginations for years
to come.

SECONDARY REFERENCES: *ChLQ* 10 (Spring 85): 43–44; *CA*
33–36; *SATA* 4; *Profiles*.

# $M$ ackay, Claire (1930–      )

When Claire Mackay was eight years old, she wrote and published her own newspaper; but it was not until over thirty years later that she became a professional writer of children's books. Born and raised in Toronto in a politically active and radical family, she graduated from the University of Toronto in 1952, married and raised a family of three boys, studied social work and counselling at the Universities of British Columbia and Manitoba, and worked as a social worker before she published *Mini-Bike Hero* in 1974. Since then she has published five more novels, one of which, *One Proud Summer* (1981), co-authored with Marsha Hewitt, won the Ruth Schwartz Award. In 1983 she received the Vicky Metcalf Award in recognition of the body of her work.

*Mini-Bike Hero* is the story of Steve MacPherson, who must hide his passionate interest in mini-bikes from his father. With the aid of a kindly motorcycle shopkeeper, he learns the skills of cross-country riding and is instrumental in saving a group of campers from a flash flood. In addition to the exciting rescue, the book is noteworthy for its presentation of the moral dilemmas Steve faces and for its communication of the joys of riding.

Two sequels are less successful. In *Mini-Bike Racer* (1975), Steve is kidnapped by an escaped convict and then rescued by his best friend Kim, who had been jealous of the publicity Steve had received for rescuing the campers. Although the tensions of friendship are well portrayed, the adventure story is somewhat sensational and contrived. In *Mini-Bike Rescue* (1982), Julie Brennan is sent to Ontario for the summer so that she can become more ladylike. The girl finally wins her family's respect when she solves the mystery of a series of robberies and rescues an old man from a forest fire and an angry bear. This book lacks the freshness of the first one in the series and, although Julie's character growth is clearly delineated, it sometimes seems secondary to the plot.

In *Exit Barney McGee* (1979), the thirteen-year-old hero feels abandoned after his mother remarries and has a child. He runs away to Toronto, where he finds his father, an alcoholic living in a rundown Toronto boarding house. He comes to understand the good points of the man who ran out on his mother and himself, but more importantly, he realizes that his true home is back with his mother, stepfather, and stepsister. The book is very strong in its portrayal of the conflicting emotions and loyalties Barney experiences, and it reflects Mackay's understanding, gained during her years as a social worker, of the emotional difficulties faced by many young people today.

*One Proud Summer* is based on events surrounding the Quebec Textile Workers strike of 1946. Thirteen-year-old Lucille Laplante becomes involved in the labour dispute and joins the strikers. Frightened and unsure at the beginning, she develops courage as she fights the ruthless attempts to suppress the strike. The book has been carefully researched, but reads like an historical tract, with the characters generally portrayed as good if they support the workers and bad, or misled, if they do not.

The fourteen-year-old heroine of *The Minerva Program* (1984) has a poor self-concept. When she is chosen to be a member of a special computer class she feels she has found her niche. However, her happiness does not last, as she is accused of using the computer to alter her marks. In her search for the culprit, she learns that she has been guilty of misunderstanding several of her classmates and teachers. She also develops a much closer relationship with her working mother.

Claire Mackay brings to her writing a tremendous sensitivity to the feelings of young adolescents. She understands the conflicts and uncertainties they experience, the joy they take in activities they love doing, and their painful realization of the difficulties faced by the adults who seem to control their lives.

SECONDARY REFERENCES: *Canadian Author and Bookman* 58 (Summer 83): 10; *SATA* 40.

---

## MacKenzie, Jean (1928–      )

"It's a place that triggers a story. I respond to the atmosphere, and when I know something interesting has happened there, I'm ready to go." That is how Jean MacKenzie described the impetus behind her two children's novels, *Storm Island* (1968) and *River of Stars* (1971). Born in Traynor, Saskatchewan, she grew up in Vancouver, and has spent the rest of her life in British Columbia, including a year and a half as a nursing assistant at a Native hospital in Bella Coola. She had always wanted to be a writer, and when she began reading to her sons she felt that "I could write a better book than some of those I was sharing with them."

*Storm Island* is set on a tiny lighthouse island north of Vancouver Island. When twelve-year-old Ray Lewis is sent to live with his aunt, uncle, and younger cousins, he feels lost and insecure, and worries about arousing the anger of his moody uncle. However, after a storm destroys the house and the family shelters in a nearby cave, Ray exhibits his bravery and resourcefulness. Although the plot is relatively thin and the character of the uncle insufficiently developed, MacKenzie successfully communicates her feeling for the desolate grandeur of the island.

*River of Stars* is the story of the clash between Native and white cultures and of a Native boy's growth to a mature understanding of his people's traditions. During the summer that he works to earn money to buy a fishing boat, Andy Hill must face the hostility of whites. His greatest supporter is an old Native, Ambrose, who "belonged in a time that was gone. He was a leftover." From him, Andy learns about his people's past. The key scene takes place in a hospital as the dying and impoverished Ambrose holds a potlatch, giving Andy his most precious gift, the Native name that had been intended for his dead grandson.

MacKenzie has referred to *River of Stars* as an interim project, a book she wrote only because there were no Native writers yet ready to tell their story. However, it has achieved the status of a minor Canadian classic, combining the author's knowledge and love of Canada's West Coast and her respect for Native cultures.

SECONDARY REFERENCES: *TCCW* 1; *Profiles 2*.

## Major, Kevin (1949–        )

Although widely praised as a young adult author, Kevin Major objects to the classification because it unnecessarily limits his readership: "I write about young people, not exclusively for them." Furthermore, it detracts from his artistic seriousness: "Many reviewers have the notion that anyone who writes novels that appeal to young people must in some way be less of a writer than, say, someone who writes purely 'adult' fiction. I want my work to be judged on its quality, on how well it works as a piece of fiction. A well-written book is a well-written book, no matter who it appeals to."

Major's first published work, *Doaryloads* (1974), and his novels — *Hold Fast* (1978), *Far from Shore* (1980), *Thirty-six Exposures* (1984), and, but to a lesser degree, *Dear Bruce Springsteen* (1987) — are products of his Newfoundland heritage. He was born in Stephenville, the youngest of seven children. Family life, a major focus of his later writing, was close and satisfying. During high school, his writing attracted the attention of an English teacher, who predicted that he would one day write a book. Although he enrolled in pre-medicine at Memorial University — "I guess you didn't think of being a writer in those days" — he was not certain that he wanted to be a doctor. After seven months of travelling, he decided to become a teacher so that he could write in his spare time. He earned a BSc and began teaching in the outports.

*Doaryloads*, an anthology of Newfoundland fiction and poetry, was a direct result of teaching in a coastal community. Major realized that his students had no material that told them about their own history and culture. Therefore, he edited the anthology and illustrated it with his own photographs in order to preserve for them the island province's unique ways.

Teaching also focused Major's writing ambition: "I saw that there were very few novels that had characters in any way like the students in my classes. The settings were very foreign, the plots of little relevance to their lives." Having decided to write a novel from the viewpoint of a Newfoundland teenager, he gave up full-time teaching and became a substitute teacher in 1976. He kept up his determination even though no publisher accepted his first attempt. His next one, *Hold*

*Fast*, won several awards — the CACL Medal, Canada Council Prize for fiction, Ruth Schwartz Award, and inclusion on the Hans Christian Andersen Honours List. His later books did not excite equal praise, but *Far from Shore* won the Canadian Young Adult Book Award.

Major's first three novels are distinctive blends of Newfoundland local colour and the universal problems of adolescence. He has, in fact, indicated that his main objectives are "to say something about growing up generally (the problems, joys, frustrations that are universal) and to portray life in present-day Newfoundland outport society," which he feels has "changed drastically...since Newfoundland joined Canada."

The presentation of Newfoundland life in the novels focuses on destructive changes. Life in the Newfoundland outport of Marten, presented through the eyes of fourteen-year-old Michael, is somewhat idyllic in *Hold Fast*. He identifies it with family ties and a closeness to nature gained through such traditional practices as squidding with his father and grandfather. Sent to live with his dictatorial uncle after his parents are killed by a drunk driver, he discovers what modern concerns have done to traditional Newfoundland values. Obsessed by possessions and the desire to dominate others, his uncle alienates his own children as well as Michael. Furthermore, Michael's outport habits of speech and interest in nature mark him as a "baywop," an outsider continually scorned by the urban teenagers. Only by running back to Marten does he find meaning: he realizes that he can "hold fast" to himself through memories of his father and grandfather and by living with caring relatives in the outport.

The traditional life that provides solace in *Hold Fast* is a victim of modern economic conditions in *Far from Shore*. Christopher Slade changes when his father, who has become chronically unemployed and has taken to heavy drinking that threatens the survival of the family, heads to Calgary to find work. Left without guidance and the visible signs of love, Chris loses interest in school, fails, and begins running around with a heavy-drinking, rowdy group. He eventually gets into trouble with the law. Furthermore, his mother comes close to having an affair with her boss. Only the return of the father provides some restoration of order. The novel implies, however, that unless the father finds work soon, the family will have to leave Newfoundland in order to avoid deterioration.

*Thirty-six Exposures* does not present as detailed a look at Newfoundland life, but it is permeated with the despair of young people who feel that they will have to leave the island to have a chance of secure employment and meaningful lives. The death of Trevor in a car crash on graduation night symbolizes the self-destruction of the island's youth, who have lost hope of a future. The young protagonist's departure for Europe suggests that youth must look elsewhere for meaning.

*Dear Bruce Springsteen* marks a significant and somewhat disappointing departure for Major because it uses a generic setting. The high unemployment caused by a mill closure links the novel to the portraits of Newfoundland in the previous books, but nothing else, not even Terry Blanchard's frequently ungrammatical statements, suggests that the novel is set in Newfoundland. In fact, nothing indicates that the setting is Canadian: Terry's unnamed home town could be almost anywhere in eastern North America.

Although social conditions are important in his books, Major is not merely a regionalist or a social realist. He emphasizes psychology rather than sociology, and character rather than topical problems: "The problems are never the focus of the novels. My emphasis is on how individual characters cope with the problems." To achieve this, he has adopted a different narrative approach in each work. *Hold Fast* is rather typical of adolescent problem novels in its use of a first-person narrator. Michael, however, who speaks in outport dialect, is alive and original. He has reminded reviewers of Huck Finn and Holden Caulfield, first-person narrators who have also undertaken journeys that lead to self-discovery and who have, albeit somewhat naively at times, honestly and clearly presented a vision of adult society.

Major feels that a significant problem of much of the fiction teenagers read is that it is "one-sided" because "we see everything from one point of view." A reading of Faulkner shortly before Major began his second novel provided a way for him to round out the characters and story. In *Far from Shore* he uses the Faulknerian device of multiple narrators — Chris Slade is the central narrator, but four more narrators provide additional perspectives. The device successfully conveys Chris's confusion of motives and the difficulty that others have in understanding him. A similar attempt at stylistic innovation is apparent in *Thirty-six Exposures*. The novel is divided into thirty-six sections, each like a frame of film snapped by Lorne, a student whose passion is photography. Each chapter, that is, presents a dominant feeling or an episode important to Lorne. Furthermore, Lorne's poems, interspersed throughout the third-person narrative, provide a sense of first-person intimacy. Unfortunately, Major does not accompany the formal experimentation with an equally good plot. He resolves the central problem of student rights and the morality of revenge by falling back on an improbable love story that causes the entire novel to lose thematic focus.

*Dear Bruce Springsteen* returns to a single uncomplicated viewpoint. The novel consists of letters that Terry Blanchard, a fourteen-year-old boy trying to come to terms with his parents' separation, sends to Bruce Springsteen. Springsteen provides Terry with a therapeutic outlet for his feelings about his father, his mother's new boyfriend, his problems at school, and his fears about dating. Furthermore, Springsteen's biography and lyrics help Terry to cope with his own situation, leading him to a sympathetic understanding of the feelings and needs of both his father and his mother. Although it has a predictable plot, the novel shows deep understanding of the powerful emotional role of music in the lives of teens, and provides a realistic portrait of a boy working through fears of inadequacy to maturer feelings of acceptance.

Although he has had some plotting problems, Major has generally displayed uncompromising integrity in presenting adolescent life. He is conscious of his potential audience, but he doesn't deliberately design stories to appeal to teenagers. Instead, he is "trying to keep true to the story," even to the point of giving his protagonists "considerable faults": "It's not all glorified from the point of the teenager." Another part of his commitment to truth is his conclusions. "I like to be at least a bit optimistic towards the end," he says, "but not to round them out too much because, basically, life's not like that." By stressing what the characters have learned from their experiences, these somewhat open-ended conclusions thus focus attention on characters, not problems.

The most controversial element of Major's commitment to truth, however, is his blunt use of language and his presentation of drinking, drug use, and sexual experimentation, especially in his first three novels. These topics form the local colour of adolescence, the authentic background for the central characters' struggles to comprehend themselves. Major's presentation of these is never sensationalistic, but his novels have been removed from library shelves and have not been listed by the Newfoundland Board of Education.

Some adults may object to Major's novels, but those willing to read him will find insights into contemporary teens. Teens reading him will find challenging narrative forms and an understanding of the universality of the problems besetting them. All readers will discover novels that bring alive a colourful part of Canada and yet speak forcefully about modern life anywhere in North America. Major has already achieved a significant literary reputation. If he can return to the high standards and originality of his first two novels, he may yet become one of the most important authors of juvenile life.

SECONDARY REFERENCES: *Profiles 2; BIC* (Dec. 84): 24–25; *ChLQ* 10 (Fall 85): 140–41; *SATA* 32; *CA* 97–100; *CLC* 26.

# *Markoosie (1941–        )*

*Harpoon of the Hunter* (1970), the first novel to be written by a Canadian Inuit, is the work of a northern bush pilot, Markoosie, who began writing after reading an Inuit autobiography published in a Canadian government magazine distributed in the North. His adventure-survival saga first appeared in the Inuit periodical *Inuttituut* and was later translated into English and appeared in book form. It has since been published in several languages, receiving high critical acclaim. Markoosie has published a second story in *Inuttituut*, entitled "Wings of Mercy," about an Inuit and a white man who survive the rugged Arctic after an airplane crash. It has not appeared in book form.

*Harpoon of the Hunter* is the story of sixteen-year-old Kamik who joins his father and a party of hunters to destroy a rabid polar bear. Although the animal is finally killed, so too are all the other hunters. The youth, alone and without dogs, makes a long, difficult journey back to his people. Reunited with them, he joins his small village in its move to

a larger community across a wide, swift-flowing river. However, during
the dangerous passage, his mother and new wife are drowned, and Kamik, drifting on a loose ice floe, kills himself in despair.

The book is a consciously, although somewhat roughly, crafted and
structured novel. When Kamik finally kills the bear, he proves his
manhood by avenging the death of his father. Although Kamik's suicide shocks many non-Inuit readers, careful rereading of the novel in
the light of the ending reveals many statements, implicit ironies, and
foreshadowings that show Markoosie never intended a conventional
happy ending, that his novel is a study of grim fortitude in the face of
ever-present death.

The harpoon with which Kamik gathers food, slays the polar bear,
and finally kills himself, symbolizes the confrontation between life and
death. At one point the author notes, "By his side is his harpoon, which
can mean life or death. The harpoon which is so small, yet holds such
power."

Although descriptions of Kamik's relationship with the young woman he marries read a little like a Hollywood romance, *Harpoon of the
Hunter* is powerfully told. The narrative moves inexorably forward to
its tragic conclusion; the descriptions of the animals and landscape
give the reader a clear picture of the dangers of the environment; and
the portrayals of the men and women illustrate their courage and dignity. *Harpoon of the Hunter* has deservedly achieved the status of a
minor Canadian classic.

SECONDARY REFERENCE: *Profiles.*

# *Martchenko, Michael (1942–        )*

One reason for the popularity of Robert Munsch's books is that most of
them have been illustrated by Michael Martchenko, whom the author
has praised as "definitely crazy." Martchenko, head of design for a
Toronto advertising agency, says that, when doing illustrations, he
tries "to make them fun: a bit goofy, bizarre even...." To a large extent
he has succeeded, fusing his wild pictures to the text of the three volumes in Allen Morgan's "Matthew's Midnight Adventure Series" as
well as many of Munsch's stories. Like John Tenniel's pictures for *Alice
in Wonderland* or E. H. Shepard's pictures for *The Wind in the Willows*,
Martchenko's seem to be definitive: they shape our responses and linger in memory. In fact, a good deal of the humour in these books is directly attributable to them.

Martchenko's illustrations owe much to those in the comic books he
avidly read in his native Carcassone, France. His characters are relatively simple, outlined in black, and often identifiable by a salient feature, such as Matthew's curly red hair. He uses bright watercolours,
which make his pictures visually exciting. Martchenko's composition
enhances this excitement in two ways. First, he generally keeps backgrounds simple, often eliminating them entirely in order to focus on

Munsch, Robert. THE PAPER BAG PRINCESS. Ill. by Michael Martchenko. Toronto: Annick Press, 1980. Reprinted with permission by Annick Press Ltd.

foreground action. Secondly, he fills the pictures with mood-creating details, such as the jumbled mess of the bedroom in the opening picture of *Matthew and the Midnight Turkeys* (1985).

Martchenko's cartoon-like drawings are not simple illustrations of the text but, especially in his pictures for Munsch's books, humorous expansions of it, presenting details not mentioned in the text. For example, in *The Paper Bag Princess* (1980), Martchenko creates an absurd anachronism by picturing the haughty Prince Ronald dressed in a crown, tights, medieval boots, and a tennis sweater, and holding a racquet. Similarly, in *The Boy in the Drawer* (1982), he shows only the tail and ears of the cat in the flooded kitchen, and in *Thomas' Snowsuit* (1985), winner of the Ruth Schwartz Award, he makes the hair of the school principal grow progressively whiter, thereby graphically indicating increasing frustration.

Martchenko also frequently employs what he calls a "little visual vignette," a graphic addition to the story's conclusion. Thus, the last picture of *Jonathan Cleaned Up* (1981) shows the mayor's office becoming a subway stop, something implied but not definitely stated in the text. In *David's Father* (1983), the picture of a giant, hairy leg gives concreteness to the punchline about meeting the grandmother. At the end of *Fire Station* (1983), the picture of Sheila dragging Michael to a police station implies that they will have more comical trouble and shows that Sheila has been undaunted by her adventure.

Martchenko has said that, before beginning an illustration, he always asks, "If I were a kid what would I want to see? What would appeal to me?" His answers have been both popular and consistently amusing.
SECONDARY REFERENCE: *QQ* 51 (Oct. 85): 12.

# *Martel, Suzanne (1924– )*

Suzanne Martel is a born storyteller. As a little girl growing up in her native Quebec City, she, together with her sister and author Monique Corriveau, created a long series of fantasies about the Montcorbier family. The stories took place in the imaginary kingdom of Gotal, which resembled the India of Rudyard Kipling, one of the girls' favourite authors. After she was married and began raising a family, Martel began writing stories for her six boys, often using them as central characters. Two of her books won major awards. *Jeanne, fille du roi* (1974) earned the Prix Alvine-Belise for the best French-Canadian children's book, while *Nos amis robots* (1982) won the Canada Council Prize for French-Canadian children's books. In 1976 she won the Vicky Metcalf Award. Four of her children's books have been translated into English: *The City Under Ground* (1964), *The King's Daughter* (1980), *Peewee* (1982), and *Robot Alert* (1985).

In *The City Under Ground*, two pairs of brothers living in a subterranean world built after a nuclear war discover the wonderful world above ground and are instrumental in bringing their people into a new life. In *The King's Daughter*, a French orphan girl comes to seventeenth-century New France, finds a husband and proves her courage. *Peewee* is the story of a young boy who earns a place on the local hockey team. In *Robot Alert*, an English girl living in Vancouver and a French-Canadian boy living in Montreal are instrumental in preventing the destruction of Earth by an alien death star.

Although Martel's stories encompass a variety of genres — science fiction, the historical novel, and the sports story — they reveal common themes and patterns. In each of them, there are a number of parallel characters and situations. In *The City Under Ground*, people of the un-derground and above-ground worlds are ignorant of each other's exist-ence and come to understand their need for each other; Jeanne, the King's Daughter, must leave behind Old France and her dreams of marriage to a wonderful knight for the realities of working with a stern husband in a rugged and dangerous land. Peewee learns that he can succeed against bigger opponents when he uses teamwork. In *Robot Alert*, both English and French children discover that they have common problems and that together they can prevent impending disaster.

In order to reach fulfillment, the central characters must cross frontiers and enter strange and wonderful new worlds. For Luke, Paul, Eric, and Bernard, this means leaving the womb-like security of the underground city and walking in a world erroneously believed to be filled with poisonous gases. Jeanne faces the wildernesses of Canada; Peewee, the roughness of the hockey rink. Adam and Eve do not leave the environs of Vancouver or Montreal, but they communicate with alien beings.

During their adventures, Martel's heroes discover not only their inner strengths but also the value of friendship and love. Working together and learning to accept outsiders — people of different back-grounds and cultures — they are able to grow as individuals. Although their adventures would be outside the experience of their readers, the inner development of these heroes is not unlike that of all young peo-ple. Within the exciting, action-filled plots of her stories, Suzanne Martel has captured the eternal themes of growing up.

SECONDARY REFERENCE: *Emergency Librarian* 12 (May–June 85), 49–51.

# Martin, Eva (1939–      )

Her training as a storyteller and a life-long love of reading were two of the important forces behind the creation of *Canadian Fairy Tales* (1984) by Eva Martin. Born in Woodstock, Ontario, Martin worked for sixteen years as a children's librarian for the Toronto Public Library before assuming the position of Co-ordinator of Services for Children and Young Adults at the City of Scarborough Public Library Board.

In both positions she has worked extensively as a storyteller, telling and retelling the tales that were to make up the collection *Canadian*

*Fairy Tales.* In her notes, she traces the development of the stories from the time they were first brought to the New World by French and English settlers. Within a matter of two or three generations, the European originals were adapted to the new environment, and the forest became an important setting. It was "deep and mysterious...where strange and fearsome creatures prowled and were a constant threat to the well-being of the settlers." In many of the stories, the youthful heroes and heroines journey through dangerous forests.

Four of the stories come from English sources and eight from French. In all of them, children or young adults must pass tests before they can live safely and happily. Often, as is the case of the central characters in "The Healing Spring," "The Three Golden Hairs," and "Ti-Jean and the White Cat," the stories conclude with marriage to a princess. Two of the stories, "Ti-Jean and the White Cat" and "Beauty and the Beast," bear close similarities to French folktales. Martin has made her versions shorter and more tightly organized than her sources, omitting some of the less important details. However, she captures the sense of wonder found in the originals while making the stories accessible to children of the 1980s.

# Montgomery, Lucy Maud (1874–1942)

"I cannot remember when I was not writing, or when I did not mean to be an author. To write has always been my central purpose toward which every effort and hope and ambition of my life has grouped itself." So wrote the creator of Canada's most famous literary heroine, Anne of Green Gables. Lucy Maud Montgomery was born in the little village of Clifton, Prince Edward Island, and lived close by it for all but four of her first thirty-six years.

Outwardly, she led a relatively quiet life. Her mother died when she was two, and her father moved to Saskatchewan when she was six. Maud was raised by older relatives and often felt lonely and isolated. However, she lived a richly imaginative life. She gloried in the scenery of Prince Edward Island, and in her mind she transformed it into a rich fairyland. "I had, in my vivid imagination," she was to write, "a passport to the geography of Fairyland." At age nine, she showed her father a blank verse poem she had composed, and was upset when he told her it was very blank indeed. While she was living with him in Prince Albert, Saskatchewan, "On Cape LeForce," her first published poem, based on a Prince Edward Island legend, was published in the Charlottetown *Daily Patriot*.

From 1894 to 1911, Montgomery taught school, studied English at Dalhousie University in Halifax, worked as a reporter, tended to her aged grandmother, and took an active role in church life. However, she steadfastly pursued her literary career. When teaching, she would get up at six o'clock and write for an hour in an unheated room. In 1895, she received her first payment: five dollars for a story in an American magazine. Her works appeared regularly, and she wrote that by 1904 she had earned nearly six hundred dollars from the sale of stories and poems.

Throughout her life Montgomery kept detailed notebooks of observations and ideas for stories. In 1904, reading over one of the notebooks, she came upon an entry about a couple who applied to an orphanage for a boy and by mistake received a girl. Writing in her spare time over the next year, she created *Anne of Green Gables*, and saw it rejected four times. Returning to it two years later, she sent a revised version to the Boston firm of L. C. Page. It was quickly accepted and published on June 20, 1907. In her journal for that day, she wrote: "Today has been, as Anne herself would say, 'an epoch in my life.' My book came today, 'Spleet-new' from the publishers. I candidly confess that it was to me a proud, wonderful, and thrilling moment. There, in my hand, lay material realization of all the dreams and hopes and ambitions of my whole conscious existence — my first book. Not a great book, but mine, mine, something which I had created." The book sold well and was received favourably. Within the year the publishers had requested a sequel.

*Anne of Avonlea* was published in 1909, and two more books, *Kilmeny of the Orchard* (1910) and *The Story Girl* (1911), appeared before her marriage to Ewan Macdonald, a Presbyterian minister, in 1911. After a honeymoon in England and Scotland, the couple settled in Leaskdale, a small community fifty miles from Toronto. They lived there until 1926, when they moved to Norval, which was closer to Toronto.

After her marriage, Montgomery combined the responsibilities of a minister's wife and young mother with her profession as author. In addition to a book of poems and two adult novels, she wrote seventeen more books for children. Eight are about Anne and her family: *Chronicles of Avonlea* (1912), *Anne of the Island* (1915), *Anne's House of Dreams* (1917), *Rainbow Valley* (1917), *Further Chronicles of Avonlea* (1920), *Rilla of Ingleside* (1921), *Anne of Windy Poplars* (1930), and *Anne of Ingleside* (1939). *Emily of New Moon* (1923), *Emily Climbs* (1925), and *Emily's Quest* (1927) are about Emily Byrd Starr. Pat Gardiner is the heroine of *Pat of Silver Bush* (1933) and *Mistress Pat* (1935). Other children's books were *The Golden Road* (1912), *Magic for Marigold* (1929), *Jane of Lantern Hill* (1937), and *The Road to Yesterday* (1974).

Although wealthy and famous, Montgomery was not completely happy as an author. The continuing demands for sequels about Anne made her feel a prisoner of her heroine. Moreover, during the 1920s she was involved in lengthy and costly law suits against her publisher, who, she charged, had illegally published a group of her stories. At home, she does not seem to have liked the life of a minister's wife. She died in Toronto and was buried in Cavendish Cemetery, Prince Edward Island.

The opening sentence of *Anne of Green Gables* epitomizes the life of Anne Shirley and, in many ways, those of Montgomery's other heroines. "Mrs. Rachel Lynde lived just where Avonlea main road dipped down into a little hollow, fringed with alders and ladies' eardrops and traversed by a brook that had its source way back in the woods of the old Cuthbert place; it was reputed to be an intricate, headlong brook in its earlier course through those woods, with dark secrets of pool and cascade; but by the time it reached Lynde's Hollow it was a quiet, well-conducted little stream, for not even a brook could run past Mrs. Rachel Lynde's door without due regard for decency and decorum...." The stream, lively, independent, and somewhat impulsive, slowing down as it nears civilization, is like the heroines who mature and accept the social values represented by Mrs. Lynde.

For Anne Shirley, the lonely and talkative Nova Scotia orphan, maturity makes her an established member of her Prince Edward Island community, wife of a doctor and mother of a big, usually happy family. However, the road to maturity is not easy for Anne. The early books treat the stages of her development, recounting the setbacks she experiences and the ways in which she learns to understand herself and her community.

When Marilla Cuthbert agrees to keep the talkative and insecure orphan girl early in *Anne of Green Gables*, Anne starts to be socialized. She begins making friends for the first time in her life, calling them "kindred spirits"; she frequently disagrees with both adults and children, finding herself often in trouble because of her active imagination, her impulsiveness, and her fiery temper.

However, Anne doesn't always blunder; she is good, honest, loyal, and responsible, and her most responsible act takes place after Matthew's death, when she gives up a college scholarship so that she can help Marilla keep their home. Some critics feel that in making the heroine grow to responsible young adulthood, the author was compromising, giving in to accepted attitudes towards fiction for girls: she replaced the imaginative, spontaneous little girl with a much more ordinary, socially acceptable young woman.

*Chronicles of Avonlea* presents a year in the life of the seventeen-year-old teacher. Idealistic and full of theories at the beginning of the year, she is still prone to mishaps. Gone, however, is the spontaneous, ingenuous Anne of the first novel. Her adventures seem contrived, and her good-natured altruism seems almost too good to be true. The same criticisms can be levelled against *Anne of the Island*, the account of her years at college.

In *Anne's House of Dreams* the long-awaited marriage to Gilbert Blythe occurs. However, before her marriage there are many conflicts and delays, which the author seems to have employed to prolong the time before the great event. When Anne and Gilbert move into their new home, he begins his medical practice and she cultivates "kindred spirits." During the story, she is able to pave the way for unhappy Leslie Moore to marry author Owen Ford, and she helps Captain Jim publish his book, which becomes the sensation of the season. The later books add little to the heroine's portrait. Montgomery's increasing dislike for writing sequels perhaps accounts for the lessening power of the later books.

Montgomery's second best-known heroine, Emily Byrd Starr, central character of *Emily of New Moon, Emily Climbs*, and *Emily's Quest*, bears some resemblance to Anne: orphaned as a young child, she must move to a new home where, with pride and determination, she achieves happiness. At the end of the third book, she finally and after many misunderstandings, marries the man she has long been interested in. Like her creator, Emily is an author, struggling to achieve success in spite of obstacles she faces as a Canadian writer and a woman.

Specific places are also very important for many of Montgomery's other heroines as they were for Anne. Pat Gardiner, in *Pat of Silver Bush* and *Mistress Pat*, hates change, and early in her life she announces, "I don't want to love anyone or anything but my own family and Silver Bush." However, she must accept many changes — births, deaths, marriages, and, most important, the destruction by fire of her beloved home. For Jane Stuart, of *Jane of Lantern Hill*, happiness comes only when she moves away from her matriarchal grandmother and socialite mother to spend a summer on Prince Edward Island with her father.

Montgomery's heroines do not mature in isolation. They have best friends who are very important and, although it may take them time to realize it, each, with the exception of Jane, has a male companion for whom she is ideally suited. The heroines are also surrounded by older people who influence them and who, in turn, are influenced. The crusty Marilla and shy Matthew are, as it were, brought to life by the little girl they have adopted. Emily gradually wins the heart of her aloof Aunt Elizabeth.

The Prince Edward Island landscape has a great influence on the heroines. On the drive from the station with Matthew, Anne reacts imaginatively to each locale, giving each a new name that, for her, captures its spirit. Emily comes to realize how important New Moon is for her, and Pat names all the fields and groves around Silver Bush. The dreariness of Toronto's misnamed Gay Street depresses Jane; Lantern Hill gives her a new vitality.

In spite of the large number of books Montgomery wrote, she is best remembered for one book and its title character. In *Anne of Green Gables* she undoubtedly created her finest work. Mark Twain called Anne "the dearest, and most loveable child in fiction since the immortal Alice," and the book's admirers have come from many countries, including Japan, where young school children annually delight in reading it. The success in the United States and Canada of the 1985 television special attests to its continued popularity and vitality.

Reasons for the popularity of *Anne of Green Gables* are easily discovered. The central character is fresh and original. She is unconventional, unlike the prim and proper girls who peopled the majority of later nineteenth- and early twentieth-century children's books. The events she becomes involved in are often funny and always moving. The characters she encounters are deftly, vividly portrayed. In addition, beneath the realistic portrayal of Anne and her Prince Edward Island setting is one of the most enduring plot structures of children's literature: the search for security and self-fulfillment. Like the orphans of so many fairy tales, Anne earns her right to a "happy ever after" ending. It is not just the structure of the orphan story that makes the book so appealing; it is also the skill with which the author has dressed the framework, fleshed out the skeleton. In developing the character of Anne and giving her a full life, Montgomery has created the only book of Canadian children's literature that has a secure, established position as an international children's classic.

SECONDARY REFERENCES: *CCL* 3: 4–70; *CCL* 30: 5–20; *CCL* 37: 5–17; *CLR* 8; *Dalhousie Review* 63: 488–501; Mollie Gillen, *The Wheel of Things* (1975); *OCCL*; *Studies in Canadian Literature* 9,2: 158–68; *TCCW* 1; *Yesterday's Authors of Books for Children* 1.

# Morgan, Allen (1946–     )

The major motif and the central plot device of the majority of Allen Morgan's books, including his most successful ones, is the dream. Through dreams, his young protagonists are able to come to terms with their worlds, often overcoming the arbitrary restrictions imposed by adults.

Born in New York City, Morgan studied at Swarthmore College, New York University, and Carnegie Tech Drama School. A conscientious objector during the Vietnam war, he came to Canada in 1968 without graduating. Because of his education and interest in drama, he became a cofounder of *Théâtre Passe Muraille*. He received a BEd with a specialty in early childhood education from the University of British Columbia and taught kindergarten in Surrey, British Columbia, and in Toronto. He became a Canadian citizen in 1974. Morgan has published an adult novel, *Dropping Out in 3/4 Time* (1972), and has had some adult plays produced, but since 1980, when he became a full-time writer, he has devoted most of his attention to works for children.

Morgan's children's books fall into three groups: easy readers, novels, and picture storybooks. The easy readers, part of the Kids-Can-Read series, are limited by a controlled vocabulary. All three use the dream motif to depict a child's understanding of his or her relationship to the world. *Christopher and the Elevator Closet* (1982; illustrated by Franklin Hammond) and its sequel, *Christopher and the Dream Dragon* (1984; illustrated by Brenda Clark), are dream journeys that resemble *pourquoi* tales because they explain such natural phenomena as rain, thunder, lightning, and the phases of the moon. *Molly and Mr. Maloney* (1982; illustrated by Maryann Kovalski), a series of three connected stories, presents life from the viewpoint of a child for whom fantasy is real.

For competent readers, Morgan has written two books suitable for fourth to seventh grade children. *The Kids from B.A.D.* (1984) is a series of six linked stories about the Barton Avenue Detectives, a group of children who solve a number of crimes. Most of the stories are implausible escapist fiction — the stuff of childish daydreams — but one, the story of a boy who steals so that he can have money to bribe people into liking him, contains both the crisp characterization and thematic focus absent in the other stories. *Beautiful Dreamer* (1982) is a problem novel about a twelve-year-old girl who feels alienated because she is unable to make significant financial contributions to her family. Using dream sequences to conclude all but the first and last chapters, the novel successfully explores Katie's feelings of frustration and inadequacy.

Morgan's easy readers and novels have had respectable sales, but his reputation depends upon his picture books. In them he has focused his wit and used to best advantage his dream journey structure. His most satisfying books are those in the "Matthew's Midnight Adventure" series, *Matthew and the Midnight Tow Truck* (1984), *Matthew and the Midnight Turkeys* (1985), and *Matthew and the Midnight Money Van* (1987), all whimsically illustrated by Michael Martchenko. Each book follows the same pattern. During the day, something happens to Matthew that inspires a series of adventures "just after midnight." The next morning, Matthew tells his beleaguered mother about his adventures and provides her with some physical sign of them. The first in the series is the most tightly plotted. Matthew, having lost a toy van and having been refused red licorice for dessert, goes out after midnight with a tow-truck driver who believes licorice builds muscles. When Matthew awakens the next morning, he has his van, and his mother, hearing of the need for red licorice, takes him to the store. In *Matthew and the Midnight Turkeys*, Matthew, criticized for his behaviour during the day, joins a group of turkeys, whose silly manner of playing and eating satirizes adult-imposed rules of decorum. He leaves an unusually messy kitchen for his mother to discover the next morning. In *Matthew and the Midnight Money Van*, he goes to a midnight mall to buy a Mother's Day present, which he discovers the next day hidden in a box of cereal.

Morgan's other picture storybooks are less successful, lacking the energy and wit of the Matthew books. *Daddy-Care* (1986; illustrated by John Richmond) is simply an extended joke reversing the normal pattern of adult-child relationships. *Sadie and the Snowman* (1985; illustrated by Brenda Clark) is an uninspired and predictable story of a girl who saves some melted snow from a snowman to form the basis of a new snowman the following year. *Barnaby and Mr. Ling* (1984; illustrated by Franklin Hammond), designed as a kind of fairy tale about an elephant and a peanut man who run away from a circus to live out their dreams, falters on the sentimentality inherent in its open-ended conclusion, an overt invitation for the reader to join the characters in their dream. *Nicole's Boat: A Good-Night Story* (1986; illustrated by Jirina Marton) suffers from the same problem. Its initial sections are folkloric in structure as, in turn, a crow, a cow, and some kittens join Nicole on her boat sailing "to the end of the day." Each makes a contribution to the boat (the illustrations show it altering in size and changing in design), which eventually reaches the sea. The book ends with the narrator-father inviting the sleeping Nicole to bring back to him stories of all that she sees on the sea of night. Obviously designed as a soporific to lure children into sleep, the book lacks a plot that would invite rereading or make it satisfying except at bedtime.

Allen Morgan's work is uneven in quality. His books often succumb to sentimentality, especially those with open-ended conclusions. His best work, the "Matthew's Midnight Adventure" series, uses the dream motif evident in most of his books, but he uses it, without winking and nudging at his audience, to create an ironic view. To children, that is, he presents Matthew's comical adventures as real, but permits the adult to see them as imaginative dream journeys. In this way, the books can repeatedly satisfy both children and the adults who read and reread to them.

SECONDARY REFERENCE: *QQ* 51 (Aug. 85): 32.

# Mowat, Farley (1921–        )

Farley Mowat is unique in being a writer almost as popular with children as he is with adults. An internationally successful author who has cultivated a reputation for being colourful and controversial, he approaches the task of writing for children with a distinctly moral attitude: "A good book for youngsters can influence the whole future life of the young reader.... I happen to believe that it is an absolute duty for good writers to devote a significant part of their time and talent to writing for young people." For Mowat, the task is "of absolutely vital importance if basic changes for the good are ever to be initiated in any human culture." Although obviously concerned that literature convey a message, Mowat is not forbiddingly didactic. He has, in fact, on numerous occasions insisted that he is, first and foremost, a storyteller: "In another time I might have been a Saga-man. Perhaps that's really what I am today."

Mowat, presented with the Vicky Metcalf Award in 1970, has written four books for children, but at least two others have found an audience among them. His books suitable for children fall into three groups. First are three children's adventure novels — *Lost in the Barrens* (1956), *The Black Joke* (1962), and *The Curse of the Viking Grave* (1966) — that obviously suit Mowat's sense of saga, for they are filled with perilous and exciting adventures and with deeds of heroism. Next are two stories of domesticated animals, *Owls in the Family* (1961), a children's book, and the adult work upon which it is based, *The Dog Who Wouldn't Be* (1957). The third group, best represented by *Never*

*Cry Wolf* (1963), concerns wild animals and people's relation to them. All of these are dedicated to storytelling as a way of advancing the ecological, anthropological, and historical concerns that dominate Mowat's work.

The concern for nature is evident throughout Mowat's books. Born in Belleville, Ontario, he spent a significant portion of his well-travelled childhood in Saskatoon, where he came to know the Prairie and its wildlife. By the time he was thirteen he was writing a regular newspaper column on birds. When Mowat was fourteen his great-uncle, Walter Farley, an amateur ornithologist, took him along on a field trip to The Pas to study arctic birds, introducing Mowat to the northern setting of *Lost in the Barrens*, and igniting in him a lifelong passion for the North. After serving with the Canadian army during World War II, Mowat returned to Canada and began studying biology at the University of Toronto. While working towards his BA at the University of Toronto, he was hired by the federal government to study the wolf and caribou situation in Keewatin. Fired for becoming involved in the problems of the Native peoples of the area, Mowat began work on a short story that formed the basis for his first book, *People of the Deer* (1952), a controversial chronicle of the vanishing Ihalmiut, the inland Inuit of the Barrens.

The concerns for the North developed in his various excursions there and expressed in *People of the Deer* form the underpinnings for two conventional Arctic survival stories, *Lost in the Barrens* and its sequel, *The Curse of the Viking Grave*. *Lost in the Barrens*, which won both the Governor General's Award for juvenile literature and the CACL Medal, and was named to the Hans Christian Andersen International Award Honors List, is far more successful artistically and thematically. A maturation tale, it is the story of Jamie Macnair, a white orphan, and Awasin Meewasin, the son of a Cree chief, who are forced to spend the winter on the Barrens when they foolishly become separated from a hunting party. In order to survive, they must understand themselves, each other, and the resources of the seemingly hostile land. They discover, as Awasin makes clear, that if man humbly submits to nature, even arctic nature will nurture him: "If you fight against the spirits of the north you will always lose. Obey their laws and they'll look after you." In addition to the ecological theme, the novel treats themes of racial prejudice and tolerance. Jamie, at first impatient of some Native beliefs, becomes more mature and more capable of survival as he comes to accept traditional Native wisdom.

In *Lost in the Barrens*, Mowat uses conventional characterization and events, but it is still exciting and meaningful reading. *The Curse of the Viking Grave*, which Mowat has called a "potboiler" and "a really bad piece of work," uses the same materials but lacks a meaningful narrative. Threatened with being sent to the south for schooling, Jamie, accompanied by Awasin, Peetyuk, and Angeline, Awasin's sister, flees from the police (we learn at the end that they do not want, as he thinks, to put him in an orphanage) and heads north to find a Viking treasure. The novel contains speculation about the Norse discovery of Canada, discussion on the plight of the Ihalmiut, and even a denunciation of white treatment of the Natives, but none of this is well integrated into the plot. Even the curse of the title, which has no effect on anyone, weakens the book by making the traditional Inuit seem somewhat foolish.

In his other adventure, *The Black Joke*, Mowat eschewed the attempt at packing the tale with relevance and created a gripping tale of piracy during the Depression. Three boys with different ethnic backgrounds heroically recover a ship that a wily businessman has taken away from an honest Newfoundland fisherman.

Mowat's tales of domesticated animals lean to humorous narrative. *The Dog Who Wouldn't Be* is an episodic biography of Mutt, a mongrel who "concluded that there was no future in being a dog." An eccentric animal who learned to walk fences like a cat, proved to be a "Prince Albert retriever" who would even bring back stuffed birds from the hardware store, and rode happily in the rumble seat while wearing driving goggles, Mutt is a source of joy and hilarious consternation for his owners. *Owls in the Family* highlights the amusing antics of two owls. The more outgoing one, Wol, receives most attention: he contributes a dead skunk to the family dinner, frightens a minister, and follows Billy (the Farley persona in this version) to school. Central to the book is a nostalgic look at boyhood when one could be close to nature and find in it friendship and happiness that one thought could never end.

Somewhere between the fictional adventure tales and the fictionalized animal autobiographies is *Never Cry Wolf*, an account of the wolf study that changed Mowat's life. An attempt to deflate the myth of the wolf as a ferocious killer, the book uses both realistic reporting of animal behaviour and pointed satire to make its case. The account of wolf behaviour, realistic and closely observed in the tradition of Roberts and Seton, shows that the wolves do not wantonly kill but actually keep the caribou stock healthy by removing its weaker members. The satire is double-pronged. Part of it is directed at governments and bureaucracies, which foster the wolf myth and refuse to accept the lessons learned by observation. Part of it is directed at Mowat himself as a naive believer in the myth. His change of attitude in the face of the government's resistance to change is a powerful appeal for men to respect nature for what it actually is instead of fearing it for what it might be.

As an adventure writer, Mowat relies on the trusted formula of the journey into troubles that test and mature young boys. His characters are not psychologically deep, but they do work as vehicles for communicating Mowat's love of nature and his respect for the rights of all people, but especially Natives. Mowat's nonfiction has often been attacked as exaggeration, but it is undeniably entertaining and often educational. Certainly he has added to Canadian literature animal characters who linger in the memory, and he has been instrumental in making many adults and children sensitive to the claims of nature. Above all, he has shown that adventure is everywhere and has achieved his goal of bringing to young readers "the feeling that life is very much worth living."

SECONDARY REFERENCES: *Profiles 2*; *TCCW 2*; *CCL* 5/6: 40–51; *Canada Writes!*

## Muller, Robin (1953–      )

When Toronto-born author-artist Robin Muller was a teenager, he took a summer job and discovered his calling. Working in a publisher's warehouse, he spent hours browsing among the books and realized that he would like to write and illustrate stories. In high school he edited an alternate newspaper that printed poetry, fiction, and reviews, and during the 1960s he lived for four years in Toronto's Yorkville district, selling his paintings on the street. Later he built a career as a successful artist, exhibiting paintings in Canada, the United States, and Europe.

It was not until 1982 that his first book, *Mollie Whuppie and the Giant*, was published. Like Muller's two succeeding works, *Tatterhood* (1984) and *The Sorcerer's Apprentice* (1985), it is an adaptation of a traditional tale. Although each of the stories is from a different European country and each deals with a different type of central character, the three books share several characteristics. None rigidly follows sources, Muller often supplying original plot material and characterization. All focus on the growth to maturity of young characters who successfully pass tests. In each, strong female characters play important roles. Finally, in all of the books Muller's illustrations contribute significantly to tone and characterization.

In portraying the British folktale heroine Mollie Whuppie, Muller emphasizes her cleverness and courage from the opening scene. But she is not just a clever trickster: she has other people's interests at heart. She willingly exposes herself to danger so that her sisters can have fine husbands.

Muller's twenty full-page black-and-white illustrations emphasize the heroic dimensions of Mollie's character. Although in nearly every illustration she is the smallest figure, she is by no means the meekest: her facial expressions, body language, and position in relation to others indicate her leadership. Mollie's facial expressions are particularly effective in portraying her varying emotions.

The title character of the Finnish Tale *Tatterhood* is also a strong heroine. Born to a mother who had disobeyed a witch's instructions, the girl is wild and boisterous, riding a goat about the palace, banging a huge wooden spoon, and yelling. But she is devoted to her younger sister, and when, as a result of the mother's foolishness, a group of

Muller, Robin. MOLLIE WHUPPIE AND THE GIANT. Richmond Hill:
North Winds Press, 1982. Published by Scholastic-TAB Ltd.

witches take her sister's head and replace it with a cow's head, she fearlessly sets out to recover it. At the conclusion of the story she has earned the love of the prince she marries.

Muller's full-colour illustrations are major vehicles of characterization. The ineffectual mother wanders around with melancholy, fearful, or distraught looks; Belinda, lovely, good, and passive, is generally seen smiling gently. In each illustration a different expression reveals the heroine's changing emotions. At first she is merely wild looking, a very large uncontrolled baby. But she smiles happily at her baby sister, an indication of the love that will take her on her dangerous voyage. Along the way she is angry, determined, pensive, and, when she first sees her prince, intrigued. At the end she is pictured as a beautiful, radiant young woman. She no longer wears the green hood that provided her nickname; now she wears a royal blue gown and her shining black hair cascades over her shoulders.

*The Sorcerer's Apprentice* bears little similarity to the German tale from which it takes its name. Although it deals with a poor boy who seeks work from a sorcerer and is warned not to read the books of magic spells, it is, as Muller has remarked, really about the value of learning to read and write. In the opening paragraph, readers are told that Robin, although he was poor and had no trade, "was clever and brave and, what was more, he could read and write." When he learns that the sorcerer plans to take over the neighbouring kingdom, Robin uses these skills, risking terrible punishment to save the day. Once again a strong heroine is instrumental in the resolution of the conflict. The wizard's dove, a princess wickedly transformed to keep her from claiming the throne, helps Robin and gives him the advice necessary for him to grow into the mature young man he is at the end.

Muller's ink- and pencil-crayon pictures represent his best use of illustration to enhance mood, theme, and characterization. For example, the first and last illustrations are in sharp contrast. As he wanders through a dark, terrifying forest at the story's beginning, Robin is small, vulnerable, and somewhat bewildered. Finally, as he stands at the edge of the meadow beside the princess, he is a stronger, wiser individual.

Although Muller has published only three children's books, he has revealed not only his artistic abilities but also his talents as a visual and verbal reteller of traditional tales. He is certainly deserving of the reputation he has quickly established.

# Munsch, Robert (1945–        )

Although he is one of the most successful authors of children's books in Canada, Robert Munsch is not really a writer. Munsch does not, that is, sit down to compose literary works for publication. From conception to final publication, his books have roots deep in the oral tradition of storytelling, beginning as tales delivered to audiences of children. Not

Munsch, Robert. THOMAS' SNOWSUIT. Ill. by Michael Martchenko.
Toronto: Annick Press, 1985. Reprinted with permission by Annick Press Ltd.

all are planned in advance. By observing his listeners' reactions, Munsch modifies his tales, removing things that fail and refining things that work. Eventually he commits the most successful to writing. Not surprisingly, given this genesis, Munsch insists that his books "always have to be read aloud."

Born in Pittsburgh, Pennsylvania, Munsch earned a BA in history from Fordham University, an MA in anthropology from Boston University, and an MEd in child studies from Tufts University. Munsch has said that he began telling tales in daycare centres while working on his MA, but that he really learned his craft when working at a childcare centre in Coos Bay, Oregon, where he told stories without using books in order to keep the children on their cots at nap time. He learned to be inventive because the children constantly demanded new tales. In 1976, he moved to Canada and taught in the Department of Family Studies at the University of Guelph before he decided to devote himself full-time to practising his art in books, recordings, and, of course, appearances as a storyteller.

Munsch, who estimates that his repertoire of stories now numbers five hundred, is acutely aware of the difference between storytelling and writing. "When you storytell," he says, "you have your presence there and it's possible to keep kids interested in a story that isn't publishable." The appeal of many of Munsch's stories, in fact, depends heavily on facial expressions, body movement, and strange noises: "A lot of my oral style," he says, "is sound effects." Furthermore, his recordings, *Robert Munsch: "Favourite Stories"* (1983) and *Murmel Murmel Munsch: More Outrageous Stories* (1984), reveal that for him storytelling is something of a communal performance. By lingering over the initial sounds of the words "yes" and "no" or by cueing his audience to repeated phrases with a slow, drawn-out mouthing of the first part of the phrase, he gets children to participate in the telling.

Munsch admits that "you lose a lot of that in the translation to book form." He tries, however, to give some sense of the language in his later books. The speech of the giant in *David's Father* (1983) — except where indicated, all of his books have been illustrated by Michael Martchenko — is thus presented in italicized capital letters to suggest his size. When he yells, the letters are dark, large, and slightly distorted, as if they were shaking on the page. In *Thomas' Snowsuit* (1985), Munsch typographically indicates both childish defiance and the way he stretches out words: "NNNNNO." For the most part, however, Munsch's texts lack printed symbols for the various voices, cries, and sounds he adds when telling the tales himself.

What does survive translation to the printed page is a style that owes much to traditional folktales. In particular, Munsch uses repetition of phrase and episode as the primary building-blocks of his stories. In *Mortimer* (1983), for instance, the obstreperous Mortimer is characterized by the memorable chant, "Bang-bang, rattle-ding-bang, goin' to make my noise all day!" Episodic repetition, with the last episode being a climactic variation, is evident in *50 Below Zero* (1986), in which Jason finds his sleepwalking father on the refrigerator, then on the car, and finally outside frozen. A final twist comes when Jason, having thawed and secured his father, ends up sleepwalking himself.

The secret of Munsch's appeal is not, however, in his use of repetition but in his development of plots that comically exaggerate a child's dilemmas. Munsch told an interviewer for the CBC's *The Journal* that children identify with his stories because "my stories are about everyday experiences for kids — going to bed, getting new clothes, getting dirty, having a new baby, cleaning up their own rooms — they're about everyday experiences, only the kids win."

The very best of his stories are hero tales in which the child achieves victory through bravery and wit. *Mud Puddle* (1979; illustrated by Sami Suomalainen), his first published book, shows the pattern. By personifying a mud puddle and making it a villain, this story hilariously makes literal the kind of excuse children offer for getting dirty so often. Jule Ann is bathed by her mother and dressed in clean clothes again and again, but a mud puddle always leaps on her. The story is completely satisfying in technique and theme. Repetition of the basic episode suggests Jule Ann's growing frustration and the power of her antagonist. Cumulative repetition — the mother adds a new body part for special washing each time — indicates the extended time required to restore Jule Ann to cleanliness after each attack. The conclusion is symbolically appropriate. It shows that Jule Ann has matured enough to learn that soap destroys dirt and that she no longer has to rely on mother to keep her clean.

Perhaps the most engaging of his hero tales and one likely to become a Canadian classic is *The Paper Bag Princess* (1980), a witty modern variation on the traditional dragon tale. Elizabeth, a princess wearing a paper bag because a dragon burned all her clothes, tracks down the dragon, tricks it into fatiguing itself, and rescues her captured fiancé, Prince Ronald. The conclusion, a twist on romantic fairy tales, provides a significant statement about appearance and reality. When Prince Ronald arrogantly tells her to come back when she is not so messy, she rejects him as a "bum" and decides not to marry him. In stressing the girl's heroic determination and wit, the story thus shows that a person's worth is not obvious from appearance.

Another successful hero tale is *Jonathan Cleaned Up, Then He Heard a Sound, or Blackberry Subway Jam* (1981), a satire on bureaucracies, in which Jonathan outwits the mayor after the city declares that Jonathan's house is a subway stop. Other hero stories, such as *The Dark* (1979; illustrated by Sami Suomalainen), about a child's fear of the dark; *The Boy in the Drawer* (1982), about a tiny boy who grows when people attack him and completely disappears when they express love for him; and *Murmel Murmel Murmel* (1982), about a girl who tries to give away a baby that has mysteriously appeared in her sandbox, do not succeed.

Silliness and exaggeration are central to another group of Munsch's tales. Typically in these, adults, unable to maintain composure, end up running around in frenzied circles when opposed or confused. Children maintain perfect control. The most entertaining are *Mortimer*, in which a sequence of adults unsuccessfully try to get Mortimer to be quiet and go to sleep, and *Thomas' Snowsuit*, winner of the Ruth Schwartz Award, in which a teacher and a principal who are trying to get Thomas to wear a snowsuit end up wearing each other's clothes. Adults as well as children will recognize the situation in *I Have To Go!* (1986), in which young Andrew, who has to pee at the most awkward times on a trip to grandmother's, insists he doesn't need to go to the bathroom at bedtime and ends up wetting the bed. In *Moira's Birthday* (1987), a party gets wildly out of control when Moira, against her parents' wishes, invites everyone in her school. Unlike her parents, Moira is perfectly capable of coping with the situation.

In contrast to the inspired silliness of these books are mechanical stories like *Angela's Airplane* (1983), about how Angela accidentally flies a plane, and *Fire Station* (1983), about how Michael and Sheila, on a visit to a fire station, are accidentally taken to a fire. Such stories lack satisfying resolutions to conflict; they stop instead of concluding.

*Millicent and the Wind* (1984; illustrated by Suzanne Duranceau) and *Love You Forever* (1986; illustrated by Sheila McGraw) are Munsch's only books without humour. The former, the story of a lonely child who gets the wind to bring her a playmate, is a hackneyed, sentimental tale. The latter, an attempt to show the continuity of parental love over the generations, becomes mired in sentimentality. Both books show by negative example that Munsch needs the humour of exaggeration to make his tales work.

At his best, Munsch, winner of the 1987 Vicky Metcalf Award, tells entertaining stories that succeed as books. The hero tales and the silly tales satirizing adult-child relationships amuse both children and adults. Memorable in language and structure, they invite further readings.

SECONDARY REFERENCES: *Profiles 2*; *CCL* 33: 46–47; *QQ* 48 (May 82): 37; *BIC* 10 (Dec. 81): 5; *TCCW* 2.

# N ewfeld, Frank (1928–          )

"When I first consider a book I'm going to design or illustrate, I don't think page by page. Instead, I visualize a concertina — I see all the pages stretched out one after the other. I make thumbnail sketches on long strips of paper, trying to find the overall rhythm of the book. Each illustration has to be seen in terms of all those that come before or after it." This is the approach of Frank Newfeld, Canada's foremost book designer and the illustrator of two of the most popular of all Canadian children's books, Dennis Lee's *Alligator Pie* (1974) and *Nicholas Knock* (1974).

Newfeld, who was born in Czechoslovakia, became interested in art after his family moved to England in 1937. He remembers that he spoke with an accent, but that there was no noticeable accent in his drawings. He studied at the Brighton School of Art and the Central School of Arts and Crafts in England and later at Atelier 17 in Paris. He worked briefly as a costume designer at a London theatre, but left the job, he says, when both he and his employers recognized his limited future in the profession.

Newfeld moved to Canada in 1948 and for several years taught art at high schools and colleges in Toronto. He also established himself as a book designer, winning many international awards. During the 1960s and 1970s he held the positions of Art Director, Vice President of Publishing, and member of the board of directors for the firm of McClelland and Stewart. He published his first picture book, *The Princess of Tomboso*, an adaptation of a French-Canadian fairytale, in 1960. However, it was not until 1974 that he illustrated his next children's books, *Alligator Pie* and *Nicholas Knock*. For his work on *Alligator Pie* he was named to the prestigious Hans Christian Andersen International Award Honors List, and for his illustrations to *Garbage Delight* (1977), his third collaboration with Dennis Lee, he received the Ruth Schwartz Award. *Simon and the Golden Sword* (1976) was his own adapted and illustrated version of an oral tale he had heard while travelling in New Brunswick. His most recent illustrated book for children, *The Night the City Sang*, a collection of Christmas poems by Peter Desbarts, appeared in 1977.

*The Princess of Tomboso* reveals the essential features of Newfeld's art, but in an undeveloped form. Often several illustrations appear on a page, providing a visual parallel to the repetitive language of the folktale. However, in abridging the text of this story about a youngest son who outwits a clever and greedy princess, he omits important elements of characterization: the two older brothers' desire for wealth and power and the princess's greed for apples, a trait that leads to her undoing. The highly stylized illustrations fail to reveal the personalities of the characters.

The design and illustrations for *Alligator Pie* and *Nicholas Knock* reveal Newfeld's art at its finest. He did not see the poems until they were in their final form and, with one or two exceptions, in the sequences in which they were to appear in the published volumes. He began his task with a basic premise: "The book is the author's, not the illustrator's." Thus, in dealing with individual poems, he did not try to extend the meanings in the way that an author-illustrator might with his own work: "I didn't want to interrupt the poem. I wanted to let the poet finish the poem and then let the children look at the picture. In many ways, what I was trying to do in the illustrations was to present a reaction to the poems, not an interpretation."

For *Alligator Pie*, Newfeld saw his job as responding to the play of the young child, the joys of youthful imagination, and the sense of security in the familiar world — all elements contained in the poems. The cover depicts a gaily coloured balloon carrying four passengers: an alligator, two children, and a Mountie. Their happiness as they float upward hints at the sense of liberation found in the book. The green of the endpapers is not only appropriate for alligators, but also for the natural vitality of the child's spirit.

The continuity of the themes in the book is reinforced by the visual patterns of circles and arcs. The dominant circle is the sun, which illuminates the children's achievements, their escapes from limitations. Many of the arcs are rainbows of happy colours.

Although *Nicholas Knock* is a companion volume, its tone is a contrasting one: in many of the poems repression and restriction stand in the way of the speakers' searches for fulfillment. The visual differences to *Alligator Pie* are immediately apparent. Instead of a full-colour, full-page cover illustration, there is an orange cloth cover with a hooded executioner standing in the corner, his arms folded over an enormous axe. Beside him, the chopping block reads, "For Nicholas." The endpapers are a dull brown rather than a lively green, and brown is the dominant colour in many of the illustrations. We find nowhere the gaiety, the sense of discovery, or the idea of the child controlling his own destiny. Instead, there are hints of punishment, containment, and dullness. While the motifs of circles and arcs are also found in *Nicholas Knock*, the circles most often create impressions of confinement. The sense of loneliness found in many of the poems is emphasized by the fact that seventeen of the illustrations depict only a single living figure.

The illustrations for "Nicholas Knock," the title poem, reveal Newfeld's great skill in using colour, design, and spacing. Six of the illustrations are brown, and brown dominates the other two, as is appropriate for the generally sombre tone. The rectangle is the dominant figure, serving as border to five of the pictures; a near rectangle surrounds another. Like the illustrations, Nicholas is often boxed in by the adults of the poem. In the first illustration, Nicholas's house is grimly angular, the trees are bare, and there is no sign of life in the house or on the street.

After the hero is led to the Supreme Court for refusing to deny his friend, two rectangular illustrations with solid backgrounds present

disapproving doctors and policemen. The pressures of the adults surround Nicholas just as the illustrations surround the text. An illustration stretching across the bottom of two pages contains a variety of
military personnel advancing, all firing weapons, which once again reinforces the idea that Nicholas is subject to incredible pressures. No
illustration shows the lonely Nicholas at the end patrolling Bloor
Street searching for his friend. Instead, the final illustration, a small
one at the end of the poem, is of a gavel. At first, it might seem to be
reinforcing the idea of adult power. More probably, it is meant to emphasize the command given by the poet to the reader: if you should see
Nicholas, "Don't bother him! He's hunting for / A silver honkabeest."

*Simon and the Golden Sword*, the only picture book for which
Newfeld has created both words and text, is a folktale about a youngest
son who, in spite of being scorned and mistreated by his older brothers,
passes a series of dangerous tests, rescues a princess, earns a golden
sword, and inherits his father's farm. Because he had complete control
of visuals and verbals, Newfeld was, he remarked, "able to balance the
pictures and text as I pleased. I made the pictures tell more of the story
and I could leave elements out of the words." The book is more successful than *The Princess of Tomboso* in embodying the stylized quality of
folktales. Contrasts in facial expressions and body language reveal the
differences between the brothers. The opulence of the castle is balanced against the poverty of the little farm.

The opening and closing illustrations are particularly effective. As
Simon and his brothers leave the farm, they are placed at opposite
sides of the picture. Simon, wearing plain clothes and carrying a bundle on a stick, smiles at his brothers, who look disdainfully at him over
their shoulders. They wear foppish eighteenth-century clothing. The
illustration is bare of other details. At the conclusion, the brothers
occupy the same positions on the page. However, Simon is now in the
foreground, embracing his father, who points at the other brothers as
they slouch away. Between the two groups is a sunflower plant whose
bright colour symbolizes Simon's new prosperity and happiness.

Although Newfeld as the illustrator of others' texts acknowledges
his responsibility to the author, he feels his greatest responsibility is to
the child who is the reader/viewer. "You could say," he has noted, "that
there are four books in every volume I've worked on. One is by the creator of the words; another, by the illustrator; a third results from the
marriage of the pictures and the text. But the most important is the
fourth one which is created by the reader. I have a real responsibility to
the children who read the books and look at my illustrations. I have to
give them freedom to react and to add to the pictures in their own
minds. Only when they can and do accomplish this do I really feel I've
been successful."

SECONDARY REFERENCES: *BIC* 6 (Nov. 77): 9–11; *CCL* 17: 3–19;
*CCL* 39/40: 72–79; *Profiles; SATA* 26; *TCCW* 2.

# Nichol, b[arrie] p[hillip] (1944–        )

One of the leading experimental writers in Canada, bp Nichol was born in Vancouver. After receiving an Elementary Basic Teaching Certificate from the University of British Columbia in 1963, he taught for a year and then moved to Toronto, working first as a book research-er and then as a therapist. He has also been a scriptwriter for the *Fraggle Rock* television series. Best known for his concrete and sound poetry — especially through his participation in the Four Horsemen, an experimental poetry performance group — bp Nichol has explored the physical, aural, and syntactical properties of language. In 1971 he received the Governor General's Award for his poetry for adults.

Although they are not at all experimental, most of bp Nichol's children's books display the same love of sound and rhythm that is characteristic of his adult works. This is particularly evident in *Giants, Moosequakes & Other Disasters* (1985), an enlarged and slightly revised edition of his first children's work, *Moosequakes and Other Disasters* (1981). Heavily dependent on rhyme and alliteration, many of the poems are reminiscent of the bouncy schoolyard chants in Dennis Lee's *Alligator Pie*. The poems here, however, are aimed at a much wider range of ages, and their nonsense humour is sometimes awk-wardly forced. Still, the collection has some bright moments and con-tains some works that demand reading aloud.

Nichol's other children's books are single, unified works. *ONCE: A Lullaby*, a repetitive, rhythmic bedtime book in which a number of ani-mals make characteristic sounds before falling asleep, has been issued twice. The 1983 Canadian edition, with simple, spare drawings by Ed Roach, pales before the lavish American edition of 1986, which con-tains richly detailed, full-colour pictures by Anita Lobel. *The Man Who Loved His Knees* (1983) is an unusual prose fable crudely illustrated by bp Nichol himself. It tells of George, a man who learned to love his knees — and ostensibly himself — even more once he discovered that he could put his knees to use helping a stationary flower to move around and be happy. Nichol's most sucessful children's book, *To the End of the Block* (1984), illustrated by Shirley Day, is a simple rhymed poem about a father and daughter taking a walk. This is a unified work because the pictures complement the text, illustrating actions not mentioned by the words and thereby adding humour to the situations. The conclusion is open-ended: the text ends in mid-sentence, and the picture shows the tired but happy father sitting to think about whether he will again walk "one more block" with his indefatigable daughter. This ending emphasizes the rhythmic, repetitive action of the story as well as the characters of both father and daughter.

Nichol strains to be funny or meaningful in his work for children past the second grade. He is far more successful in writing for preschoolers. His strength is his sensitivity to the sounds and rhythms of language, and his ability to create works that are a pleasure to read aloud.

SECONDARY REFERENCES: *CLC* 18; *CA* 53–56; *OCCL*.

## Nichols, Ruth (1948–          )

When she was a young child, Ruth Nichols created a series of fantasy/ adventure cycles about her dolls; when she was fourteen, she received a Government of India prize for a one-hundred-page biography of Catherine de Medici; in 1969, when she was twenty-one, she published *Ceremony of Innocence*, an adult novel, and *A Walk Out of the World*, a children's novel; and by the time she was thirty, this precocious and dedicated writer had published three more children's novels: *The Marrow of the World* (1972), winner of the CACL Award; *Song of the Pearl* (1976); and *The Left-Handed Spirit* (1978). Born in Toronto, she received a BA from the University of British Columbia and MA and PhD degrees in Religious Studies from McMaster University.

Early in her life Nichols decided she wanted to be a writer; but like many aspiring authors, she received many rejection slips before *A Walk Out of the World* was published. A fantasy that reveals the influence of J. R. R. Tolkien and C. S. Lewis, it is the story of Judith and Tobit, a lonely and unhappy sister and brother who are mysteriously transported into another world. They engage in a dangerous and important quest to help restore the rightful rulers to the throne. Judith takes the initiative, announcing, "I do not know how we were brought here, but I know why. It is we who must end Hagerrak's reign. Only so will the circle be made complete." During their successful adventure they mature and grow in self-knowledge. Judith, who during much of the novel had wanted to remain in the alternate universe, realizes that her place is back in this world, with the parents who love her.

Like *A Walk Out of the World*, *The Marrow of the World* deals with children transported into an alternate universe. However, the characters are older, and the problems they face are more complex. Linda and Philip are teenaged cousins who spend their summers at a Northern Ontario lake. The boy admires his cousin's strength of character and wonders about her identity — she is an orphan. When they are transported into the world of Linda's birth, Linda's supernatural powers grow, and Philip is virtually powerless to control or help her as she struggles to define her identity and her loyalties. At the conclusion, she has resolved her conflicts, and Philip has learned an important lesson: "No human being can possess another." Even though he loves her, he must allow her to choose her own identity.

In *Song of the Pearl*, Nichols departs from the conventions of high fantasy. Writing for older readers about a heroine who must confront her complex and conflicting attitudes to her personality, Nichols needed a looser form of fantasy, one which allowed deeper analysis of character. The heroine, Margaret Redmond, dies early in the novel. Seventeen years old, she is filled with anger and hatred towards herself and her uncle, whose lustful advances she had encouraged. The action of the novel takes place in heaven, where Margaret is told, "You must read the riddle of yourself." During the course of the action she encounters earlier reincarnations of herself, and faces her responsibility for her actions and attitudes in those lives. When she is reborn at the end of the novel, she has the self-knowledge necessary to lead a fulfilling life. The novel marks a significant advance in Nichols' writing because she deals with difficult emotions and conflicts and gives new depth to themes she has been treating since her earliest works.

In *The Left-Handed Spirit*, which also traces a young woman's growth to maturity, Nichols uses a different genre, the historical novel. Set during the reign of Emperor Marcus Aurelius, it is the story of Mariana, an orphan who has no knowledge of her parents or her exact age. When she learns that she possesses healing powers, the gift of the god Apollo, Mariana is both frightened and angry. Only when she is kidnapped by Paulus, an ambassador from the Chinese court, and taken to China does she realize that her gifts are not for herself alone and that she is responsible for the consequences of her actions. Although not literally fantasy, the novel employs many elements found in the earlier works: the influence of powerful supernatural forces, the journey through strange exotic lands, and the confrontation with earlier states of existence.

In her essay "Fantasy: the Interior Landscape," Nichols makes several observations that cast light on the techniques, themes, and characters of her works. Writers of fantasy possess special ability; they have "somehow preserved a *habit of access* to the subconscious which has become unfortunately rare in modern culture." As a result they are able to draw on powers that the rationalistic, mechanistic modern world has repressed or ignored, powers that must be used if the individual is to be healthy and complete. Fantasy embodies these forces and thus "can provide an instinctive correction...to the excesses of the dominant culture." In reading a fantasy, one is sharing the author's awareness of "the essential coherence, wonder, and loving energy which he perceives to permeate existence." Reading has the result of awakening the reader's awareness of these forces within himself.

An examination of the characters, actions, and settings of Nichols' four novels for children and young adults indicates the basic nature of the inner qualities that must be faced and understood if human fulfillment is to be achieved.

Each of Nichols' major characters is young, isolated, and lacking in self-knowledge. She has said, "The youth of my heroes has always been merely a guise for the questing soul." Their ages are also symbolic of their states of being. Even Margaret, who in earlier incarnations has been married several times, is not yet mature, a state symbolized by the fact that, when she dies, she is only seventeen years old. Only after her long journey across the Near and Far East does Mariana of *The Left-Handed Spirit* achieve true adulthood.

The incompleteness of these characters is partially indicated by the fact that they are exiles from their homes. Tobit and Judith have literally descended from an exiled king; Linda has been transported to our world by her evil half-sister; Margaret is a wanderer; and Mariana feels rootless during her long absence from Rome. As a result of their long, arduous, and dangerous quests the characters discover their true homes.

Particularly in *A Walk* and *The Marrow*, the events in Nichols' novels are exciting and often dangerous, but as Margaret is told, "the journey lies within," and the events provide characters with opportunities for inner growth. Judith and Tobit, playing instrumental roles in the restoration of the rightful king, learn to respect each other's differences and to acknowledge responsibilities to other people. Linda's task is more difficult; in searching for the marrow that will give health to her evil half-sister, she discovers and controls the tremendous power she has over others. Before she can exorcise the hatred and anger that she possessed when she died, Margaret must realize that "power enthralled her. Its existence seemed sufficient for its use." With it she had made herself and the men in her lives miserable; yet she had refused to acknowledge her responsibility for her and their situations. Mariana does not wish to be a healer, and she responds with fear, anger, and bitterness. Love for Paulus (who in *Song of the Pearl* has appeared as Paul) is an ennobling experience that she accepts only gradually and reluctantly. Only when the characters confront the depths of their realities, only when they are in touch with the powers of the subconscious and recognize them, can they achieve fulfillment and completeness. In telling their stories Nichols, like the fantasists she so admires, is telling the universal story, the story of discovering who one is and where one belongs.

SECONDARY REFERENCES: *CCL* 12: 5–19; *Junior* 4; *OCCL*; *Proceedings of the Fifth Annual Conference of the Children's Literature Association* (ChLA Publications, 1979), 41–48; *SATA* 15; *TCCW* 1; *TCCW* 2.

## Nutt, Ken (1951–        )

Ken Nutt was enjoying a successful career as an artist and an art teacher in Stratford, Ontario, when his friend Tim Wynne-Jones suggested they collaborate on a book for children. The result, *Zoom at Sea* (1983), and its sequel, *Zoom Away* (1985), both winners of the Howard-Gibbon Medal, have made Nutt one of Canada's most sought-after book illustrators. Born in Woodstock, Ontario, Nutt studied art at York University and moved to Stratford in 1979. His adult art, which has been widely exhibited, is very different from his work for children. People who come to see cats like Zoom, he has noted, will be surprised by the serious, message-oriented quality of his paintings.

Copyright Ken Nutt 1983 from ZOOM AT SEA by Tim Wynne-Jones. Illustrated by Ken Nutt. A Groundwood Book, Douglas and McIntyre.

In the "Zoom" books, both Wynne-Jones and Nutt wanted to capture the strange fantasy world experienced by the title hero, a small, rather ordinary cat. To achieve the desired effect, Nutt created black-and-white drawings, not unlike those used in the fantasy picture books of American artist Chris Van Allsburg, using graphite, with occasional watercolour washes beneath and with acrylics to highlight. As a result, the firmly realized physical details found in the pictures radiate a strangeness that suggests magical power. In the books, both words and pictures create a mixture of the homey and familiar with the unusual and fantastic.

In both "Zoom" books, the opening illustrations depict the feline hero in the ordinary world of his home. In *Zoom at Sea* he is playing with the water in his kitchen sink; in *Zoom Away* he lies on his back in an easy chair, knitting. However, when he enters Maria's house, he moves into a strange new world. Nutt's illustrations are of a very large house filled with mysterious shadows and passageways. From the house Zoom goes to the sea or the North Pole, and as he does so he enters into a world of bright light and distant horizons. Nutt implies that the passage through Maria's house is from the ordinary to the fabulous. His adventure over, the cat returns to Maria's house, and in *Zoom at Sea*, back to his own place. Ken Nutt's pencil drawings are a perfect complement to Wynne-Jones's slender text, providing visual details and, more importantly, adding to the sense of wonder and magic inherent in the plot.

Nutt has created fifteen pencil drawings for Paul Fleischman's *I Am Phoenix: Poems for Two Voices* (1985), a collection about birds. In illustrating poems rather than a narrative, Nutt faced a different challenge: he had to capture the rhythm and symbolism of the language of the individual pieces. He succeeded very well. The pictures for the opening and closing poems, "Dawn" and "Owls," each shows a bird at the window: the first, a finch with grey light behind it; the last, an owl with a cloudy, moonlit sky outside. The design of each of the pictures parallels the pattern of the corresponding poem. For example, that for "Sparrows" has sixteen birds on the faces of playing cards, with each card showing a different activity. The accompanying poem suggests the variety and vitality of sparrows and their movements.

Nutt's most recent illustrations, published under his pseudonym Eric Beddows, are for David Day's *The Emperor's Panda* (1986), a legend-like novel about the world's first panda and his relationship with a poor shepherd, Kung. The forty-five pencil sketches, ranging from full page to tiny illustrations tucked into the text, reproduce the stylistic formality of Chinese art, while at the same time depicting the warm relationship between the panda and the boy.

At a time when the large majority of children's picture books are published in full colour, Ken Nutt has achieved great success with monochromatic illustrations. With his subtle use of design, details, and light and shade, he has caught the spirit of the texts with which he

is working, has added his own sensitive understandings of them, and has ably communicated these to his viewers.
SECONDARY REFERENCE: *QQ* 51 (Oct. 85): 4.

# O huigin, sean (1942–        )

Since the publication of *Scary Poems for Rotten Kids* (1982), sean o huigin has been delighting children and worrying some adults who object that his poems assault conventional standards in both taste and poetics. In *Poe-Tree: A Simple Introduction To Experimental Poetry* (1978), an essay reprinted as part of *Well, You Can Imagine* (1983), o huigin indicates that he has abandoned capitalization and all punctuation. He considers them artificial conventions that get in the way of the individual's personal experience and interpretation of the various meanings of a poem. Concerned with the exploration of language in poetry, he turned to writing for children because, he has said, "I like people who work at reading a book, who crawl inside it and use their imaginations."

Born John Higgins in Brampton, Ontario (he changed his name after his first visit to Ireland, where he now lives), o huigin has claimed he is a high-school dropout. He joined Toronto's artistic community and participated in many "happenings," helped to found the New Writers' Workshop, and collaborated on "Cricket," Toronto's first multi-media event. He began working with children in 1969 as part of the Inner City Angels, a private group that sent artists into the schools. He continued to give workshops but did not start writing his own children's poetry until 1978.

Despite its experimental surface, much of o huigin's work is really traditional light verse. He gives it a touch of the ghoulish in his tales of ghosts and monsters in *Scary Poems for Rotten Kids*. His emphasis is on the bizarre in *Blink (a strange book for children)* (1984), in which a child finds himself in two places at once, and in *I'll Belly Your Button in a Minute!* (1985), in which a boy finds a little man crawling out of his navel. In *The Dinner Party* (1984) he presents a delightfully revolting meal that begins "with bits of / skin / the type you'd / find a / rat within." Although many have criticized the free verse in these books as too confusing for children, the rhyme, repetition, sound, and visual shape are adequate guides for most children. Two books, *Pickles, Street Dog of Windsor* (1982) and *Pickles and the Dog Nappers* (1986), are light narratives about a dog who speaks in free verse.

Although noted for his humour, o huigin has also written two serious works: *Atmosfear* (1985), an anti-pollution cautionary poem, and *The Ghost Horse of the Mounties* (1983), the first children's poetry book ever to win the Canada Council Prize. Based on an episode in 1874, in which a violent thunderstorm stampeded the horses of the first Mounties in Manitoba, *The Ghost Horse of the Mounties* is as much an evocation of atmosphere as it is a narrative. The narrator compels the reader to imagine himself alternately a horse and a Mountie. Full of repetitions of ideas, words, and sounds, the poem creates a dream-like state and evokes both pathos with the separate deaths of the horse and Mountie, and grandeur with their united apotheosis, when the horse carries the rider into the sky.

A number of o huigin's poems are intended for oral presentation and simply do not work on the printed page. Sometimes the poems seem to be divided into extremely short lines for arbitrary and quirky reasons. For the most part, however, o huigin has shown that his free verse is an ideal medium for comic poetry. In *The Ghost Horse of the Mounties*, he has shown that it is also suitable for sophisticated and serious work. SECONDARY REFERENCES: *BIC* 13 (Dec. 84): 6–8; *QQ Books for Young People* 1 (Feb. 87): 1, 3.

# P aperny, Myra (1932–        )

Myra Paperny has used childhood memories, the experiences of her parents and in-laws, and careful research to create two novels that graphically present the Alberta of earlier eras. The daughter of a Jewish Russian emigrant, Paperny was born in Edmonton, but spent time as a child in a small Alberta town and in British Columbia. She received a BA from the University of British Columbia in 1953 and an MSc in Journalism from Columbia University the following year. As a teacher of creative writing, first at Mount Royal College, Calgary, and then at the University of Calgary, Paperny felt guilty that she had not published any fiction, so she determined to prove she could write a novel. Her first novel, *The Wooden People* (1976), won the Little, Brown Children's Book Award and the Canada Council Prize. Her second, *Take a Giant Step*, appeared in 1987.

Paperny's novels ring out changes on the theme of the artistic son and the stern, domineering father. In *The Wooden People*, which opens in the year 1927, Teddy Stein is the sensitive, artistic child whose father seems a "tyrant" because he forbids his son all things associated with the theatre. Teddy, however, defies his father by secretly developing his "own private world," a puppet theatre. The novel is very slow in developing the tense confrontation between Teddy and his father, and the resolution of the conflict is contrived, but it pictures historical conditions clearly and portrays with sensitivity the lonely child seeking refuge in his imagination.

In *Take a Giant Step*, it is the child who rejects the world of art. Buzz Bush, a violin prodigy, wants to do what ordinary boys do, but his domineering father, afraid Buzz will injure his hands, won't let him play ball or ride a bike. Again, the device setting up the resolution to the problem is implausible and awkward. After an abortive effort at running away, Buzz comes to terms with his talent and his unique individuality when his father shows him that he can use the instrument to express himself. A denser novel than *The Wooden People*, *Take a Giant Step* paints more fully its social world, the early years of World War II, describing polio scares, scarlet fever quarantines, and the upheaval of families who lost relatives in combat.

Paperny's major weakness is her plotting: she falls back on the clichés of adventure to resolve conflicts, thereby undermining characterization and injecting sentimentality into her novels. Her major strength is her creation of a tangible historical world that contributes to the problems affecting the relationships between adults and their children.

SECONDARY REFERENCES: *SATA* 33; *CA* 69–72; *QQ* 43 (Jan. 77): 18–19; *Profiles 2*.

# Penrose, Gordon (Dr. Zed)
# (1925–        )

Dressed in a white lab coat, sporting large round glasses, his eyebrows exaggerated with grease pencil and his white hair mussed up, Gordon Penrose is Dr. Zed, the archetypal image of the brilliant, absent-minded scientist. As Dr. Zed, Penrose is one of North America's most entertaining and stimulating educators. Through his monthly columns in *OWL* magazine, his books, his appearances on the *OWL/TV* series, and his numerous public performances, he has made scientific enquiry fun for children.

Although he plays the part perfectly, Penrose did not create Dr. Zed. That honour belongs to the *OWL* magazine staff, who invented him as the fictional author of its staff-written science column. In 1977, when the magazine decided to hire a specialist to write the column, they chose Penrose, who had both impeccable credentials as an educator and a dramatic flair that excited children.

Born in Hamilton, Ontario, Penrose trained there to be an elementary school teacher. He later received a BA from the University of Western Ontario and BEd and MEd degrees from the University of Toronto. During his 32-year career, he taught in both elementary schools and teachers' college. In the twelve years prior to his retirement in 1981, he was a master teacher in science for the York County Board of Education in Aurora, Ontario. In November 1981, he was named a Fellow of the Ontario Institute for Studies in Education, the first elementary school teacher to be so honoured.

Although Penrose is probably at his best as a performer because he can directly involve the audience in his experiments, his columns and books share the wit, energy, and clarity of purpose that make his performances so successful. His books, *Dr. Zed's Brilliant Book of Science Experiments* (1977), *Dr. Zed's Dazzling Book of Science Activities* (1982), and *Magic Mud and Other Great Experiments* (1988) are collections of simple experiments using readily obtainable materials. Deliberately aimed at ten-year-olds, the experiments are safe, clearly written, and practical: Penrose tests them thoroughly to ensure that children will be able to obtain the desired results. The cartoons of Linda Bucholtz-Ross, who, Penrose says, "captures the spirit of the experiments from the children's viewpoint," crowd the page, giving it energy and excitement. They also provide a device for working in jokes and explanations that would distract from the clear presentation of instructions for performing an experiment.

By illustrating scientific principles in a concrete or dramatic manner, Dr. Zed has shown children that science is not something remote from daily life. Because following directions is important to completing his experiments successfully, he has also subtly implanted in them the

notion that reading is a key to both pleasure and knowledge.
SECONDARY REFERENCE: *QQ* 48 (Feb. 82): 38.

# _R_ eaney, James (1926–    )

James Reaney has said about drama that "you've got to have an underlying legend or myth or pattern that makes the whole thing work dynamically." Accordingly, he has used the patterns of folktales or the conventions of Greek comedy to produce some of the most unusual and stimulating plays ever written for Canadian children. He has also exercised his mythic and pattern-making techniques in two novels, although not as successfully. Reaney has been the winner three times of the Governor General's Award for his adult writings — twice for poetry and once for drama. He was born in South Easthope, Ontario, a small community near Stratford, and received BA, MA, and PhD degrees from the University of Toronto, where his supervisor, Northrop Frye, stimulated his interest in myth and patterns. After teaching for several years at the University of Manitoba, Reaney took up a post in the English Department, University of Western Ontario. Devoted to developing new forms of modern drama and to exploring the dramatic presentation of local history and legend, Reaney began holding regular theatre workshops, out of which came some of his children's plays.

Reaney wrote the four plays in _Apple Butter and Other Plays for Children_ (1973) as "a set which should guide a child's imaginative and community development through to the end of high school." These plays show his two approaches to children's stories. The two for younger children are more heavily patterned, exhibiting the repetition of words and episodes typical of folktales. In _Apple Butter_ (first produced 1965), an amusing puppet play, the title hero, whose respect for nature is evident in his kindness to a tree and a cow, becomes mythically identified with the ripening of fruit and the solving of human problems. _Names and Nicknames_ (first produced 1963) uses a transformation legend: spite and envy turn mean old Grandpa Thornberry, who ruins children's lives with derogatory nicknames, into an actual thornberry. Filled with poetic repetitions and catalogues, the play effectively uses a chorus to celebrate the beauty of naming.

The plays for older children are looser in plot and leave space for improvisation. _Geography Match_ (first produced 1967) was conceived, Reaney admits, as "a shamelessly patriotic play." A race across Canada between two rival schools provides the framework for repeated choric catalogues celebrating Canadian history and geography. _Ignoramus_ (first produced 1967), a companion piece, is what Reaney calls "an Aristophanes Old-Comedy type of play where you have lots of comic chorus work and grotesque farcical combats." Its patterns are formed from parallel scenes satirizing the war between traditional and progressive systems of education.

Two of Reaney's adult plays, _Listen to the Wind_ (first produced 1966) and _Colours in the Dark_ (first produced 1967), are accessible to high-school students.

Reaney has collaborated on two musical works for children: *Let's Make a Carol: A Play with Music for Children* (1965), with music by Alfred Kunz; and *All the Bees and All the Keys* (1973), a folkloric tale with accompanying music by John Beckwith.

Reaney's novels use the same two approaches to storytelling that his plays do. In *The Boy with an R in His Hand* (1965), a fictional account of the smashing of William Lyon Mackenzie's printing press in 1826, Reaney's insistence on "lots of patterns" weakens the novel. Parallel scenes, such as the poor man being hanged for stealing a cow and the influential Tories being merely fined for wrecking the press, do advance the theme, but other patterns, such as Alec's accidental falls into the water and the preposterous story of the bear who saves the boy who had freed him, violate the historical realism developed in much of the novel. *Take the Big Picture* (1986), a novel for slightly older readers, is bolder and freer. This comic novel uses a story-within-a-story technique to mix a number of elements, including a pattern based on that of Scheherazade's uncompleted tales and a mythic transformation of the Sasquatch into a god of retribution. The novel does not quite hang together because it attempts too much, but it has a number of fine comic moments and is especially successful in celebrating the gripping power of story.

Reaney is an artist willing to take chances. He sometimes goes to extremes with his repetitions and his mythic and folkloric patterns, but all of his works have stimulating sections. He is a major force in Canadian children's drama, breaking new ground with his exuberant, rhythmic language, his use of the chorus, and his loose structures that encourage improvisation. Less successful in his fiction, he is, nevertheless, a writer who combines a strong ethical sense and a playful intelligence. In both drama and fiction, he has produced work that entertains while challenging children.

SECONDARY REFERENCES: *TCCW* 2; *SATA* 43; *OCCL*; *CCL* 29: 4–24; Ross G. Woodman, *James Reaney* (1971).

# Reid, Barbara (1957–        )

When she was growing up in Toronto, Barbara Reid enjoyed reading picture books. But it was not until she attended an art school presentation at her high school's career day that she decided to become an artist. After attending the Ontario College of Art, Toronto, she illustrated textbooks and the works of such authors as Mary Blakeslee (*It's Tough To Be a Kid*, 1983), Betty Waterton (*Mustard*, 1983), and Mary Alice Downie (*Jenny Greenteeth*, 1984). In 1984 she illustrated the book that brought her national attention, Edith Chase's *The New Baby Calf*. Her pictures for Joanne Oppenheim's *Have You Seen Birds?* (1986) earned her the Canada Council Award for Illustration.

The illustrations for both *The New Baby Calf* and *Have You Seen Birds?* are made of plasticine, a medium Reid discovered at art school.

Oppenheim, Joanne. HAVE YOU SEEN BIRDS? Ill. by Barbara Reid. Richmond Hill: North Winds Press, 1986. Published by Scholastic-TAB Publications Ltd.

In one of her classes she was required to copy a well-known work of art in another medium. After several attempts at recreating Botticelli's "The Birth of Venus" using tissue paper, she tried using plasticine, and the results pleased both her fellow students and her instructor. After preparing the plasticine art for her children's books, Reid frames the completed picture in an acrylic box so that it will not soil. Then her husband, Ian Crysler, photographs the illustration using strong lighting to cause the shadows that create a three-dimensional effect. Indeed, one of the strong points of the plasticine illustrations in Reid's picture books is the tactile impression conveyed to the viewer.

The fourteen full-page illustrations that accompany Edith Chase's poem in *The New Baby Calf* focus on the newly arrived animal, but also show the loving environment into which he has been born. In ten of the pictures the mother is present, licking the calf clean, feeding him, and watching solicitously as he takes his first tentative steps and then begins exploring the world. The emphasis is on new life, and often there are other young animals. Presiding over the farm is the benevolent farmer, who cares for all of the animals as the cow does for her calf. Reid's illustrations provide a valuable complement to the simple poem of forty-nine lines: the poem focuses on the calf and its reactions to life; the pictures reinforce the themes of love and life.

Reid's illustrations for *Have You Seen Birds?* make a far greater contribution to the total effect of the book than do those of *The New Baby Calf*. Joanne Oppenheim's poem begins with the question of the title and then invites the reader to consider the tremendous variety of birds in the world. Although the names of specific birds are not given, they are divided into groups of opposites: birds of city and country, day and night, winter and summer, land and water. In the illustrations, Reid depicts specific birds that fit into the general groups and reinforce the poem's impression of variety.

The book is superbly designed: the individual pages and the relationships between the pages contribute to the overall effect. Different sizes, numbers, and arrangements of the pictures on a double-spread suggest the size of the individual birds and the relationships between them. Page design is constantly varied so that viewers become aware of the differences between the types of birds and their environments. In nearly every illustration a part of the bird — wing, beak, leg — extends beyond the blue plasticine border. These are not museum specimens, dead and rigid in glass cases, but living birds that cannot be tied down or contained within the picture frames. The book opens and closes with a visual joke, one not mentioned in the poem. A cat is looking out the window as the text says "Have you seen birds?" He is not seen again until the end of the book, when he jumps away from the window, back to the safety of the room. He has seen birds, but he has not caught any. Maybe their numbers and variety, along with the size of some of them, have frightened him away.

Reid's success as a children's book illustrator is not merely a result of her using a novel medium. It is a result of her ability to use plasticine

to give added dimensions of meaning and feeling to two short and relatively simple poems.
SECONDARY REFERENCE: *QQ* 51 (Oct. 85): 11–12.

# Reid, Dorothy (?–1974)

Most Canadian children quickly recognize such legendary British and
American heroes as King Arthur, Robin Hood, and Paul Bunyan. If
they recognize Nanabozho, the hero-god of the Ojibway people, it is
probably because of *Tales of Nanabozho* (1963), the CACL Award-win-
ning collection of stories by Dorothy Reid. Born in Edinburgh, Scotland, she attended school and later taught in rural Saskatchewan. In
1940 she moved with her husband to Geraldton, Ontario, where she
was made a member of the library board and became interested in the
Ojibway legends of the area. After moving to Fort William (now
Thunder Bay), she worked as a children's librarian from 1956 to 1967.
She was a popular storyteller and her radio program, "The Magic
Carpet," was heard on local radio for ten years. Undoubtedly that is where
many of the stories that later appeared in her book began to take shape.

Stories of Nanabozho are found amongst the Ojibway people
throughout the western Great Lakes region. Although nearly all of the
tribes have legends accounting for his miraculous birth and for his departure from active participation in the lives of human beings, most of
the tales are about unrelated events in his life. Both trickster and hero,
he often gets himself into trouble, but he sometimes helps his people in
their struggles with the environment and with their enemies. His actions also account for many of the physical characteristics of the world
as it is now.

In *Tales of Nanabozho*, Reid takes several of these legends and
shapes them into a biography, beginning with the hero's birth to a mor-
tal woman and the immortal spirit of the West Wind, and ending with
his sinking into a long-lasting sleep in the middle of Thunder Bay.
Early in his life, his mischievous traits predominate. Although he does
steal fire for his old grandmother, he spends most of his time attempting to gratify his excessive appetite, often with disastrous results.
However, after journeying to the Prairies to battle his father, he is told,
"You must return to your people. You have the power and knowledge to
help them greatly. Go and do good." This he does, starting with the re-
creation of the world, which had been destroyed in a great flood caused
by the evil Windegoes. Although Nanabozho does good, he is finally
defeated by the coming of the white people, the treachery of the Sioux,
and the weakness of his own people. In his great sleep he is "awaiting
the time when the Great Spirit will need him once more and bring him
back to life. Then he will arise and continue his appointed work for all
the people of his land."

By giving the tales biographical shape, Reid has made *Tales of
Nanabozho* more accessible to non-Native readers. However, she
remains true to the spirit of her originals, capturing the humour of

many of the episodes and the mixed nature of the hero. Unlike many early twentieth-century children's collections of Native legends, which attempted to make them into European fairy tales and which were often written in old-fashioned poetic prose, Reid's collection reflects the culture from which the stories are taken and at the same time captures the interest and imagination of contemporary young readers.
SECONDARY REFERENCE: *Profiles*.

# Richler, Mordecai (1931–        )

"Isn't there something of yours we are not too young to read?" The question asked by the children of Canadian novelist Mordecai Richler provided the impetus for the creation of one of the best-loved Canadian children's novels of the 1970s, *Jacob Two-Two Meets the Hooded Fang* (1975). The Montreal-born author of such comic and satiric novels as *The Apprenticeship of Duddy Kravitz* (1959), *Cocksure* (1963), and *St. Urbain's Horseman* (1971) — the latter two winners of the Governor General's Award — found the stories he occasionally read to his children boring and often didactic. Of course, his own novels were beyond their comprehension at the time. So, like many other well-known adult writers, he set about to create his own children's story, drawing on adventures of his own children and their life in London, England, where they had lived until 1972.

The title hero of *Jacob Two-Two Meets the Hooded Fang*, who is loosely based on the author's youngest son, suffers from feelings of inadequacy, and repeats things twice to gain attention. Running away from an unfriendly greengrocer, he falls asleep and dreams he is instrumental in releasing thousands of inmates from the children's prison and in revealing that the dreaded Hooded Fang, a wrestler turned prison warden, is a soft-hearted person. The book was published in England, the United States, and Canada, became a great success, and received the CACL Award. It has since been made into a motion picture starring Alex Karras as the Hooded Fang, and into a musical play.

This short novel takes the form of the circular dream journey in which the central character's problems are confronted and overcome during the dream. Richler's achievement is in the vitality of characterization and in the humour he infuses into his narrative. He is adept at capturing Jacob's view of the world, particularly of the adults in it. They are overwhelming, unreasonable, and tyrannical, treating him at best with benign neglect, or at worst with bullying nastiness. The plot moves quickly; presentation of the hero's development is clear and crisp. The story is marred by some inconsistency, most notably in the viewpoint of two chapters in which the dreamer himself is not present. Generally, younger children can identify with Jacob, older ones can enjoy the mocking of adults, and grownups can recognize in the older characters elements of their less desirable selves.

In spite of the success of *Jacob Two-Two Meets the Hooded Fang* —

the author laughingly noted it had outsold many of his well-known adult novels — Richler stated two years after its publication that he had no plans for a sequel. However, in 1987 *Jacob Two-Two and the Dinosaur* appeared. The hero, now eight years of age, receives the gift of a lizard brought back from Africa by his parents. The new pet is really a dinosaur, and it grows to monstrous size. Although the boy and his pet are devoted to each other, the rest of society is outraged, and the two flee across Canada to the Rocky Mountains where they hope to find a mate for the dinosaur. The book is a disappointment, lacking the *élan* and the sparkling satire of the first book. Jacob, who seems to have lost the respect he had gained at the end of the first novel, undergoes little character development; the satire of various adults, including the prime minister, is gratuitous; and elements of the plot are forced.

Richler's position in Canadian children's literature is secure, but it rests only on his first book, *Jacob Two-Two Meets the Hooded Fang*, a work that is not only a Canadian classic but an international favourite as well.

SECONDARY REFERENCES: *CCL* 15/16: 31–37; *CL* 78: 6–8; *OCCL*; *SATA* 27; *TCCW* 2.

# Roberts, Sir Charles G. D. (1860–1943)

Born in Douglas, New Brunswick, Charles G. D. Roberts spent much of his childhood reading and observing the wildlife around his home, activities that provided valuable training for the books that later established his reputation in the field of children's literature. In his "Prefatory Note" to *The Watchers of the Trails*, he referred to his childhood: "The present writer, having spent most of his boyhood on the fringes of the forest, with few interests save those which the forest afforded, may claim to have had the intimacies of the wilderness as it were thrust upon him."

Roberts attended the University of New Brunswick, where he received his BA and MA. He served as a school headmaster, editor of a Toronto weekly, and Professor at Kings College, Windsor, Nova Scotia, and was a member of the British and Canadian armed forces during World War I. Before moving to Toronto in 1925, where he lived until his death in 1943, he spent extended periods in New York, Europe, and London. He was knighted in 1935.

A prolific writer, Roberts published twenty books of poetry, four collections of short stories, seven novels, and twenty-three books of fiction for children. The novel *Red Fox* (1905) and such collections of short animal stories as *The Kindred of the Wild* (1902), *The Watchers of the Trails* (1904), *Kings in Exile* (1909), and *Wisdom of the Wilderness* (1922) established Roberts, along with Ernest Thompson Seton, whom he greatly admired, as one of the foremost creators of realistic animal stories for children.

Underlying Roberts' animal stories is a carefully thought out philosophy and methodology, one which he explained in detail in several of his prefaces. In "Introductory: The Animal Story," the preface to *The Kindred of the Wild*, he notes that the modern animal story is the product of an evolutionary storytelling process extending back to primitive times. Cavemen, he hypothesizes, must have frequently recounted their hunting exploits and perilous encounters with savage beasts. However, with greater sophistication, human beings developed a literary tradition in which the animals symbolized human characteristics and moral concerns. Domestic animal stories of the nineteenth century combined with growing scientific studies to rekindle an interest in detailed, precise observation of wild animals, observation that he notes was brought to a high degree of accuracy and artistic skill in the stories of Seton.

Roberts went far beyond giving accurate descriptions of his animal characters: "Having got one's facts right, — and enough of them to generalize from safely, — the exciting adventure lies in the effort to 'get under the skins'...to discern their motives, to understand and chart their simple mental processes." While he did not think that the mental faculties of animals were anywhere as fully developed as those of human beings, he did believe that they possessed the powers of rational thought.

Roberts was most interested in studying and portraying the superior members of each species, the "kings" or "masters" as he often refers to them in book or story titles. In the "Preface" to *Red Fox*, he notes of the title hero, "He simply represents the best, in physical and mental development, of which the tribe of the foxes has shown itself capable.... Once in a while such exceptional strength and such exceptional intelligence may be combined in one individual. This combination is apt to result in just such a fox as I have made the hero of my story." Roberts' animal characters are every bit as heroic to him as are human actors in adventure stories.

Because Roberts repeatedly dealt with the same types of characters and actions in his animal stories, an understanding of his themes, characters, and techniques can be gained from a reading of one representative collection, *The Kindred of the Wild*, and his best-known animal biography, *Red Fox*.

In *The Kindred of the Wild*, his greatest interest is in superior animals: "The Lord of the Air," "the great bald eagle who ruled supreme over all the aerial vicinage"; Hushwing, an owl of "tameless spirit"; and "The King of the Mamozekel," a magnificent bull moose. Each possesses superior size and strength, skill in hunting, and overall daring, courage, and wisdom. Roberts also admires animal mothers, whose role is not only to give birth and thus to insure the continuity of life, but also to protect and train their young so that they can grow to adulthood. "Wild Motherhood" is an account of a cow moose who leaves the herd to protect a calf who has fallen into a pit and is being stalked by wolves. Although she is successful at keeping her enemies at bay, she is later shot by a hunter who needs fresh meat for his wife and baby. Roberts suggests that the greatness of the King of the Mamozekel results not only from his inherent superiority, but also from the benefit he received from his mother's careful tutelage.

For each of Roberts' noble animals, the most dangerous enemy is man. "Whenever any individual of the wild kindreds, furred, feathered, or finned achieves the distinction of baffling man's efforts to undo him, his doom may be considered sealed." The backwoodsmen, as Roberts calls his hunters, stalk their prey for three reasons: they need fresh meat for their families; they wish to prove their "woodcraft," their cunning, against animals whose cleverness challenges them; and they respond to their hunting instincts. Although admiring the skill and determination of his human hunters, Roberts' greatest respect is for people who prefer to study nature without killing. A recurrent character is "the Boy," a solitary individual who quietly and sympathetically observes the wild kindred.

In *Red Fox*, Roberts combines character types and themes found in his short stories into a tightly unified biographical narrative. The novel opens with a scene that illustrates the interrelatedness of life and death. To save his newly born pups, a wily old fox, "a very Odysseus of his kind for valor and guile," leads a pair of dogs on a long and devious chase away from the den before being killed. One of the pups early shows his superiority, combining instinct, native intelligence, and the ability to learn from his mother's teachings and his own experiences to survive the many perils that overcome three of his siblings. He quickly learns about the danger from human beings and about ways either to avoid or outwit them. The two people who most interest Roberts are Jeb Smith, a backwoodsman who prides himself on his skill as a hunter, and a youngster, "the Boy," who prefers to use his woodcraft to study the animals.

The central portion of the novel focuses on the mature life of Red Fox as he mates with a vixen who, like him, has superior mental abilities, protects his young, and proves his cleverness in surviving a particularly harsh winter and his leadership in leading his family and other animals to safety during a forest fire. However, his superiority creates problems. He develops "that self-confident pride which so often proves a snare to its possessor." Moreover, his skill in raiding barnyards and evading human and canine trackers increases the determination of Jeb Smith to shoot him: "It was inconsistent with his reputation as a woodsman to let the wily and audacious fox go any longer triumphant over gun and dog and trap."

The Boy convinces Smith that it would be better to trap than shoot the fox, and the two work together to capture him. But Red Fox is released in the American South, where he is to be the prey for a fox hunt. He must summon all his cleverness and strength to escape with his life.

Extremely popular during the earlier decades of the twentieth century, Roberts' animal stories are not widely read today. As the dominant interests of young people have changed, the relative simplicity of Roberts' plots, characters, and themes seem old-fashioned. There are also limitations inherent in Roberts' treatment of his subjects. Although he emphasizes the animals' cleverness and heroism, he cannot engage in overly complex characterization without running the danger of humanizing them. Not surprisingly, the reader of several of his stories begins to see the formula underlying each one.

Nonetheless, in *Red Fox* and his best short stories, Roberts' achievement is considerable. The New Brunswick settings are fully realized; his heroic beasts become three-dimensional characters; and the life-and-death nature of the conflicts in which the animals become involved raise the plots to the level of high, sometimes tragic, drama.

SECONDARY REFERENCES: *CL* 26: 22–32; *CL* 84: 18–29; *CCL* 2: 23–37; *CCL* 30: 33–41; *OCCL*; *SATA* 29; *TCCW* 1.

# S aunders, [Margaret] Marshall (1861–1947)

Margaret Marshall Saunders published close to thirty novels, but today she is remembered for only one, *Beautiful Joe* (1894), the autobiography of a dog. Translated into fourteen languages, this novel quickly sold over a million copies and has been reprinted in Canada as recently as 1985. Saunders, who was born in Milton, Nova Scotia, attended boarding school in Edinburgh, and studied French in Orleans, began her writing career with publication of a romance for adults, *My Spanish Sailor* (1889). *Beautiful Joe* was the winning entry in a contest sponsored by the American Humane Association. She followed this with a number of animal stories, including *Beautiful Joe's Paradise: A Sequel to Beautiful Joe* (1902), *Alpatok: The Story of an Eskimo Dog* (1906), *Golden Dicky: The Story of a Canary and his Friends* (1919), and *Bonny Prince Fetlar: The Story of a Pony and his Friends* (1920). She also wrote a number of girls' stories with human protagonists.

*Beautiful Joe* is the last historically significant work in a style of animal writing that was to be superseded by the more realistic animal stories of Ernest Thompson Seton and Charles G. D. Roberts. Written in imitation of Anna Sewell's *Black Beauty* (1877), it is narrated by Beautiful Joe, a dog who has been mutilated by his cruel master. Episodic rather than tightly plotted, the story is relentlessly didactic, Joe faithfully reporting long discussions about the proper methods of keeping a variety of pets and about the need for respect for wild animals. The story also links the causes of abstinence and animal rights: the villains who abuse animals are drinking men who come to bad ends. Finally, it is unabashedly sentimental.

*Beautiful Joe* is stiff and artificial in its dialogue, weak in characterization, and conventional in its episodes, but it is undeniably earnest in its appeal for respect for "dumb animals." Now mostly an historical curiosity, it represents an outmoded way of treating animals and of addressing children.

SECONDARY REFERENCES: *OCCL*; *OCChL*; *CCL* 34: 31–40.

# Seton, Ernest Thompson (1860–1946)

"If there be one man, since St. Francis of Assisi, whom all the kindreds of the wild have cause to bless," declared Sir Charles G. D. Roberts, "it is Ernest Thompson Seton." Seton was, according to Roberts, "chiefly responsible for the vogue of the modern 'Animal Story'," a form that "resulted in a more sympathetic and understanding humane attitude toward our inarticulate kin." Seton did not number himself among the saints, but throughout his long career as an artist, naturalist, lecturer, and writer, he tried to share his passion for nature, to educate people about the ways of wild creatures, and thus to interest them in the cause of conservation.

Seton, born Ernest Evan Thompson in South Shields, County Durham, England, came to Canada with his family in 1866, living first on a farm near Lindsay, Ontario, and then in Toronto. *Two Little Savages; Being the Adventures of Two Boys Who Lived as Indians and What They Learned* (1903), a fictionalized version of his boyhood experiences, shows how intensely he responded to nature and to native lore. Upon graduation from the Ontario School of Art (now the Ontario College of Art), Toronto, he began studies at the Royal Academy, London. Illness forced him to return to Canada, where he studied wildlife on his brother's homestead near Carberry, Manitoba. Publication of his studies led to his appointment in 1893 as the official naturalist by the government of Manitoba. A serious naturalist all his life, Seton later won both the prestigious U.S. National Institute of Science Elliott Gold Medal and the John Burroughs Medal for his four-volume *Lives of Game Animals* (1925–28). Nevertheless, Seton also continued with his artistic career, winning a major prize at a Paris exhibition and illustrating numerous works for American publishers.

After 1896 he made his home in the United States, where, in 1902, he founded the Woodcraft Indians, a forerunner of the Boy Scouts of America, which he also helped to found in 1910, serving as Chief Scout until 1915. He wrote a number of books for these groups, including *Rolf in the Woods: The Adventures of a Boy Scout with Indian Quonab and Little Dog Skookum* (1911), an historical novel designed to teach children the elements of woodcraft and the customs of Native Indians.

His autobiography, *Trail of an Artist-Naturalist* (1940), is not completely reliable on all phases of his life, but it does explain the complicated matter of his change of name. Briefly, he came to believe he had claim to a Scots title and therefore adopted what he called the "ancient family surname of Seton."

Seton's celebrated animal stories are the most notable and enduring legacy of his lifelong passion for nature. His first collection, *Wild Animals I Have Known* (1898), was immensely popular, and he followed it with more than twenty volumes, either collections of tales or novellas. The most notable of these are *The Biography of a Grizzly* (1900), *Lives of the Hunted* (1901), *Monarch, The Big Bear of Tallac* (1905), and *Animal Heroes* (1906).

In his prefaces, he articulated both his philosophic premises and his artistic methods. He announced his central tenet in *Wild Animals I Have Known*: "...we and the beasts are kin." He concluded: "Since, then, the animals are creatures with wants and feelings differing in degree only from our own, they surely have their rights." Once a hunter himself, he was particularly concerned with the right of wild creatures to live without being wantonly hunted by men. He increasingly portrayed hunters as villainous or deranged. For example, in "The Winnipeg Wolf," included in *Animal Heroes*, Fiddler Paul kills the mother and siblings of Garou, the wolf of the title, in order to collect a bounty. Abusive humans then cruelly exploit Garou. Ironically, Garou eventually kills Paul, thereby suggesting that nature is a moral force that exacts retribution from man. Similarly, in "Krag, the Kootenay Ram," a powerfully haunting tale from *Lives of the Hunted*, Old Scotty, who obsessively stalks and kills the magnificent Krag, is himself killed by an avalanche.

Seton recognized that violence and death were inevitable in the lives of all wild creatures. He said in *Wild Animals I Have Known* that "the life of a wild animal *always has a tragic end.*" In *Lives of the Hunted*, he added that "there is only one way to make an animal's history un-tragic, and that is to stop before the last chapter." He implied that violence in nature was part of the Darwinian process by which the fittest survived and transmitted their genes to their offspring. He thus describes the death of Molly Cottontail in "Raggylug," one of the tales included in *Wild Animals I Have Known*, by pointing to her son: "She lives in him, and through him transmits a finer fibre to her race." In another story in that collection, "Redruff," he says of the death of some young partridges, "The weakest, by inexorable law, dropped out."

In order to evoke sympathy for his subject as a tragic victim, Seton concentrates on the animal hero, defined in *Animal Heroes* as "an individual of unusual gifts and achievements." The animal hero is not just a member of its species, but possesses a discrete personality and superior abilities, usually because of its superior size; it is a natural leader, a suitable protagonist for a tragic fate. These characteristics are evident, for instance, throughout the stories in *Wild Animals I Have Known*: the "poor old hero," Lobo the Wolf, "King of the Currumpaw," is larger and more cunning than all others; Silverspot the Crow is the wisest, strongest, and bravest of his band; Molly Cottontail is "a true heroine" because she sacrifices her life to save her son; the Pacing Stallion is "an image of horse perfection and beauty, as noble an animal as ever ranged the plains" and is more powerful and elusive than any other horse; Redruff the partridge is "the biggest, strongest, and handsomest of the brood...." Seton also ensures the tragic stature of these animals by ennobling their behaviour. The "inevitable tragedy" comes for the outlaw Lobo because he is loyal to his mate. Silverspot and Molly Cottontail are dedicated teachers who pass on their wisdom. Although "good fathers are rare in the grouse world," Redruff is an exemplary parent. Vixen the Fox poisons her captive young because she cannot endure to see it deprived of its rightful freedom. Similarly, the Pacing Mustang so values his freedom that he commits suicide by going over a cliff once he is captured.

Seton develops character and dramatic interest in controversial ways. He insists that the stories in *Wild Animals I Have Known* are true, but he also admits that he "pieced together some of the characters" from the exploits of a number of individuals. His admission that he used composite portraits has led some to question the authenticity of other elements in his stories. For example, Seton occasionally reports animal conversations. He attempts to maintain his claim of recording truth rather than inventing details by insisting that he has observed animal behaviour long enough to act as a translator of their sounds and actions.

Although frequently charged with anthropomorphising animals, Seton never went to the extremes evident in Anna Sewell's *Black Beauty* (1877) or Margaret Marshall Saunders' *Beautiful Joe* (1893), in which the animal narrators possess remarkable vocabularies, an ability to transcribe human speeches, and a tendency to moralize about human and animal behaviour. Seton convinces us with his third-person narration that he is treating real animals, not costumed people. His presentation of animal psychology stresses basic feelings of hatred, loneliness, hunger, and pain, not emotions or ideas more suitable to humans. He avoids the generalized nature study by making his characters interesting as individuals and their stories gripping as struggles for survival. Although he occasionally slips into stridency when pleading for animal rights or when preparing for the tragic climax of a story, for the most part he uses a simple, direct style that is equally effective in communicating information and tense drama. As a result, his stories have a continuing freshness absent in those by Roberts. As Roberts said on a book Seton sent to him, Seton is still "the King of the craft of the wild kindred."

SECONDARY REFERENCES: *SATA* 18; *CA* 109; *OCCL*; *OCChL*; *TCCW* 1; *TCCW* 2; Jeffrey M. Heath, ed., *Profiles in Canadian Literature 5* (1986).

---

# Sharp, Edith Lambert (1917–        )

Keen observation of the central British Columbia landscape in which she grew up, extensive historical research at the Smithsonian Institution, and a sensitivity to the history and customs of Native people — these are the ingredients Edith Sharp used in creating *Nkwala* (1958), winner of the Governor General's Award for Children's Literature. Born near Carroll, Manitoba, Edith Sharp grew up in Penticton, British Columbia, and studied at the Vancouver School of Art and the Smithsonian Institution in Washington, D. C. She has worked as a freelance writer and teacher of creative writing. *Nkwala* is her only work for children.

Set in the early nineteenth century before the coming of the white people, *Nkwala* deals with the struggles of the title hero, a member of the Spokane tribe, to find a meaningful role in his society. Twelve years old, he has tried unsuccessfully to complete the vision quest that will give him "his guardian spirit, his song, and his name." His personal problems are compounded by difficulties in the tribe, which, because of a great drought, must leave its home of many generations and journey to the area that is now Penticton. At the novel's conclusion, Nkwala is instrumental in resolving both his own conflict and that of his tribe. While seeking his vision on a lonely mountainside, he hears the enemy approaching, warns his people, and plays a major role in bringing peace between them and the Okanagans. The work is sometimes marred by stilted, "poetic" language, and the portrayal of the friendship between Nkwala and a lost dog reads like the standard material of many boys' stories. However, the author generally combines precise historical accuracy with a moving account of the tensions the boy experiences, both as a person at the edge of maturity and as a member of his culture.

SECONDARY REFERENCE: *TCCW* 1.

## Smucker, Barbara (1915–          )

Barbara Claasen Smucker is a novelist who dramatizes the conflicts within minority groups and between them and society at large. She comes by her concerns quite naturally: she belongs to the New Order Mennonites, a minority group that does not believe in the complete withdrawal from the world practised by the Old Order Mennonites. Consequently, she understands both the attitudes towards minorities sometimes held by those outside and the powerful tensions that can develop between those who seem at first glance to have much in common.

Born in Newton, Kansas, Smucker has had a varied career. After graduating with a BS in journalism from Kansas State University in 1936, she has worked as a high-school teacher, a reporter, a children's librarian, and a college librarian. She came to Canada in 1969 when her husband, a Mennonite minister and professor of sociology, accepted a post at the Mennonite Conrad Grebel College in Waterloo, Ontario.

Before her arrival in Canada, she published three novels. *Henry's Red Sea* (1955), about the escape of Mennonites from Russia to Paraguay after World War II, and *Cherokee Run* (1957), about the Mennonite migration from Kansas to Oklahoma, were written to teach Mennonite children their history. *Wigwam in the City* (1966; republished as *Susan*, 1972), the story of a Native family moving from a reservation to Chicago, deals with contemporary events and with people outside the Mennonite community.

Since taking up residence in Canada, she has published five more novels, the major work upon which her reputation depends. *Underground to Canada* (1977), which received the Brotherhood Award from the National Conference of Christians and Jews, is a dramatic account of Blacks escaping from slavery in the southern states to freedom in Canada. *Days of Terror* (1979), winner of both the Canada Council Prize and the Ruth Schwartz Award, is about the persecution and emigration of Russian Mennonites after the Revolution. In *Amish Adventure* (1983), a contemporary story, a boy spends time on an Amish farm after he is injured in an auto accident. *White Mist* (1985) is a time-shift fantasy in which two Natives travel back to the nineteenth century to discover and accept their relationship with the exiled Natives of Michigan and to learn reverence for the land. *Jacob's Little Giant* (1987), her least dramatic novel, is a gentle tale about a small Mennonite boy who matures and gains respect when he successfully raises some giant Canada geese.

Smucker structures her novels to investigate beliefs and values. "I like my story heroes to have difficult goals to win," she has said, "and to strive for values that are the very best in our society." Thus, in most of her novels, her child heroes undertake a journey that leads to new understanding of themselves or their group and to a symbolic affirmation of values, particularly Christian values.

The pattern is clearly evident in *Underground to Canada*, which was at least partly inspired, she has said, by a passage from a speech in which Martin Luther King talked about the coded language of the slaves: "Heaven was the word for Canada...." Jullily, a black slave, undertakes a journey from the earthly hell of the American South to the earthly heaven of Canada, which represents for her an opportunity for freedom and human dignity. Her journey tests her courage and compassion and provides strengthening grace, in the form of the assistance she receives along the way. Smucker depicts Christian charity, one of her primary values, by contrasting the good deeds of the saintly Abolitionists, who risk their own freedom and lives, with the mindless brutality of Sims, the slave hunter and overseer, who, as even Smucker admits, is a "sort of a stereotype bad man." Finally, Jullily's successful journey to freedom also symbolizes the journey of life itself, suggesting Smucker's belief that God watches over believers. Smucker does not, however, allow the pattern to violate historical accuracy. She is quick to point out, therefore, that Canada is only relatively a heaven for the escaped slaves. They are not welcome in white schools, and their lack of education makes them unfit for many jobs.

A similar pattern and meaning are evident in the journey of *Days of Terror*, in which Canada, the goal of the Mennonite migration, stands for political and religious freedom, and thus, happiness and godliness. In this case, however, Smucker conducts a much more complex study of the effect of beliefs and values. Thus, although she does not excuse the racism of the Russians who hated the German-speaking Mennonites, she shows how Mennonite aloofness exacerbated the prejudice. Smucker's New Order belief that religious values and participation in the state can coexist are expressed by wise old Grandfather Penner, who says that, once in Canada, "We must not withdraw from the native people as we have done in Russia." Furthermore, Smucker uses the story of Otto Neufeld, a member of a Mennonite Self Defence League that took up arms to defend the community, to show how the pressure of circumstances affects principles. She also contrasts the moral inflexibility of the community with the sensitivity and devotion to private conscience of Otto's brother, Peter. Peter is the only one who keeps in touch with and remains true to Otto after the group permanently ostracizes him.

In *Amish Adventure,* Smucker varies the journey pattern. Ian McDonald journeys from Chicago to an Amish farm near Waterloo, where the hardships of farm life test him, and the kindness of the Amish opens his eyes, helping him to discover his own abilities and his desire to become a farmer. Because he is not Amish, his journey continues beyond the farm. Counterbalancing this pattern is the circular journey of John Bender, who has left his Amish home on adventures but comes back accepting that home as the ideal place for him. The climactic community barn-raising symbolizes the solidarity of the group. The fact that John Bender "seemed to be holding the whole structure together" shows that only the voluntary participation of young people will ensure the survival of the group. Still, Smucker's plot indicates problems with inflexible adherence to rules. John returns, after all, only because an outsider, Ian McDonald, is willing to tell him about his father's misfortunes. Furthermore, John's sister, who left to be a nurse, continues to be shunned because she never does repent. By presenting issues from the perspectives of both the Amish and the outsider, Smucker makes us feel the hard steel of faith and the pain it occasions for both sides.

In *White Mist,* Smucker uses the journey of two outsiders to explore values. May Apple Appleby, who denies her obvious Native ancestry, and Lee Pokagon, a Native bitter about the way whites have treated both Natives and their lands, are mysteriously shifted into the nineteenth century. When they return to the present, the pride in their ancestry, developed from their adventures, impels them to offer white people the ecological vision of the Natives: "If we destroy the earth, we destroy ourselves. We are one with the earth." The novel lacks a satisfyingly dramatic conclusion, but the pattern suggests that people have to go deeply into their heritage, into their identities, in order to face the modern world with confidence and purpose, and that individuals must stand up for their beliefs.

*Jacob's Little Giant,* a novel for much younger children, does not depend on such dramatic journeys, nor does it explore such large moral issues. Jacob Snyder, a Mennonite boy small for his age, tires of being "Little Jakie," a name that suggests incompetence and insignificance. Although heavy-handed in its repetitions of Jacob's identification with Little Giant, the smallest of the goslings he raises, the novel succeeds in using Jacob's journeys between the pond and other settings, particularly his home, to show how he gains maturity and acceptance. By beginning and ending with the migratory journeys of geese and by presenting significant stages of their life cycle, the novel also conveys a reverence for nature.

As a writer Smucker has weaknesses, most attributable to the didacticism that has been a part of her writing from the beginning. Her dialogue is often contrived: characters present information as if they were lecturing from the pulpit or in the classroom. Her villains, such as Sims, the slave trader in *Underground to Canada,* Mahkno, the anarchist in *Days of Terror*, and Pete Moss, the teenage troublemaker in *Amish Adventure*, often speak and behave implausibly. Smucker also has trouble making characters other than the Mennonites and Amish seem psychologically plausible. In *Amish Adventure*, for example, she attempts to contrast characters who accept responsibility and tolerate differences, but neither Ian McDonald's obsessive guilt for being in the car that crippled Ezra Bender nor the cowardliness of the driver is convincing.

Nevertheless, Smucker also has compensating strengths. As the bibliographies appended to her major novels indicate, she is a meticulous researcher who is particularly skillful in reconstructing history. Thus, even her weakest novel, the fantasy *White Mist*, is redeemed by her portrayal of life in a nineteenth-century logging camp. It is *Underground to Canada* and *Days of Terror*, however, that support her belief "that there are so many exciting things happening in history and that it doesn't have to be dull." Smucker is not a narrow sectarian. At her best, she is a Christian novelist who shows the need for tolerance and compassion in the treatment of all peoples. Her sympathetic look at lives not normally treated in Canadian children's literature shows that Canada's cultural mosaic can provide fitting material for intelligent fiction.
SECONDARY REFERENCES: *CCL* 22: 4–14; *CCL* 25: 18–25; *SATA* 29; *Profiles 2*; *TCCW* 2.

# Stinson, Kathy (1952–      )

Kathy Stinson has been both a teacher and a parent, and she has used her experiences, along with childhood memories, to create books for preschool children: *Red Is Best* (1982) and *Big Or Little?* (1983), both illustrated by Robin Baird Lewis; *Mom and Dad Don't Live Together Any More* (1984), illustrated by Nancy Lou Reynolds; *Those Green Things* (1985), illustrated by Mary McLoughlin; and *The Bare Naked Book* (1986), illustrated by Heather Collins. Although she had enjoyed writing as a child, Stinson chose a career as a teacher, working for five years in an elementary school in Toronto before raising her two children. With the encouragement of her children, friends, and members of the Children's Book Centre, she submitted her first book, *Red Is Best*, based on her daughter's preference for red socks, to several publishers. Accepted by Annick Press, it received the IODE Book Award and has been translated into seven languages.

Stinson's first three books present children's simple but nonetheless significant responses to elements of their lives. The narrator of *Red Is Best* steadfastly refuses her mother's suggestions that she choose clothes of different colours. In *Big Or Little?* the speaker experiences the difficulties of being in between: big enough to do up zippers and tie shoes, but too small to ring door bells. In *Mom and Dad Don't Live Together Any More*, a small child ponders her parents' separation.

*Those Green Things* is a question and answer session between a child and her parent. Every time the young speaker asks what something is and receives a factual answer, she replies that she had thought the object was something imaginary and fantastic. In mock frustration, the mother finally creates a fantasy answer herself: "Those green things on the porch are Martians. They are coming to take me to Mars so you can't ask me any more questions about those green things." *The Bare Naked Book* discusses the various parts of the body, including genitals, each time asking the child reader, "Where is your...?"

In addition to the illustrations, which are excellent complements to the texts, Stinson's books succeed because of their sensitive use of very simple language to capture children's emotions. Even in *The Bare Naked Book*, which at first might appear to be merely a listing of body parts, the words build up a rhythm that expresses the child's joy of exploring body parts and the pleasure of repeating words. The adjectives preceding the repeated nouns suggest that different people look different, although all possess the same body parts.

In her five short books, Stinson has established herself as a significant author of books for preschoolers. Not only has she presented the world as they experience it, but she has done so in sensitive, poetic language.

# *Stren, Patti (1949–      )*

Patti Stren has won critical respect for her blend of urbane wit and sentiment in a series of books illustrated with appealingly quirky, cartoon-like drawings. A native of Brantford, Ontario, she graduated from the University of Toronto and worked with autistic children in Israel before studying at the Ontario College of Art and the New York School of Visual Arts. She began her career by illustrating two works by Rosemary Allison, *I Never Met a Monster I Didn't Like Colouring Book* (1973) and *Yaaay Crickets!* (1973). She has also illustrated Phyllis Green's *Eating Ice Cream with a Werewolf* (1983). She is at her best when she is both author and illustrator, for she then controls the interplay between her idiosyncratic, unconventional drawings and her relatively simple, straightforward text.

All of Stren's work explores some facet of the related themes of friendship and self-acceptance. In *Hug Me* (1977), Elliot Kravitz, the first of Stren's heroes who must adjust to being different from the crowd, is a porcupine who longs for a friend to hug and finally meets Thelma Claypits, a female porcupine. *Hug Me* is a minor classic because it presents a universal theme and because the combination of clear, direct prose and witty illustrations saves it from its inherent sentimentality. Seemingly constructed out of the least possible number of lines and enhanced with only a single colour, the deceptively childlike drawings concentrate attention on Elliot and develop his personality. As in her later books, Stren's pictures here work in one of two ways. Sometimes they illustrate the action directly, picturing exactly what is written, with words from the text included, cartoon-fashion, in the drawing. At other times the drawings amplify the text with commentary.

For instance, one picture shows Elliot trying to hug a flower, an act not mentioned in the main text. The flower explains to another that Elliot is lonely, while yet another, separated from all the rest, says, "I know how he feels."

Stren's other picture books follow the pattern of *Hug Me*, although none is quite as successful in blending elements. *Bo, the Strictor That Couldn't* (1978), an early work illustrated with colourful watercolours, explores peer pressure and individuality through the story of a snake who would rather kiss his enemies than squeeze and eat them. In *Sloan & Philamina; Or How To Make Friends with Your Lunch* (1979), an anteater and an ant become friends. In *I'm Only Afraid of the Dark (at Night!!)* (1982), an arctic owl overcomes the fear of the dark that makes him distressingly unlike others when he is befriended by a girl owl with the same problem. *Mountain Rose* (1982) is the tale of a girl who is teased for being big but who finds happiness and identity as a world champion wrestler. Weak in focus, it lacks the clear development of theme and the sharp wit that distinguish the other books.

Stren has pursued her theme of the search for identity in two novels. In *There's a Rainbow in My Closet* (1979), Emma Goldberg, a girl with a passion for painting, is brought to a deeper appreciation of her artistic talent, and hence, her own individuality, when her unconventional grandmother comes to take care of her. Dialogue and characterization, particularly of the impossibly ideal grandmother, are weak, the thematic strands never quite fuse, and the story occasionally succumbs to sentimentality. Nevertheless, the novel is humorous and does provide unusual insight into the artistic sense of a child.

*I Was a 15-Year-Old Blimp* (1985) is Stren's only book without illustrations. A rather conventional problem novel, treating bulimia, an eating disorder suffered by girls who vomit and purge themselves with laxatives in order to control weight, it is the story of Gabby Finklestein, a fat girl who dreams of romance but endures humiliating mockery. Sentimental and predictable, the novel has obvious flaws, but it is quite readable because of its simple, conversational prose and because Stren extends the identity crisis theme beyond the issue of obesity.

Only partially successful as a novelist, Stren has demonstrated that she is an important picture-book artist. Universal and serious in theme, but simple and humorous in presentation, her picture books entertain both children and adults.

SECONDARY REFERENCES: *CLR* 5; *SATA* 41; *QQ* 45 (Oct. 79): 8.

# *Suzuki, David (1936–      )*

David Suzuki is recognized by millions of Canadians for his work as host of two major television series, *The Nature of Things* and *A Planet for the Taking*, both of which have also been shown on public television in the United States. He has thus become a leader in popularizing scientific knowledge, in promoting public awareness of scientific issues, and in advocating enlightened government policy affecting science and scientific education.

Born in Vancouver, Suzuki was interned with his Japanese parents during World War II, an experience he has only begun to talk about since the publication of his autobiography, *Metamorphosis: Stages in a Life* (1987). He received his university education in the United States, graduating with a BSc from Amherst College in 1958 and a PhD in genetics from the University of Chicago in 1961. After taking up a post at the University of British Columbia, he quickly established a reputation as one of Canada's leading scientists. Concerned with making the public aware of science, he began his broadcasting career in 1971 with his first television series, *Suzuki on Science*. He also developed a popular radio series, *Quirks and Quarks*, in 1976.

With the assistance of Barbara Hehner, Suzuki has produced a series of scientific discovery books suitable for children 8–12 years old: *Looking at Plants* (1985), *Looking at Insects* (1986), *Looking at Senses* (1986), and *Looking at the Body* (1987). Uniform in design and concept, each book divides its subject into parts. Each part has a brief introduction and suggested activities to make concepts graphic and comprehensible. For example, *Looking at the Body* explores the various organs and systems of the body, explaining such things as how the sense of touch works and how we digest food. Although the books in the series generally cover their topics adequately, *Looking at the Body* avoids all mention of human reproduction and the reproductive organs. The activities in the book range from demonstrations of the way the lungs work to tests of memory.

Suzuki, together with Eileen Thalberg and Peter Knudson, has also produced *David Suzuki Talks about AIDS* (1987). Based on a special edition of *The Nature of Things*, this book is a frank and useful discussion suitable for junior and senior high-school students.

Suzuki's *Looking at* books, like the Dr. Zed books of Gordon Penrose, mix information with activities and make children participants in the process of scientific discovery. Children can learn from and enjoy books by either, but those who find the crowded pages of the Dr. Zed books too juvenile may prefer Suzuki's books with their clean format and use of simple line drawings for illustrations. And while Penrose's books may appeal to those children who want information about an eclectic variety of topics, Suzuki's books may appeal instead to children who prefer a more thorough treatment of one topic. In any case, Suzuki has provided good sources of accurate and entertaining scientific knowledge.

# *T* ait, Douglas (1944–       )

Douglas Tait is Canada's most successful non-Native illustrator of the familiar West Coast Native legends. But he did not intend to become an artist or a children's book illustrator. He was not even born on the West Coast, but in Medicine Hat, Alberta. He grew up there and in Deep River, Ontario. While an engineering student at the University of British Columbia he met painter Harry Savage, who interested him in painting. He studied for a year at the University of Chile and graduated from the Vancouver School of Art before taking a position as a graphic designer at Simon Fraser University.

His first commission as an illustrator came from McClelland and Stewart, who invited him to furnish a series of drawings for Paul St. Pierre's *Chilcotin Holiday* (1970). Shortly after that he met Christie Harris, a noted reteller of West Coast Native legends, and over the next decade illustrated eight of her books, including *The Trouble With Princesses* (1980), for which he received the Howard-Gibbon Medal.

Speaking of the role of the illustrator, Tait has said that the pictures "must be an integral part of the whole, not just filler." When he receives a manuscript, he reads it carefully, deciding which parts he wishes to illustrate. He then checks the distribution of pictures through the text, making sure that they are spaced at regular intervals, makes a final decision on specific pictures to create, engages in extensive research, and meticulously prepares the final illustrations.

In depicting scenes from the West Coast Native legends, Tait faced a challenge: he had to depict the landscape accurately — people, artifacts, and animals — while at the same time communicating a sense of the supernatural forces and beings that influenced the lives of the people. These legends were not fanciful, imaginary fairy tales but part of the sacred history of a traditional people, records of events in which the human, the natural, and the supernatural frequently interacted. At the centre of this world is the Native village, which Tait has presented with precise, meticulous accuracy. On one side is the dark, tangled forest, a place of mists and shadows, home of wild animals and fearsome supernatural beings; on the other, the sea, equally terrifying and magnificent. Many of Tait's illustrations of forests are, as it were, seen from the eyes of the stories' participants. Huge trees and tangled undergrowth seem to contain mysterious shapes in their shadows. The human figures in the sea scenes appear small and vulnerable.

The central conflict in most of Harris's legends is between human and supernatural beings. In depicting the supernatural characters, Tait has captured the power they possessed and the fear they inspired in the people. His pen and ink drawings precisely delineate the distorted and exaggerated features; light and shade imply the spirit power emanating from them.

In addition to *The Trouble With Princesses*, Tait has also illustrated the following books by Christie Harris: *Secret in the Stlalakum Wild* (1972), *Once More Upon a Totem* (1973), *Sky Man on the Totem Pole?* (1975), *Mouse Woman and the Vanished Princesses* (1976), *Mouse Woman and the Mischief Makers* (1977), *Mouse Woman and the Muddleheads* (1979), and *The Trouble With Adventurers* (1982). He has illustrated Margaret Bemister's *Thirty Indian Legends of Canada* (1973), Lois McConkey's *Sea and Cedar: How the Northwest Coast Indians Lived* (1973), Maria Campbell's *People of the Buffalo: How the Plains Indians Lived* (1976), and Anne Simeon's *The She-Wolf of Tsla-a-Wat* (1977). SECONDARY REFERENCES: *Profiles 2*; *SATA 12*.

# Takashima, Shizuye (1928–       )

"Rambo-type, violence-oriented stories are doing great harm to the young. If we as adults wish to have a better world with fewer wars, with less of the usual human failures to care for one another, then we should all make greater efforts to expose our young to beautifully illustrated books, well-written ones which will set their hearts on fire so that they will aspire toward excellence all through their lives." These thoughts of Vancouver-born artist Shizuye Takashima could well serve as an introduction to her own book, *A Child in Prison Camp* (1971), winner of the Howard-Gibbon Medal. In it, she draws on her own experiences as a Japanese-Canadian during World War II. Like thousands of her people, she was interned in central British Columbia, denied her rights as a Canadian citizen, and treated as a prisoner. Years later, after she had moved to Toronto, received a degree from the Ontario College of Art, and become an internationally acclaimed artist, she accepted the invitation of publisher May Cutler to describe her childhood in words and pictures.

*A Child in Prison Camp* is loosely autobiographical: Takashima was two years older than she portrays herself in the book, and she had four brothers, not one. She is thus presented as the vulnerable youngest child of three, a more universally recognizable character type. The story becomes a universal one of loss and restoration. The narrator, expelled from a place of security, survives a journey through an unknown land supported by a loving family and community, her own hopeful personality, and the beneficent forces of nature.

The events are carefully structured to emphasize several themes, three of which dominate: the injustice of the historical events and the bitterness they caused; the strong sense of family and community that gave the displaced people the strength to endure; and the abiding, restorative power of nature. The book does not avoid discussing the injustice of the actions of the Canadian government, but it emphasizes the tensions created for the Japanese families themselves. Families turn against each other depending on whether their loyalties are determined by Canadian citizenship or Japanese heritage. The anger and bitterness constantly well up in the narrator's father, especially when, near the end of the war, his family refuses to agree to his plans to return to Japan. However, the families do survive in the alien wilderness of central British Columbia, celebrating traditional festivals, producing Japanese dramas, and helping each other in times of need. For all of them, especially Shichan, the author's persona, nature exerts a positive influence. Many of the events described take place when Shichan, alone or with one or two others, responds to the natural beauty around her.

Takashima's verbal and visual artistry give her presentation of these universal themes the status of a Canadian classic. Events are perceived through the eyes of the young narrator, and the reader/viewer experiences her bewilderment, hopes, and fears. There is little authorial comment; instead, details sensitively chosen and presented evoke the various emotions. Vignettes, such as the visit to the Exhibition grounds where the Japanese are housed in animal barns, the confusion and anger at the railway station, the terror at watching a family's house consumed by fire, and the preparations for the O-bon festival, give the reader a clearer sense of events and emotions than generalized statements would. The eight watercolours accompanying the text reinforce the themes. The frontispiece illustration of the O-bon festival held against the backdrop of the Rocky Mountains introduces the ideas of community and nature; the picture of the bucket brigade vainly fighting the house on fire emphasizes the hazards of their lives; the concluding illustration underscores the theme of love and joy that dominates. As Shichan and her mother stand in the shallow waters of the lake, doing their laundry for the final time, the sun shines down on them through a break in the clouds, its rainbow hues a symbol of the new hope they feel as they prepare to leave their temporary home for a new life in Ontario.

SECONDARY REFERENCES: *Profiles 2*; *SATA* 13.

# Taylor, Cora (1936–        )

"I'd written a short story for my creative writing class at the University of Alberta. During a roundtable discussion I began to see that I had too complex a theme and more characters than I could handle in a short story. Over a period of years, it evolved into a children's novel." This novel is *Julie* (1985), winner of both the Canada Council Prize and the CACL Award. It is the first novel by Cora Taylor, a resident of Winterburn, Alberta, and native of Fort Qu'appelle, Saskatchewan. Attending a small school, where the library was tiny and old, Taylor grew up mainly on a diet of old classics, such as Charles Kingsley's *The Water Babies*. It wasn't until her husband gave her a copy of W. O. Mitchell's *Who Has Seen the Wind* that she first came into contact with an author whose work was to influence her novel profoundly and from whom, in the 1970s, she was to take a course at the University of Alberta.

"Julie had been different from the beginning." This statement early in Chapter One embodies both the character of the title heroine and her central conflict. Julie Morgan is a seer. At an early age, she amazes her family with the long, involved stories she tells, her unusual sensitivity to nature, and her ability to discuss scenes that have happened long before she was born. Warned by her mother that she must distinguish between the real and the imaginary, and partially rejected by her brothers and sisters, Julie is forced to face her special talents by Granny Goderich, an ageing family friend who also has psychic powers. At her deathbed, the old woman tells the girl, "That's how it is with us, Julie. We're not sure what to do...we're afraid. We don't know what to do and so we do nothing, nothing at all. Sometimes that's right, there's nothing we can do, sometimes.... There comes a time when we have to act, like you did tonight. You have to decide and that's when the gift can be terrible."

Although Julie tries very hard to be normal at school, she cannot deny her powers; and when she sees an Egyptian Ship of the Dead sailing in the clouds above the farm, she realizes that her father is in grave danger. Galloping across the fields on the back of an unbroken stallion, she rescues her father, who has been trapped beneath his tractor. Hours later she has a presentiment of his imminent death and, remembering Granny Goderich's confession that the denial of her own powers had caused the death of her son, Julie wills her father to live. She has accepted her differences, along with the joys and the tremendous burden of responsibilities these will give her.

Like W. O. Mitchell's *Who Has Seen the Wind*, *Julie* is more than a Prairie novel. Although, like Mitchell's novel, it captures a sense of the mystic powers of the Prairie skies and lands, it uses this sense to reinforce its powerful theme: the great difficulties faced by the individual who is made different because of special powers. The work is also about "sisterhood," for, although Julie feels closest to her father, the most intricate relationships are between the female characters. Julie has been visited in dreams by her paternal grandmother, a woman who was also reputed to have had special powers; at school, the librarian, Miss Johnson, encourages the girl to read special books; Granny Goderich, as we have seen, reveals to Julie the special responsibilities of her powers; and finally, Julie's mother comes reluctantly to acknowledge these powers. Ultimately, however, Julie is alone. Yet, alone though she is, Julie is smiling at the conclusion of the novel, for she has understood and come to terms with her powers. Her smile is one of joy.

# *Thurman, Mark (1948–     )*

Any biographical sketch of Mark Thurman would have to be subtitled "A Portrait of the Artist as Educator." A native of Toronto who graduated from Central Technical School, Thurman now teaches weekly classes at the Toronto School of Art. He also devotes almost half of his time to conducting workshops for elementary school students, seeking to open up their imaginations by demonstrating how they can express their ideas and feelings through drawings. Thurman reaches far more children, however, through the stories and books he illustrates.

Thurman is probably best-known for *Owl* magazine's "Mighty Mites" series, which is designed to make natural science interesting to children. Together with Emily Hearn, who writes the text, Thurman researches the topics, then devises stories that follow the adventures of three children; these children can shrink to a very small size to explore miniature facets of the natural world. He presents these facets in pen-and-ink panels, comic-book style. In *Mighty Mites in Dinosaurland* (1981), a book-length adventure, the children visit Alberta's Badlands and end up going back in time, where they learn all about the dinosaurs who once roamed the region.

The Mighty Mites opened the door for Thurman to do illustrations for other educational work. Joan Bodger's *Belinda's Ball* (1981) is a book designed to teach Piaget's concept of object constancy. He has illustrated both of Emily Hearn's books teaching children about the humanity of the physically disabled, *Good Morning Franny, Good Night Franny* (1984) and *Race You Franny* (1986). His paper cutout illustrations for the first of these are particularly clever in their use of perspective. It is only in the fourth picture that we get any sign that Franny is in a wheelchair, allowing children to develop an identification with her before they realize she is disabled. The fifth drawing, showing the world from Franny's viewpoint, intensifies the identification.

Thurman has both written and illustrated a number of books. *Who Needs Me?* (1982) is ostensibly designed to teach children about interdependency; it invites children to make up sentences showing relationships and to colour the line drawings. Far more substantial are Thurman's animal tale picture books for children aged three to eight. The "Douglas the Elephant" series includes *The Elephant's Cold* (1979; revised 1985), *The Elephant's New Bicycle* (1980; revised 1985), *The Lie That Grew and Grew* (1981; revised 1985), and *The Birthday Party* (1981; revised 1985). The books in the "Two Pals on an Adventure" series are *Two Pals on an Adventure* (1982; revised as *Two Pals*, 1985), *City Scrapes* (1983; revised 1985), *You Bug Me* (1985), *Old Friends New Friends* (1985), and *Two Stupid Dummies* (1986). Both series use simple stories to teach children such concepts as sharing, accepting disappointments, and learning to believe in oneself even when people say mean things. Thurman has revised many of these because the morals were awkward and heavy-handed. In illustrating these gentle and often amusing tales, he uses vibrant watercolours, and he frequently omits backgrounds to create a focus on the antics of the characters. Thurman has also started placing jokes for adults in his pictures: in *Two Stupid Dummies*, Doctor Zighound Froid the Fourth reads a book entitled *Id Did It*.

Thurman's most recent book is *Cabbage Town Gang* (1987), an illustrated, partly autobiographical novel about growing up in a housing project in the 1960s. Slow-paced and with too many trivial episodes receiving belaboured attention, its best moment is a tense scene in which the hero decides not to cheat on a test.

Thurman has described himself as "a philosopher who paints," and he is unapologetically didactic. Some may find his morals heavy-handed and simplistic, but at his best he creates animal tales that bring an amusing light to bear on problems all young children have encountered.

SECONDARY REFERENCE: *QQ* 51 (Oct. 85): 7–8.

# Toye, William E. (1926–        )

William Toye is one of Canada's most respected editors and authors. He has written two children's histories, *The St. Lawrence* (1959) and *Cartier Discovers the St. Lawrence* (1970), both winners of the CACL Award, and has collaborated with Elizabeth Cleaver on four retellings of Native Canadian folktales. However, Toye did not specifically intend to be a children's writer. Born in Toronto, he loved reading as a child and decided he wanted to enter the field of publishing. After graduation from the University of Toronto in 1948, he joined Oxford University Press, rising to the position of Editorial Director.

In order to have children's books to publish, he collaborated with Clarke Hutton on *A Picture History of Canada* (1956), and later wrote *The St. Lawrence*, drawing heavily on first-hand accounts to give children a lively, immediate account of the country's past. *Cartier Discovers the St. Lawrence* uses the journals of the explorer and is illustrated by Laszlo Gal.

He undertook the difficult job of rewriting Native legends, he has said, because he wanted Elizabeth Cleaver, whose art he greatly admired, to have books to illustrate. Their four collaborations are *The Mountain Goats of Temlaham* (1969), *How Summer Came to Canada* (1969), *The Loon's Necklace* (1977), and *The Fire Stealer* (1979). Although the books are most noted for their illustrations, the spare texts are very successful, combining a European narrative structure not found in the original legends with a sense of the originating Native culture. *The Loon's Necklace* won the Howard-Gibbon Medal.

Five of the children's books Toye edited have also won major awards. *Glooskap's Country* (1955) by Cyrus Macmillan, *The Golden Phoenix* (1958) by Marius Barbeau and Michael Hornyansky, *Tales of Nanabozho* (1963) by Dorothy Reid, and *The Double Knights* (1966) by James McNeill each received the CACL Award. Elizabeth Cleaver's illustrations for *The Wind Has Wings* (1968), compiled by Mary Alice Downie and Barbara Robertson, were awarded the first Howard-Gibbon

Medal. In 1972 Toye received the Vicky Metcalf Award for his distinguished contributions to Canadian children's literature.
SECONDARY REFERENCE: *Profiles 2*.

# Traill, Catharine Parr (1802–1899)

*The Canadian Crusoes: A Tale of the Rice Lake Plains* (1852; later retitled *Lost in the Backwoods*) by Catharine Parr Traill was the first major example of a form considered to be quintessentially Canadian: the outdoor adventure tale. Born in Kent, England, Mrs. Traill was a member of an immigrant family that made a significant contribution to Canadian letters. Her brother Samuel Strickland was author of *Twenty-seven years in Canada West* (1853), and her younger sister Susanna Moodie published numerous works, including *Roughing It in the Bush* (1852). Before moving to Canada in 1832, Mrs. Traill had written *The Tell Tale* (1818), a collection of children's tales, and several didactic and pious works, the most notable of which is *The Young Emigrants; or, Pictures of Canada* (1826), an epistolary novel based on the Canadian experiences of family friends.

An accomplished botanist as well as a pioneer who endured many hardships, Mrs. Traill wrote a number of adult works instructing others in the natural wonders of Canada and showing them how to turn the wilderness to their use. Her most famous adult works were *The Backwoods of Canada* (1836) and *The Female Emigrant's Guide* (1854; later retitled *The Canadian Settler's Guide*). The combination of accurate description of wilderness conditions and practical advice for survival found in these adult works also appears in *The Canadian Crusoes*. An attempt to impart practical instruction by pleasing readers with a survival tale, her story shows how three adolescents, two boys and a girl, survive in the forest for three years because of their previous knowledge, the instruction in survival techniques provided by a friendly Mohawk princess, and their sustaining Christian faith. In the end, the children, who became lost because they were careless and did not think sufficiently of others, are wiser and more thoughtful because of their adventures.

The story suffers from overt didacticism evident in the cataloguing of the flora of the region, complete with Latin names in the footnotes, from stilted, pious dialogue, and from an explicit attempt to make the wilderness adventure an allegory of life. It is, however, notable for its symbolic use of marriages between a Scot and a French Canadian and between the Mohawk princess and a white boy; Mrs. Traill thereby signals her hope that Canada will be a land of united aspirations and domestic harmony. The work is also notable for establishing the pattern of the circular journey into the wilderness testing ground that is the basis of novels by such modern Canadian wilderness writers as Farley Mowat and James Houston.

SECONDARY REFERENCE: Jeffrey M. Heath, ed., *Profiles in Canadian Literature 3* (1982): 25–32.

## *Truss, Jan (1925–     )*

Born in Stoke-on-Trent, England, Jan Truss grew up in a family that, although very poor, stimulated an interest in books and other cultural activities in all of its children. Truss won scholarships to a grammar school and then to university. After graduating with a teacher's certificate from Goldsmith's College, University of London, in 1945, she taught in the tough docks area of Liverpool and then in the British reform school system. She emigrated to Canada in 1957 and began a lengthy career teaching in Alberta. She received a BEd from the University of Alberta in 1962. Truss has written a number of stories for radio and magazines, but her published work for children consists of three plays and four novels.

Two of her plays are explorations of moral issues in Canadian history. *A Very Small Rebellion*, first produced in 1974 and published in *Ooomerahgi Oh and A Very Small Rebellion: Two Plays for Children* (1978), presents sympathetically the struggle of Louis Riel and his Métis followers to defend their lands and rights against the encroachments of settlers supported by the federal government. *The Judgement of Clifford Sifton*, produced in 1974 and published in 1977, uses a device similar to that popularized in Charles Dickens's *A Christmas Carol* to examine anew the settlement of the West. After his death, Sir Clifford Sifton (1861–1929), a politician often celebrated for his aggressive promotion of immigration, hears the voices of Conscience, Truth, and History challenge his accomplishments. At the end, the audience is asked to judge whether Sifton was justified in making some pay a high price in suffering so that people like those in the audience could benefit. Her other drama, *Ooomerahgi Oh*, a fantasy for preschoolers first produced in 1974, shows Mimi, the youngest of three children, maintaining her love of home in the face of enticements to wander into the wide world with the Traveller, an evil magician who enslaves the rest of the family.

In her novels, Truss treats social and moral difficulties faced by young people, generally focusing on the way characters handle the pressure of severe problems and thereby discover their identities and their relationship to others. Because it combines an historical essay and fiction, *A Very Small Rebellion* (1976) is an unusually powerful outgrowth of the play of the same title. Sections of the essay, an account of the Riel rebellion written by Jack Chambers, alternate with Truss's fictional account of the efforts of some Métis and Natives to resist eviction from their homes. The fact that the youths who are the focus of the story are staging Truss's play about Riel intensifies our sense of the continuity of historical conditions. Although the protesters

lose their battle, as did the followers of Riel, the youthful Métis acquires a new pride in his heritage.

Truss's other books are problem novels focusing on the difficulties of
talented young girls. *Bird at the Window* (1974), winner of the first
Search for a New Alberta Novelist Award in 1972, is a frank account of
teenage pregnancy that straddles the border between adolescent and
adult fiction. Eighteen-year-old Angela Moynahan, a lonely "brain" at
school, refuses to allow her unexpected pregnancy to interfere with a
long-planned trip to Europe. After the baby is stillborn, she returns to
Canada, where her father has just died, and tries to gain control of her
life. A tense psychological study that weaves themes of death, rebellion, liberation, and identity throughout, it does not judge Angela but
shows how she gradually comes to understand not only herself but also
her mother and the social pressures that often control people's lives.

*Jasmin* (1982), winner of the Ruth Schwartz Award, uses the
familiar pattern of the journey into the wilderness to show a young
girl's growth in identity. Jasmin Marie Antoinette Stalke, oldest of
seven children living in a squalid two-room farmhouse, runs away to
live in the woods when she can no longer bear the burden of looking
after her siblings and the noise and lack of privacy that prevents her
from doing her homework. During her journey she learns that she is a
talented artist who can gain acceptance outside of her family because
of her ability. The novel successfully presents events from the point of
view of several characters in order to provide a richer understanding of
Jasmin and the conditions against which she rebels.

*Summer Goes Riding* (1987) attempts to give sociological and psychological depth to the conventional horse story. Charlotte Mauney, a
Nebraska farm girl who longs for a horse so that she can become a
championship rider, matures as she learns to deal with jealousy and
thwarted ambition. The novel suffers from strained symbolism in the
mechanical gothicism of Charlotte's identification with an ancestor
killed by a horse and in the implausibility and heavily veiled eroticism
of Charlotte's transforming immersion in a river. Nevertheless, it contains some powerful sequences, especially its presentation of Charlotte's shock after a tornado destroys her home and all chances of obtaining her horse. A note of realistic hope prevents undue pessimism at
the conclusion: Charlotte's friends provide her with opportunities to be
around horses, and she determines to continue working for her dream.

Truss is an uncompromising artist who is at her best in her novels.
In them she deals with tough social and moral issues without preach-
ing or resorting to blatant didacticism. Her greatest strength is her
creation of characters who are fully convincing as people who have
problems. Her problem novels are thus meaningful pyschological
studies.

SECONDARY REFERENCES: *Profiles 2*; *CA* 102; *TCCW* 2.

# W *allace, Ian (1950–     )*

"My books all seem to deal with 'Very Last First Times'. But I wasn't conscious of this fact until a librarian drew it to my attention." So spoke Ian Wallace about the visual and verbal content of his five children's books. In *The Sandwich* (1975; illustrated by Angela Wood), *The Christmas Tree House* (1976), *Chin Chiang and the Dragon's Dance* (1984), *Very Last First Time* (1985; text by Jan Andrews), and *The Sparrow's Song* (1986), he combines his artistic talents, love of story, and sensitivity to the problems children face as they grow up. Born in Niagara Falls, Ontario, Ian Wallace studied graphic design at the Ontario College of Art and worked in advertising before, at the age of twenty-five, he rediscovered his childhood love of stories and began creating books for children.

Wallace's first two books were part of the Kids Can Press series about children of diverse cultures living in contemporary urban settings. In *The Sandwich*, Vincenzo eats his lunch at school for the first time. It is a powerfully smelling mortadella and provolone sandwich, and he is mocked by his classmates. His father explains, "Your friends laughed because it was different.... It was new to them." And he tells the boy, "You are who you are and you have nothing to be ashamed of." For Nick, the hero of *The Christmas Tree House*, "every Saturday would begin quite routinely, but once he closed the front door of his house, anything could happen." Just before Christmas, he and his new friend Gloria discover a treehouse that has been built by the dreaded local eccentric, Don Valley Rose, and learn that she is really a friendly and kind person. While these stories are relatively simple, they explore the themes of self-worth, understanding of others, and friendship that are developed more fully in Wallace's later works.

*Chin Chiang and the Dragon's Dance*, winner of the Howard-Gibbon Medal, portrays the insecurities of the title character as he prepares to participate with his grandfather in his first dragon's dance. Although Chin Chiang has waited for years for this opportunity, he fears he will fail, disappointing his parents and perhaps incurring the displeasure of the great sky dragon, thus causing a poor harvest in the coming year. Fleeing to the roof of the nearby public library, he meets Pu Yee, an old lady who, without his realizing it, helps him to practise the intricate steps of the dance. As the procession begins, Chin Chiang rushes to the street, where he joins his grandfather and the other dancers and invites his new friend to take part. At the conclusion of the story, Chin, his parents and grandfather, along with Pu Yee, celebrate a New Year's feast.

The illustrations, with their formalized designs, inclusion of several traditional religious symbols, and representation of contemporary Chinese-Canadian life, imply the importance of the community of which the boy is a part. The text simply states the importance of the dance in preparing for a prosperous new year. However, the dialogue of the grandfather, the neighbours, and the old lady make it very clear that Chin Chiang's participation will be an integral part of the success of the festivities.

His conflict is understandable. By taking his place with his grandfather and the other dancers, he will be assuming a meaningful role in his society for the first time. As his grandfather tells him, "Every dragon must have a tail as well as a head." Although Chin chooses at first to reject responsibility, he discovers that retreat is impossible. Like the wise helper in many traditional folktales, the old lady he meets subtly begins building his confidence. That his process of integration into the community has commenced is indicated in the illustration of the two dancing; the figures are in harmony as they perform the intricate steps on the library roof. The integration is completed as the family celebrates. Chin is no longer set apart from other people in the illustrations; he is in the midst of his family in a room gorgeously decorated in traditional Chinese style.

*Very Last First Time* is the first work of another writer that Wallace has illustrated. However, the story is certainly a congenial one for him, dealing as it does with a young person's engaging in an activity that integrates her into her culture. Eva Padlyat makes her first solitary journey under the sea ice to gather mussels. In planning the illustrations, Wallace deliberately chose a different style. "*Very Last First Time* could not have been painted with the same intricate detailing as *Chin Chiang*. The very nature of the culture it was portraying demanded a style that was much looser and freer to accurately reflect the Inuit society."

The words and pictures of *Very Last First Time* transform an unusual northern experience into a universal journey of maturation. The movement from village to seashore and under the ice is one away from the known and secure. As Eva wanders away from the hole in the ice she is entering the unknown. When she finds herself in darkness and hears the tide beginning to flood, she has reached the turning point of her journey; relighting her candle, she moves towards the hole, the light, her mother, and finally, the village.

Wallace's illustrations reinforce and expand on the meaning of the narrative both in the structural patterns and in specific details. Two colours dominate: yellow representing the known, secure world, and purple, representing the realm Eva enters alone for the first time. Visually the reader moves from yellow to purple and back to yellow; similarly Eva leaves her home and later returns to it. Within the story, the same movement of colour is seen. In the second structural pattern, Wallace moves from single-page illustrations in the scenes above ice to double spreads in those under ice, and back to single-page illustrations as Eva rejoins her mother.

The details of individual pictures reflect the inner experiences. Eva's home is ordinary: on the outside it is painted yellow; within there is a refrigerator and an electric stove; a picture of Michael Jackson is taped to the fridge; a box of cornflakes is on the table. But through the window can be seen purple expanses of sea ice. Once Eva has entered the underworld, she is in a place of darker hues and threatening shapes of animals and spirit creatures. Psychologically, she is confronting her fears of the unknown. The glow from the candles only slightly diminishes the darkness. When she finds herself in darkness, she covers her face in despair. Yellow has vanished from the illustration. The relighting of the candles, the return of yellow into the pictures, signals the beginning of her return to the human world. The final illustration shows her seated at the kitchen table. However, purple hues are not absent; they are found in the mussel shells, her sweater, and the sky in the window behind her. She has not left her experiences behind her. She has brought the memories of them back to the ordinary world in which she lives.

Wallace's most recent book, *The Sparrow's Song*, is set in Niagara Falls near the beginning of the twentieth century. When a mother sparrow is killed by her brother, Katie cares for the orphaned fledgling. Finally agreeing to forgive Charles for his murderous deed, she joins with him in gathering food for the bird and teaching it to fly. The crisis occurs when the children's mother insists that they liberate the growing bird. In the story, Wallace deals with a familiar theme: the chance for children to grow in understanding their world and the people in it. However, he deepens his concerns as the children confront major aspects of nature: the mysteries of life and death, and the need of nature's children to be free. Katie becomes a care giver, Charles accepts responsibility for his actions and their consequences, and the two grow in their love for each other.

The book's opening and closing illustrations deal with the themes of birth, growth, and death. The title page depicts an empty nest. The mother will never return, for she will be killed by Charles's slingshot. The baby has left the nest in the first stage of growth. In the concluding picture, the sparrow and its mate stand above their nest, proudly guarding three speckled eggs; the cycle of life is beginning anew.

The illustrations also trace the changing relationships between Katie and Charles. In the early pictures, Katie is seen alone or in confrontational situations with her brother. The transition is depicted in a wordless, two-page spread. In order to teach the sparrow to fly, they dance together, twigs and grass woven into their clothes and hair. In the background is the mystic gorge and Niagara Falls, whose spiritual powers, it is implied, are influencing the children.

Although Wallace's literary output is small, his works comprise, in words and pictures, a significant and strong vision of life. They emphasize not only the individual's need for self-worth but also the necessity for individuals to understand themselves in relation to family and friends, to their cultures, and to the powerful world of nature of which they are a part.

SECONDARY REFERENCES: *CA* 107; *Canadian Library Journal* 42 (Oct. 85): 304–5.

# Waterton, Betty (1923–          )

Betty Waterton had her first work, a poem, published in the *Vancouver Sun* when she was twelve years old. But although she worked as a newspaper reporter and television artist, the Oshawa-born writer did not see her first children's book in print until 1978. By that time she had raised a family and was living with her husband in Sidney, British Columbia. *A Salmon for Simon* (1978), illustrated by Ann Blades, was followed in 1980 by *Pettranella*, also illustrated by Blades. Waterton has since written the text for two other picture books, *Mustard* (1983; illustrated by Barbara Reid) and *Orff, 27 Dragons and a Snarkel* (1984; illustrated by Karen Kulyk), and two novels, *Quincy Rumpel* (1984) and *Starring Quincy Rumpel* (1986). In addition, she has translated and adapted into novel form the script of the motion picture *The Dog Who Stopped the War* (1985).

Waterton's stories can be divided into two groups. The first deals with young characters overcoming problems in their lives. In *A Salmon for Simon*, the title hero feels inadequate because he is the only person in his West Coast Native village unable to catch a fish. Pettranella is unhappy because she has lost the flower seeds her grandmother had given her to take from their old world home to a new homestead in Manitoba. Orff is the only member of his group of dragons who cannot fly. The characters resolve their conflicts by helping others: Simon liberates a salmon trapped in a tidal pool; Pettranella discovers that the seeds she had lost have bloomed in the wilderness and is happy that they will give joy to passing travellers; Orff finds happiness with a school of fish he has rescued from the dreaded Snarkel.

The second group of stories deals with the humorous adventures and misadventures of zany characters. In *Mustard*, an oversized and wild puppy with a penchant for trouble finds a home after he rescues a kitten from the sea. *Quincy Rumpel* and *Starring Quincy Rumpel* focus on the escapades of eleven-year-old Quincy and her unpredictable family. In the first book, the heroine, her brother, her sister, her mother, and her father, an impractical inventor, pile in their old stationwagon to travel across the country to a new home in Vancouver. Quincy is disaster prone: she locks herself on the balcony of the new house, breaks through the attic floor, cracks her brand new glasses, and gives herself a new perm — which turns out horribly. In the sequel, *Starring Quincy Rumpel*, she wants to appear on television so that she can help her father sell his latest invention, home trampolines called Rumpel Rebounders. The accounts of her escapades are told in a lively, fast-paced, and humorous fashion.

In her sensitive portrayal of the problems faced by young children and her humorous depiction of Quincy and the dog Mustard, Betty Waterton has created books that are widely enjoyed by middle and upper elementary readers.
SECONDARY REFERENCE: *SATA* 34.

# Wilson, Eric (1940–        )

"The package was ticking." Thus begins *Murder on the Canadian* (1976), the first of the Tom and Liz Austen mysteries by Eric Wilson. Each book in the series begins with a similar short, action-charged, one-sentence paragraph deliberately designed to force readers, especially reluctant ones, into continuing with the book.

Eric Hamilton Wilson was born in Ottawa, but he lived in St. John's, Montreal, Winnipeg, Saskatoon, Regina, and Kitimat because his father, a member of the RCMP, was transferred frequently. His father's occupation taught him about Canada and also gave him a love of mystery. He remembers unsuccessfully searching for crimes to solve when he was a boy in Winnipeg. After receiving a BA and teacher certification from the University of British Columbia, he spent two years in England and Scotland, working at a number of jobs, including reporter for the London Bureau of the Canadian Press, while he tried to write adult fiction. He gave up, he says, when he discovered he had "nothing to say to adults of importance." He returned to Canada and taught slow learners in White Rock, British Columbia. While watching students reject as boring the books provided for them, he developed his ideas about suitable books for reluctant readers and determined to write something his class would willingly read all the way through.

Although his students enjoyed his books when he read them aloud, Wilson had five manuscripts rejected by publishers in five years. The breakthrough came when he made a return journey to England and met Margaret Clark, a children's editor for Bodley Head. She encouraged him to continue, but she also showed him some of his problems. "She showed me that I needed to plot the stories and that I had to have a very clear moral viewpoint. I had to know exactly how I felt about the actions of my characters and the actions of people they were interacting with."

Wilson combined this advice with lessons learned from his observations of his students to devise a formula for books that would capture interest. First, he decided that the book had to be short; otherwise, students who find reading difficult and long books threatening would pass over it. Next, the story had to start immediately. His use of the dramatic opening is a calculated narrative hook, "not unlike that in a television show," designed to lure the reluctant reader into the book. He also knew that the language had to be simple and straightforward, but he did not want to go to the extreme of some controlled vocabulary texts: "I don't believe that an unfamiliar word is a roadblock in a good story."

In addition, he felt the story needed lots of dialogue for three reasons: to add interest because conversation is dramatic and active; to add to the sense of realism; to create "a lot of white space" that breaks up the dense blocks of text that frighten reluctant readers. Finally, he knew that he had to keep enticing readers, so he determined to end each chapter with a cliff-hanger that would force the reader on to the next chapter where, of course, the action would build to another suspenseful situation.

Wilson's aim in the Austen mysteries is "to combine the adventure of the Hardy Boys with the true detection of an Agatha Christie novel. The reader then becomes an active participant in the story." Not surprisingly the first one, *Murder on the Canadian*, contains references to both the Hardy Boys and Agatha Christie, and its setting and title echo Christie's *Murder on the Orient Express*. Furthermore, Wilson deliberately gives the books Canadian settings he has visited. By filling the novels with pieces of historical data and interesting facts about each setting, he hopes to educate and excite his readers about Canada. The one non-Canadian title, *Disneyland Hostage* (1982), was to be the first of a series of "international novels" presenting "other parts of the world through Canadian eyes" — those of Liz Austen — but he has apparently abandoned the project.

Wilson's mysteries fall into two broad categories. The first, the traditional adventure-mystery story, puts the hero or heroes into threatening or mysterious circumstances that demand detection and luck to survive: the emphasis in these is thrilling adventure and red-herring mysteries. This category includes *Murder on the Canadian, The Lost Treasure of Casa Loma* (1980), *The Ghost of Lunenburg Manor* (1981), *Vampires of Ottawa* (1984), and *The Green Gables Detectives* (1987). His first mystery without one of the Austens, *The Unmasking of 'Ksan* (1986), also belongs to this group, even though it does give some attention to the issue of Natives' pride in their culture. The second group uses the settings and the mystery formula to provide what Wilson calls "educational matter" that enables the books to function as "teaching vehicles" or "springboards for discussions in classrooms." In these, issues from the evening news become important thematic elements. Thus, *Terror in Winnipeg* (1979) and *Spirit in the Rainforest* (1984) express environmental concerns, the former about industrial pollution and Minamata disease, and the latter about the devastation of clear-cut logging. *Terror in Winnipeg*, together with *Disneyland Hostage*, shows terror as a misguided instrument of social reform. *Vancouver Nightmare* (1978), *Disneyland Hostage*, and *The Kootenay Kidnapper* (1983) are efforts to "streetproof" children. The first shows the sordid world of drugs that often claims runaways. The second tries to show that quiet compliance with the demands of terrorists, not hostile opposition, is necessary when one is held ransom. *The Kootenay Kidnapper*, inspired by the grisly Clifford Olson case of kidnap-murders in British Columbia, seeks to teach children the necessity of avoiding strangers, even those who seem like figures of authority. It shows some of the tricks that Olson and others have used to lure away unsuspecting children.

Wilson's plots are improbable, but he tries to give his young heroes some reality. Thus their conversations are filled with corny jokes and riddles, they constantly play practical jokes, and they govern themselves by a code that demands getting even for the jokes played on them. Most importantly, his young detectives are not improbably heroic or infallible. Tom, for example, constantly makes mistakes in identifying the villains. Wilson claims that "kids like the fact that Tom isn't Encyclopedia Brown, omniscient, highly successful." He feels that they identify with him more readily because he is an ordinary boy who "blunders around" and worries that his sister may discover something important and get glory before he does.

In addition to the mysteries, Wilson has also published two problem novels, *Susie-Q* (1978), a tough-minded exploration of class bias and teenage pregnancy, and *Summer of Discovery* (1984), which contains two parallel stories of independence, one involving a handicapped boy and the other an able-bodied one.

Eric Wilson admits that he doesn't write what he calls "capital L literature," because he is writing for a specific need. He refuses, however, to allow his publishers to indicate in any way that his books are written for reluctant readers. The result is that he has become enormously popular with both his intended audience and a much younger group of accomplished readers. Wilson's books do have flaws. In particular, his concern for action means that characterization is sometimes much too weak. Nevertheless, he has worked hard to produce books that, even when they are improbable, are carefully plotted, swift in movement, and interesting in setting. For many readers, both the reluctant and the accomplished, Wilson has succeeded in providing books that are both entertaining and informative.

SECONDARY REFERENCES: *ChLQ* 8 (Summer 83): 44–45, 34; *Profiles 2*; *SATA* 34; *CA* 101.

# Wynne-Jones, Tim (1948–        )

"His research into the history of the Mafia was a fairy tale but like any fairy tale, it was peppered with very real aspects; reality observed through a distorted glass, no less real for the distortion." This comment about one of the characters in Tim Wynne-Jones's adult novel *The Knot* (1982) could well be applied to the author, especially as a creator of children's stories and poems. In *Madeline & Ermadello* (1977), *Zoom at Sea* (1983), *Zoom Away* (1985), *Mischief City* (1986), and *I'll Make You Small* (1986), he has mixed reality and fantasy to create characters and situations that, although make-believe, reflect experiences and emotions true to human nature.

Born in Cheshire, England, Wynne-Jones grew up in Kitimat, British Columbia, Vancouver, and Ottawa. He received a BA from the

University of Waterloo and an MFA from York University, and has worked as a book designer, rock singer, lyricist for the television program *Fraggle Rock*, teacher, and children's book reviewer. His first adult novel, *Odd's End* (1980), won the Seal First Novel Prize.

*Madeline & Ermadello*, an outgrowth of an Ontario government Opportunities for Youth grant project, is a relatively slight story about the relationship between a little girl and her imaginary friend. The book anticipates two themes of Wynne-Jones's later stories: the creative power of imagination and the importance of love and friendship.

The two Zoom books grew out of the author's observations of his own water-loving cat and a desire to create a book with his friend, artist Ken Nutt. It seemed logical, the author later recalled, to send the hero to the seashore. However, that seemed to be a fairly trivial approach: "And then I thought of the enclosed quality of Ken Nutt's drawings and realized that Zoom would have to find the sea inside a magical house." In the house, Zoom meets Maria, a woman who is a kind of Jungian mother figure, a fact Wynne-Jones admits but did not consciously impose while writing. In *Zoom at Sea*, Maria lets the sea into her house and permits the hero to take a wonderful raft ride. He returns to shore and leaves her house to return home. In *Zoom Away*, he again visits Maria, goes upstairs with her in the magical house, walks through a dark passage to the North Pole, and discovers his Uncle Roy's ship, stuck in the winter ice. He then returns to Maria's house.

Although the adventures of Zoom are relatively simple, one can see their appeal to younger children. Zoom is small and inquisitive, and when he leaves his familiar home he is discovering a new world, in his case a world of imagination and magic. He must explore alone, but nearby there is the adult, Maria, providing security and, if needed, help. She is like the fairy godmother of folktales, helping the hero to help himself.

*I'll Make You Small*, like the Zoom books, sends a young person into the world of an adult; however, both the tone of the story and the significance of the child's adventure are much different. Redemption, a theme found in Wynne-Jones's adult novels, is important in this story; the boy hero is the agent of that redemption, courageously and thoughtfully entering into an unknown and frightening house to help Mr. Swanskin escape from his self-imposed isolation. In addition to presenting the boy's heroic qualities, Wynne-Jones successfully portrays a child's view of many adults.

*Mischief City* is a collection of poems in the tradition of A. A. Milne's *Now We Are Six* and Dennis Lee's *Alligator Pie*. Based on the author's observations of his son and his remembrances of his own childhood, the twenty-five poems focus on the two worlds of Winchell: the one containing his parents and baby sister, and the one he has created with his imagination. In the former, he laments the difficulty of communicating with his sister and discusses the problems of adjusting to her. His imaginary world, realized in the pictures he draws, contains monsters over which he exercises control, and his imaginary friend Maxine. "I Wasn't Angry When I Thought About Maxine," the focal poem of the collection, describes the wonderful day when he drew the girl into existence and received the praise of the baby and his parents.

The success of Wynne-Jones's books results not only from the high quality of the poems and stories he has created, but also from his close collaboration with his illustrators. His are true picture books in which the words and pictures complement each other to create the total impression. *Zoom at Sea* and *Zoom Away*, both winners of the Howard-Gibbon Medal, were written with the qualities of Nutt's illustrations strongly in mind. Victor Gad's illustrations for *Mischief City* unify the individual poems. Maryann Kovalski's pictures for *I'll Make You Small* capture the frightening quality of the house Roland enters and the feeling of vulnerability he experiences as Mr. Swanskin angrily chases after him.

Although Tim Wynne-Jones's literary output for children is relatively small, he has quickly established himself as a major Canadian children's author. His stories and poems are written with an exquisite feeling for the sounds and meanings of language and with a sense of what children enjoy. More importantly, he knows what rings true to their experience of the world; in his specific characters he has captured the universality of childhood.

SECONDARY REFERENCE: *QQ* 50 (Apr. 84): 10–11.

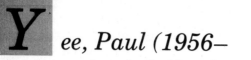

# Yee, Paul (1956– )

Paul Yee was born in Spalding, Saskatchewan, and raised in the Strathcona and Chinatown districts of Vancouver. He studied Canadian history at the University of British Columbia, graduating with a BA in 1978 and an MA in 1983, and is now an archivist for the City of Vancouver. An author of poetry, short fiction, and articles for adults, Yee turned to writing for children when a publisher asked him to produce a book about life in Vancouver's Chinatown. Believing that the request provided him with the opportunity "to portray accurately how kids lived in that neighbourhood and to give them an accurate mirror to help them grow," Yee wrote *Teach Me To Fly, Skyfighter! and Other Stories* (1983), four loosely linked stories of contemporary life. He followed this with an historical novel, *The Curses of the Third Uncle* (1986), "to immortalize and thank those who raised me and to celebrate the strengths that enable common people to overcome adversities." Although set in different times, both books examine the tense interaction of old-country traditions and new world realities.

The narratives in *Teach Me To Fly, Skyfighter! and Other Stories* provide a graphic indication of daily life in the Chinatown area, but their focus is not local colour. Each story concentrates on the psychology of the protagonists and explores the identity problems of children in an ethnic community. Although never resorting to unrealistic events, each story works to a significant climax, usually involving acceptance by the group. For example, in the title story, Canadian-born Sharon Fong symbolically comes to terms with her heritage by flying a kite made by an old Chinese man.

*The Curses of the Third Uncle* uses the framework of an adventure tale and mystery to explore the question of female identity and the possibility of individual heroism. Set in British Columbia in 1909 against the background of the conflict between those seeking to overthrow the Chinese emperor and those seeking to prevent a revolution, it traces the development of Lillian Ho. Lillian represents the possibilities in the new world. Steeped in the sword tales of the Orient and taught the ancient medical art of "breath fighting," she becomes both warrior and healer. She thus uses old-country knowledge to preserve the safety of her family in Canada. Her evil "third uncle," who represents the worst side of Chinese feudalism, constantly threatens to send her back to China, noting as he does so that "Girls in China are garbage...." Lillian displays physical courage by exposing her third uncle's schemes, but she also demonstrates maturity when she teaches her mother that China means fear and Canada means hope.

Yee's stories are neither preachy nor pretentious. Whether treating a modern or historical situation, he successfully evokes the Chinese-Canadian community and portrays his characters as significant individuals struggling to achieve a satisfying identity.

# Young, Scott (1918–        )

One of Canada's top sports journalists, Scott Young was born in Glenboro, Manitoba. After serving in the Navy during World War II, he began a newspaper career, working for *The Winnipeg Free Press*, the Toronto *Telegram*, and the Toronto *Globe and Mail*. Among his many adult books are *Hockey is a Battle: Punch Imlach's Own Story* (1969), *War on Ice* (1976), and *Hello Canada: the Life and Times of Foster Hewitt* (1985). For children he has written *The Clue of the Dead Duck* (1962), a mystery; *Hockey Heroes Series* (1974); and three hockey novels: *Scrubs on Skates* (1952; revised 1985), *Boy on Defence* (1953; revised 1985), and *A Boy at the Leafs' Camp* (1963; revised 1985).

Although the revisions for the hockey trilogy update topical references, the books remain essentially unchanged, asserting the positive values of sports current during the 1950s and 1960s, and capturing the excitement of action on the ice. In *Scrubs on Skates*, star player Pete Gordon is angry that he must play at a new high school on a team made up of inferior players or "scrubs." Only when he examines his actions and takes a more positive attitude to the other players does he really feel a member of the team. In *Boy on Defence*, a team looks suspiciously at a new player and must come to understand that teamwork is more necessary than talent. *A Boy at the Leafs' Camp* portrays the experiences of Pete's teammate Bill Spunska, a Polish immigrant trying to make the difficult transition from high-school hockey to the National Hockey League.

SECONDARY REFERENCES: *SATA* 5; *TCCW 1*.

# Zola, Meguido (1939–        )

Meguido Zola was born in Cairo, Egypt, raised in Kenya, and educated in France at the Sorbonne and in England at the University of Leeds and Bristol University. Now teaching in the Education Faculty, Simon Fraser University, Zola has produced a number of educational and scholarly works as well as a variety of children's books.

Zola's best work is derived from traditional storytelling. *A Dream of Promise: A Folktale in Hebrew and English* (1980) is a dignified bilingual retelling of a traditional tale about a boy who, after making a long journey, finds that his promised treasure is buried in the very building from which he began the journey. However, Zola's moral, which makes the entire story a symbolic allegory of the discovery of self, is too lengthy and heavy-handed. In *Only the Best* (1981), illustrated by Valerie Littlewood, Zola effectively uses the traditional structures of repetitive scenes and a cumulative climax to tell the story of a foolish father who searches everywhere for the perfect gift for his infant daughter. In the end, the father discovers, as wiser people had said, that the perfect gift, his love, was within him all along.

Zola's other books are varied. *Moving* (1983) is historical fiction. In it, a little girl comes to accept that her Mennonite community's move is a symbol of the movements that living requires. *Nobody* (1983), co-authored by Angela Dereume, uses the repetitive formula of folktales to tell the comical story of three contemporary Native children who try to convince their mother that a mysterious "Nobody" is responsible for all the mischief around the house. *My Kind of Pup* (1985), a comical monologue, is particularly successful in generating humour through Zola's verbal irony, his surprise plot twist at the end, and Wendy Wolsak's drawings, which comically contradict the boy's praise of his well-behaved pup.

Zola has also written four biographies in the "Picture-Life Series": *Gretzky! Gretzky! Gretzky!* (1982), *Karen Kain: Born to Dance* (1983), *Sharon, Lois & Bram* (1983), and *Terry Fox: "Dreams Are Made If People Try"* (1984). The last two were co-authored with his wife, Melanie Zola.

# Part II:
# Using Canadian Children's Books in the Schools

# *C*anadian Children's Stories in the Language Arts Curriculum

Introduction

If you were to survey Canadian children, you would undoubtedly discover two things: first, the majority spend considerably more time watching television than reading, and second, those who do read books read far more non-Canadian than Canadian books. These situations, particularly the latter, are especially upsetting because the last two decades have witnessed the publication of large numbers of Canadian children's books of such high quality that few children could fail to find among them works that would entertain them and enrich their lives.

One way of introducing children to the vast array of worthwhile Canadian stories is to make Canadian children's literature an integral part of the literature segment of the Language Arts programs in schools. Not only will Canadian books provide valuable examples of the use of art and language at their best, but they will also introduce children to many elements of our rich and diverse cultural heritage.

This section suggests a number of class-tested approaches and techniques for incorporating Canadian children's stories into elementary and junior high school curricula. After briefly discussing the processes of reading and the basic components of literature, we examine techniques for helping children to read picture books, short stories, and novels more fully; introduce ways of relating Canadian children's stories to those of other countries; and describe methods of using Canadian stories as starting points for student writing.

Reading: The Creation of Meaning

When we read a book, we play an important role in the creation of its meaning. Unless we actively respond to the material on the page in front of us, unless, as the reading specialists say, we actively engage with the text, we are not reading; we are only passively absorbing stimuli. A closed book, or a book to which we do not actively respond, is inert; it has no life. It is the reader who gives life to a story, who completes the process of communication that began when the writer wrote the words or the illustrator created the pictures. Good writers need and expect good readers. Between them, they form a partnership out of which real books, books created by both of them, are born.

Stories have two basic components: details, presented by words, or in the case of picture books, by illustrations, and patterns. Authors select details and arrange these into patterns. However, they do not belabour their points. They do not stop telling their stories to say, "Notice what I've just said and remember it when you read page 15 in the next chapter. If you do, you'll see that I've developed a pattern that means —." Instead, they ask that their readers perform two essential activities. Readers must notice the details and the patterns, and then they must interpret these details and patterns to give them meaning.

For example, readers of Mordecai Richler's *Jacob Two-Two Meets the Hooded Fang* should notice the specific events of the hero's waking life as presented in the first two chapters. During Jacob's dream, several of these events recur in altered fashion. Seeing the pattern, readers can begin the process of interpretation, beginning with the premise that in the dream Jacob is working out problems that bothered him in his waking life. Similarly, readers looking at the illustrations of Ann Blades' classic picture book *Mary of Mile 18* will notice that many of the pictures contain cold and dull colours, whereas others contain warm and bright ones. Colours form a pattern that communicates the changing emotions of the young protagonist, Mary Fehr.

Helping students to develop the skills that enable them to notice and interpret the details and patterns should be an important goal of Language Arts programs. Before considering methods to achieve this goal, however, we must first examine some basic elements of stories, because an understanding of these is essential for developing meaningful approaches to stories.

Essential Details and Patterns of Stories

All writing makes use of details and patterns. In literature, these are used in special, unique ways. An encyclopedia article about possible conditions of life after a nuclear holocaust will be as direct and specific as possible. A novel on this subject, like Suzanne Martel's *The City Under Ground* or Monica Hughes' *Beyond the Dark River*, will also attempt to be scientifically accurate, but the details and patterns will also be suggestive or connotative, seeking to imply character conflicts, moods, and themes. The novel will invite a reader to understand and feel the lives of characters as they confront incredibly difficult physical and psychological situations.

*Conflict: the Basic Pattern*

Every story for children must have a conflict. Without conflict, the story would lack both the tension that stimulates interest in the events and the meaning implicit in the development of those events. Near the beginning of a story, something must go wrong or be wrong; the rest of the story must show how what is wrong is set right, how the conflict is resolved. Stories have clearly defined beginnings, middles, and ends, and the details introduce the conflict, trace its development in the middle of the story, and present its resolution at the conclusion.

At the beginning of *Anne of Green Gables*, the heroine feels lonely, insecure, and unloved; at the end, she has a home, a sense of self-worth, and a circle of loving friends. In Lindee Climo's *Clyde*, the farm horse is frightened that he will no longer be needed because the farmer has bought a new tractor. His conflict is resolved when he is given the job of taking neighbouring children for rides. Between the introduction and resolution of the conflicts of these two stories, the authors include the details that show how the characters attempt to resolve the conflicts.

Mathematical problems or scientific experiments could also be said to involve conflicts. In the former, a person must come up with the correct answer; in the latter, a person must discover some new fact or law. But neither of these could be called stories. They lack the essential ingredient of stories — characters.

### Characters: the Basic Ingredient

Characters, the beings who face difficulties and must resolve conflicts, come in an incredible variety of forms in children's literature — realistically portrayed animals, as in Sir Charles G.D. Roberts' *Red Fox*; animals with distinctly human qualities and habits, as in Margaret Laurence's *Jason's Quest*; human beings from the past, as in Jan Hudson's *Sweetgrass*; human beings from other worlds, as in Ruth Nichols' *A Walk Out of the World*; and human beings similar to the reader, as in Jean Little's *Mama's Going to Buy You a Mockingbird*.

But no matter what the form, each character resolves the conflict only by finding answers to the basic questions underlying nearly every story. The most frequent and central of these questions are "Who am I?" and "Where do I belong?" These are fundamental questions for all human beings because we all need a sense of our own identity and a sense that we belong to a community. Conflicts arise when these questions are asked, and conflicts are resolved when the answers are found.

In many children's stories, the answers to the questions provide happy solutions to the conflict. Elliot Kravitz, in Patti Stren's *Hug Me*, finally meets.a true friend. Badger, in Kay Hill's *Badger, the Mischief Maker*, is reunited with his little brother. In other stories, frequently in those intended for older children or young adults, the conflict is resolved when characters accept the painful knowledge they have acquired. Both Olwen, in Monica Hughes' *Keeper of the Isis Light*, and the title heroine of Cora Taylor's *Julie* realize the pain and accept the responsibilities that are created because they are different from other people.

### Some Character Types

After we have read a large number of stories, we begin to see that some characters resemble characters in other stories. It is not just that writers are consciously imitating each other, although sometimes they do. Most probably, it is because certain kinds of characters with certain kinds of personality traits and certain kinds of problems or conflicts hold a special interest for storytellers and readers alike. By recognizing that a character belongs to a certain type, we have a framework to guide us in our understanding of him or her. Although the following list of character types in children's stories is not exhaustive, it should help the reader to recognize the major types. Readers should note that characters in a story can be classified under more than one type, and that characters of superficially different forms, such as animal characters and human beings, may nevertheless belong to the same type.

a) The outsider: orphans, newcomers to a community, people with marked physical or psychological differences, and members of minority groups fit into this category. The title heroine of Beatrice Culleton's *In Search of April Raintree*; Shichan, in Shizuye Takashima's *A Child in Prison Camp*; Anna, in Jean Little's *Listen for the Singing*; and Rose Larkin, in Janet Lunn's *The Root Cellar* are outsiders. Their conflicts are resolved when they find acceptance within a group.

b) The unlikely hero: whereas heroes like Robin Hood, King Arthur, or Superman are unquestionably superior beings, the unlikely hero is, at the beginning of a story, often rejected by others because of a perceived inferiority. During the course of a story, the unlikely hero either develops or discovers and then exhibits heroic qualities. Because of social attitudes or social conditioning, girls and women are often included in this category. Youngest children or children in a world of adults are also unlikely heroes. Examples of unlikely heroes can be found in Maria Campbell's *Little Badger and the Fire Spirit*, Dennis Lee's *Lizzy's Lion*, and Robin Muller's *Mollie Whuppie and the Giant*.

c) The trickster: this type of character is frequently found in Native folklore. Raven, Napi, Coyote, Wisakajak, Nanabozho, and Glooscap are noted examples. Tricksters are mixed characters. At times they use their cleverness to help their people, but at other times they merely wish to fulfill their selfish desires. Often they are not as clever as they think, and their schemes backfire.

d) Helpers: in many stories, the hero is a helper, using positive qualities to assist others. In a sense, in helping, the hero is answering the question, "Where do I belong?" Helper heroes assert their links to their community by strengthening that community through their deeds. As we have seen, the Native trickster, in his better moments, is a helper. Such is the case with Nanabozho in Elizabeth Cleaver's *The Fire Stealer*. Simon, in Betty Waterton's *A Salmon for Simon*, feels that he is a real member of his village after he has liberated a trapped salmon. At first, the hero in Robin Muller's *The Sorcerer's Apprentice* merely wants to make his way in the world; but, by liberating a princess, he helps to save a kingdom and makes a royal marriage.

*Actions: the Testing of Characters*
When we read good stories for the first time, we are anxious to find out what happens next and how things will finally turn out. That is because we have developed an interest in, even a sympathy or empathy for, the main characters. We want to see how they will perform — in

effect, we are examining their character development. The characters' actions need not necessarily be physical actions; they may have to pass psychological or spiritual tests if they are to resolve the conflicts.

Short stories may contain only one or two important actions, and these may be quite simple. In Elizabeth Cleaver's *The Mountain Goats of Temlaham*, a boy rescues a small goat that was being abused by other children; later, the goat, now full grown, saves the boy as reward for his earlier kindness. In *The Paper Bag Princess*, by Robert Munsch, the heroine tricks a dragon, causing him to become so exhausted that she can easily rescue a prince. The events of these stories reflect the inner qualities of the characters, qualities that lead to happy resolutions of conflicts. By rescuing the goat, the boy reveals his goodness and his respect for all living things. The princess is both clever and caring: she not only saves the prince, but she also spares the dragon.

A quick look at actions in Canadian stories might suggest that they range from the apparently small and insignificant to the apparently large and significant. In Phoebe Gilman's *Jillian Jiggs*, a little girl must tidy up her messy room; the title character of Betty Waterton's *Pettranella* loses a packet of flower seeds; in Jan Hudson's *Sweetgrass*, the heroine single-handedly nurses her family through a smallpox epidemic that strikes in the middle of winter; Kamik, in Markoosie's *Harpoon of the Hunter*, kills a rabid polar bear and later commits suicide. However large or small, each of these events is very important within the context of the story of which it is a part. Each is a vital element in the development of the conflict and the growth of the character. Attentive readers will ask of each element, "How does it help the character answer the questions 'Who am I?' and 'Where do I belong?'"

*Settings: the Places of Testing*
Every story has to take place somewhere; Canadian children's stories occur in a wide variety of settings: specific geographical locations, as in Eric Wilson's *The Lost Treasure of Casa Loma*; generalized areas, such as the Arctic in James Houston's *The White Archer*; imaginary lands, like those in Pierre Berton's *The Secret World of Og*; or dream landscapes, as in Allan Morgan's *Matthew and the Midnight Tow Truck*.

Every story must also occur at some time. Although the time is most frequently and unemphatically the present, Canadian children's stories also use other time periods as a significant part of the setting: remote and generalized periods of time, as in Roderick Haig-Brown's tale of precontact Native life, *The Whale People*; specific historical periods, sometimes associated with particular historical events, such as the 1826 smashing of William Lyon Mackenzie's printing press in James Reaney's *The Boy with an R in His Hand*; sometimes time periods associated with a set of social conditions, such as those in the early part of World War II in Myra Paperny's *Take a Giant Step*; and the technologically advanced future, as in Monica Hughes' *The Tomorrow City*. The temporal setting also includes lesser units of time, such

as morning or night and the seasons, and such special events as Easter
and Christmas. Such times may be symbolically significant. The title
hero of James Houston's *Tikta 'liktak* returns in the spring, the season
of rebirth and renewal, to find that his home, where there was once
starvation, now has abundant game. In Jean Little's *Mama's Going to
Buy You a Mockingbird*, at Christmas, the festival of giving and hope,
Jeremy Talbot gives his mother an owl carving symbolizing his deceased father's love.

Settings can make significant contributions to stories. They can provide physical backdrops for the actions, and they help to create mood.
But more importantly, they help us to understand the development of
the characters, particularly as they search for a place to belong,
because every setting can be categorized as either home or not-home.

Home is the central focus in the lives of virtually all children. And
stories for children generally involve the characters' relationships with
home. The conflicts in stories usually have the central characters
either departing from or being excluded from a home situation of love
and security. In the course of making their journeys, the characters
travel through a series of not-home settings before reaching one that is
a home. In linear journeys, the character establishes a home by travelling to a completely new place. In circular journeys, the character returns to the point of departure, which is now a home for him or her. In
either case, at the end of their journeys, after the resolution of their
conflicts, the characters are generally in a home situation, secure in
their role and position. What happens in their journeys, the actions in
which they participate and the obstacles they overcome, make it possible for them to reach their final home destination.

With the idea of home and not-home in mind, we can see why so
many children's stories contain orphans. Anne Shirley in L. M. Montgomery's *Anne of Green Gables*, Jeanne in Suzanne Martel's *The King's
Daughter*, Rose Larkin in Janet Lunn's *The Root Cellar*, or Judith and
Tobit in Ruth Nichols' *A Walk Out of the World*, do not, at the beginning of their stories, have homes, or they feel that they are outsiders in
the places where they live. Their stories are about their searches for
and earning of homes. Many other stories are about entire families
who have left their old homes and must create new ones. Barbara
Smucker's *Underground to Canada* and Mary Alice Downie's *Honor
Bound* fit into this category.

Many realistic stories dealing with family life have conflicts that focus on a breakup of harmony that transforms a home into a not-home.
In Ian Wallace's *Chin Chiang and the Dragon's Dance*, a young boy
briefly runs away to avoid joining his grandfather in a ritual celebra-
tion; a little girl and her mother are not initially successful in communicating with each other in Sue Ann Alderson's *Bonnie McSmithers
You're Driving Me Dithers;* in Claire Mackay's *Mini-Bike Hero*, a son
hides his biking enthusiasm from a disapproving father.

Although most children's stories end with the achievement or restoration of a home situation, some do not. In Monica Hughes' *Keeper of the Isis Light,* Jan Truss's *A Very Small Rebellion,* and Markoosie's *Harpoon of the Hunter,* the stories end with the characters' painful recognition that they cannot return to their old homes and that there are no new ones available.

Readers who are familiar with the elements of stories and have identified these elements in a large number of stories will possess a basic framework that can assist them in noticing and interpreting the details and patterns of each new story they read.

### The Special Language of Picture Books

Like novels and short stories, picture books contain details and patterns that the attentive reader interprets to create meaning. However, instead of focusing on the words, the reader of picture books focuses much and sometimes all of the attention on the visual elements. The details, designs, and colours of individual illustrations, and the relationships between illustrations are significant vehicles of meaning.

*Details*

Of course, the details of a picture can portray what is being narrated or described in words. If either the settings or the kinds of actions are unfamiliar to readers, the illustrations can be extremely informative. The harsh and lonely landscape of northern British Columbia is captured in Ann Blades' illustrations in *A Boy of Taché.* Stories dealing with lesser known cultures use the illustrations to depict artifacts central to those cultures. In *Akavak* and *Long Claws,* James Houston's sketches depict the costume and equipment of the traditional Inuit. In all of Elizabeth Cleaver's illustrations for Native and Inuit legends, the results of her painstaking and accurate research into traditional symbols and designs enhance the authenticity of the stories.

In addition, pictures complement, amplify, and often supplement the words of a story, conveying emotions and aspects of character not found in the words alone. The attitude of the two older brothers to their younger sibling is conveyed in the opening illustration of Frank Newfeld's *Simon and the Golden Sword.* Their faces reveal scorn; their body language expresses their rejection of Simon; their stylish clothes suggest their feelings of proud, snobbish superiority.

*Design*

Individual pictures are not merely camera-like reproductions of physical reality. Objects are carefully arranged, colours contrasted, and line patterns subtly structured to communicate aspects of the story. David Maclagan's double-spread illustrations depicting the beginning and the resolution of the conflict in Maria Campbell's *Little Badger and the Fire Spirit* exemplify the communicative functions of design. In the initial setting the lines of the landscape and the branches of the trees slope downward, drawing the reader's eyes to Little Badger, huddled miserably in the snow, his shoulders curving downward, as he awaits the arrival of his friend Grey Coyote. At the conclusion of the story, Little Badger has single-handedly acquired the fire that his people need to survive the winter. Badger is now at the top of the illustration, and the bright flowing lines coming from the fire brand create a sense of vitality.

*Colour*
Picture book artists use colour to control mood and to create visual symbolism. Elizabeth Cleaver, in *The Mountain Goats of Temlaham*, moves from bright and natural greens and golds to darker colours, especially purple, and then back to the opening colours to depict the shift in mood from happiness and contentment to extreme anger, and then back. In *Very Last First Time*, illustrator Ian Wallace uses the complementary colours of purple and yellow to symbolize the two worlds of author Jan Andrews' story. When Eva Padlyat is in the comfortable, secure, and known world of her home and village, yellow colours are dominant. As she moves towards the sea and her first solitary trip beneath the ice, more purple appears in the illustrations until, at the story's climax, the little girl is in a world almost completely purple. Her return home is a return to a yellow world, although there is more purple in the last illustration than in the first. Eva has brought the memories of her under-ice adventure back home with her.

Although many picture books employ a full spectrum of colour, dramatic effects can also be achieved using only black and white. Robin Muller in *Mollie Whuppie and the Giant* and Ken Nutt in *Zoom at Sea* and *Zoom Away* convey a wide variety of emotions through variation of lights and shades. Mollie travels through a dark forest, escapes from an evil giant's home, and finds happiness for herself and her sisters in the king's palace. Shadows pervade the giant's dwelling; the scenes set in the palace are suffused with a gentle, yet bright, light. The adventures of Zoom, the Cat, begin in the large, rambling, and magical home of Maria. Dark cross-hatching in the illustrations creates a sense of mysterious, dimly perceived areas that may contain or may lead to the strange and the unknown.

Creating a Literature Curriculum: Some
  Preliminary Considerations
The creating and reading of a story are very private and yet very public activities. They are private in that the creator working alone thinks of characters, actions, and conflicts, and puts them together, creating the right words or illustrations to communicate the story. They are private in that each receiver takes the words and pictures into his or her mind and there reacts to them. The words and pictures are drawn from the common stock of the culture that the author and the receiver share to a greater or lesser degree. A large number of children receive a great number of their stories in what are essentially public situations: with

their families in front of TV, at a play or movie, or in a classroom sitting in a group listening to an adult reading or telling a story.

Although adults should always be sensitive to the uniqueness of each child who is receiving a story in a group setting, the teachers of literature in a classroom are essentially working in a public situation; they are sharing a specific work with an entire group. One of their main goals will be to help children acquire strategies that will enable them to understand and therefore enjoy more fully the stories they receive.

Needless to say, teaching the skills of reading stories is not the same as teaching mathematical skills. A teacher does not present specifically defined processes that should lead to the only and correct answer. Teaching the strategies of reading stories provides children with ways of coming up with their own answers, answers that are their personal interpretations of the details and patterns they have noticed in a story.

Before considering ways in which elementary and junior high school teachers can develop programs for teaching skills of literary interpretation, we should consider the following important points.

1. Teachers should choose stories with which they feel comfortable. If they are not familiar with a story or if they do not like it, the chances are that they will not be successful in sharing it with a class.

2. Stories should be read aloud throughout the elementary and junior high grades. Even older children love to close their eyes and listen to well written words being well read. Moreover, several studies have indicated that students who regularly listen to good prose become better readers themselves.

3. Teachers should use a lot of picture books in the early grades AND should continue using them in the higher grades. Younger children can more easily notice visual details and patterns than linguistic ones. Later, they can develop skills with words. Older children who are presented with the many challenging picture books now available respond enthusiastically to the complex themes and conflicts communicated by the illustrations.

4. Books should be selected with instructional goals in mind. Indiscriminate reading or reading on impulse is fun. However, with only so many hours in the school week, teachers cannot share with children all the good stories they might wish to. Consequently, they should choose good and enjoyable stories that will also help children acquire reading skills for their own independent use later on.

5. The instructional component of a literature class should not be overdone. Allow children to enjoy and respond personally to a story. A few minutes of pointing out and discussing certain details and patterns, relating these to other stories, and encouraging children to create their own interpretations will do far more good than hours of quizzing and workbook activities.

6. There are no absolutely right answers in literary interpretation. But children should remember that they are listening to, looking at, or

reading someone else's words and pictures. They have a responsibility to try to find out what the storyteller is trying to communicate. Different students may offer different explanations, but their answer should be based on what IS in the story, not what they wish were in it or what they would have put in it if they had been the storyteller.

7. After children have interpreted, they should be encouraged to share their personal responses with classmates. How did they feel when they heard or read the story? Did they think it was a good or bad story? Did they agree or disagree with what the characters did? What would they have done had they been in the story? Have they ever been in similar situations, or have they ever felt emotions similar to those of the characters?

8. Finally, teachers should not be afraid to present stories that challenge children. Facing challenges leads to growth, and, as all teachers know, children constantly surprise us by their eagerness to accept challenges and to encounter them successfully.

The teaching activities that follow have been made with the above suggestions in mind. Except where specific writing activities are discussed, they have been designed for use with an entire class during a Language Arts period that could range from 15 to 20 minutes in the early elementary grades to between 30 and 40 minutes in the upper elementary and junior high grades. The emphasis in all grades is first on shared reception, through listening to the reading of stories and chapters in novels, and *then* on the shared response, through analysis and the discussion of personal reactions to selections. Teachers who frequently divide classes into smaller groups will find that group discussion in the upper elementary and junior high grades will allow more students to participate in the response to works, particularly to character development and theme as these are found in specific chapters of novels.

Noticing and Interpreting Details

The first step is to notice and interpret details as they occur. For younger children, it is generally most effective to start by noticing the details of illustrations.

After looking at the cover, title, and dedication pages of Phoebe Gilman's *Jillian Jiggs*, they can discuss the clothes the girl is wearing and the actions she is performing, and then use their observations to predict her character as they think it will develop in the story to come. On the final page, Jillian says that tomorrow everything will be neater. After looking at the details of her room and the expression on her face, students can consider such questions as, "Will the room be more tidy? If it is, how long will it stay that way?"

Studying Michael Martchenko's illustrations for Robert Munsch's *The Paper Bag Princess*, older children can compare the relationship between Elizabeth and Ronald at the beginning and ending of the story. By comparing body language, facial expressions, and positions of the characters in the earlier and later illustrations, they will be able to notice how the relationship has altered.

In some picture books, the illustrations present aspects of the story not even mentioned in the text. Ian Wallace, for example, has deliberately added a second story line in his illustrations for Jan Andrews' *Very Last First Time*, and has said that he hopes the children will "read" this story as well. When Eva Padlyat is under the ice, she is surrounded by a number of figures found in the shapes of the rocks and in the shadows. Children are invited to consider why they are there and how their actions are related to the story of Eva's "very last first time."

Just as younger readers of stories can notice and interpret the details of pictures, older children can focus their attention on the words. It is important that readers pay careful attention to opening sentences and paragraphs because these frequently introduce major elements of the narrative to follow. For example, at the start of Robin Muller's *The Sorcerer's Apprentice*, we are told: "Once upon a time, an orphan named Robin packed his belongings and set out to look for work. The fellow had no trade, but he was clever and brave and, what was more, he could read and write." Children who have discussed the title can carefully consider these two sentences, can then predict the outcome of the story, and can state which of Robin's attributes mentioned in the story's opening have led them to make their predictions.

When introducing characters, authors often imply their personalities through description of their appearance, actions, and speech. After reading Chapter 2 of *Anne of Green Gables*, in which Matthew Cuthbert meets the heroine, students in the upper elementary grades can create a character portrait of the orphan, providing details in support of their observations. Such a study might be entitled "First Impressions and Later Reflections." Students might initially take the point of view of a superficial and insensitive observer, one who had noticed only such obvious details as the girl's physical appearance, facial expressions, her penchant for chattering, and her tendency to jump to conclusions. Then students could take the point of view of someone who, having taken the trouble to get to know Anne, remembers that first day and then tries to explain to the superficial observer why the girl looked and acted as she did. As the first observer, they are noticing details; as the second, they are interpreting them.

Noticing and Interpreting Patterns

The second step in understanding stories is to see how individual details interrelate to form meaningful patterns. When we perceive the story as a whole, we understand it better. Picture books and short stories are easier to understand in their entirety because they are short. The length of a novel, which allows for greater depth and complexity, may cause difficulties for readers unable to retain all the details, let alone see and understand the patterns these create. Our discussion will thus focus on longer works.

We have already seen that the basic pattern of all stories centres on conflict and its resolution. Thus readers must recognize the beginning of a conflict and its nature; then they must remember obstacles in sequential order; and, finally, they must spot the resolution.

After reading Chapter 1 of *Jacob Two-Two Meets the Hooded Fang*, children in Grade Two or Three should be able to discuss all the things that are bothering Jacob. They can start by noticing his age and his position as the youngest sibling. Then they can list the activities he cannot perform. Finally, they can discuss his treatment by other members of the family. If teachers wish, they can invite children to compare Jacob's situation to theirs when they were much younger, or to the situations of their younger brothers or sisters. These discussions will implicitly establish the nature of the novel's conflict. After reading Chapter 2, children can consider whether Jacob feels better or worse than he did in Chapter 1, and why. After reading subsequent chapters, the class can examine how Jacob's emotional state results from the actions he performs or fails to perform. Implicitly, they are examining how he overcomes obstacles on his way to resolving his conflict.

One way of helping children to see the emerging emotional pattern of Jacob is to create a large graph (see Figure 1) on which they can mark the changes in Jacob's feelings at the conclusion of each chapter. After reading the first three chapters, the teacher can introduce the graph. Listed down the left side of the graph is a range of emotions, from "super" at the top to "saddest" at the bottom, with "sad" in the middle. Beside these can be placed sun and fog/cloud symbols. The symbol for "super," for example, will be a smiling yellow sun face. Below that will be a sun face with a less pronounced smile. Going down the chart, the sun faces change from smiling to frowning, and more and more cloud covers the face until, at the bottom, beside "saddest" only a cloud is seen, the face now completely covered.

Ask the students how they think Jacob feels before his father sends him to the store. Generally, they will agree that he feels somewhere between "so-so" and "sad." Place the appropriate symbol on the vertical line marking the beginning of the story. After a discussion of how he feels as he sets out at the end of Chapter 1, place the symbol in the area suggested by the majority of the children. If it is higher, as it no doubt will be, make sure to use a more smiling face, one covered by less cloud. Repeat the activity after each chapter, inviting the children to discuss why they think Jacob is more or less happy. When the reading of the story is complete and the graph has been filled, the children will have before them a visual record of Jacob's changing emotions as he confronts the obstacles leading to the resolution of his conflict.

Children reading Jean Little's *Lost and Found* in Grade Three or Four can use their understanding of the title to help them trace Lucy Bell's resolution of her inner conflict. Reading "lost and found" columns

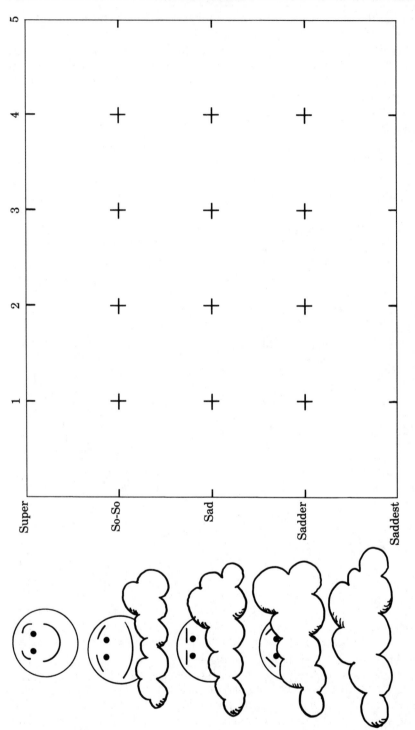

Figure 1 — Jacob Two-Two Meets the Hooded Fang

in the local newspaper and discussing the "lost and found" box in the school, they can discuss general meanings of the term. Of course, in this novel, the title refers mainly to Lucy's emotional feelings during her first three days at her new home in a new city. Discuss the idea that people can feel lost even when they know where they are physically, and have the children relate their own experiences of feeling lost.

Now the children are ready to discuss the opening chapter, which introduces Lucy's conflict. After the students have read the first chapter on their own, have them consider why, as the opening sentence states, "Lucy Bell felt lost." The teacher can then give each child a copy of the "Lost and Found" graph (see Figure 2). The first column lists the chapter numbers. On the left side of the second column appears the word "Lost," on the right, the word "Found." After reading each chapter, students place a mark somewhere between "lost" and "found" to indicate how they think Lucy feels at the chapter's conclusion. The third and largest column is labelled "Why." In the appropriate space, children can note briefly why Lucy felt more or less lost in the chapter. In addition to seeing a developing pattern, the children are explaining why they interpreted the details of the chapter the way they did.

Children in Grade Five and Six delight in the ironic actions of the trickster figure. When his tricks prove successful, they can identify with his feeling of superiority over the victim. When the tricks backfire, they feel superior to the trickster. In *Badger, the Mischief Maker*, Kay Hill weaves the adventures of the Micmac trickster into a novel in which the egocentric self-seeker develops into a kind, considerate helper. The conflict begins when the demi-god Glooscap hides Badger's little brother so that Badger will become too busy searching for him to play tricks. It is important for students to recognize that a defect in Badger's character, his love of playing tricks for his own pleasure, precipitates the conflict, and that it will be resolved only when Badger reforms. His reformation will lead to a joyous reunion with Little Brother.

In examining the individual episodes that take place as Badger travels around the countryside searching, students will notice that he continues to play tricks, creating ironic situations. Careful attention will enable readers to trace the methods by which Badger executes his tricks. They will be able to notice that he often exhibits a keen understanding of human nature, playing on the character weaknesses of his victims to achieve success. They will also be able to see the reasons for his failures. When he uses his wits to aid him in the search for his brother, when his motivation is good, he generally succeeds, but when his motivation is purely selfish, he does not.

However, in addition to studying individual episodes, students should examine how these fit into a pattern related to his character development and the resultant resolution of the conflict. One way of assisting them to see this pattern is to create a large "picto-map," an illustrated map indicating the places he visits and the events that occur in each location (see Figure 3). On an initial reading, it is only

Chapter Lost                    Found                    Why?

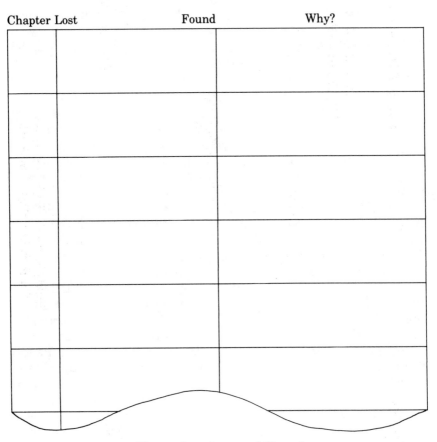

Figure 2 — Lost and Found

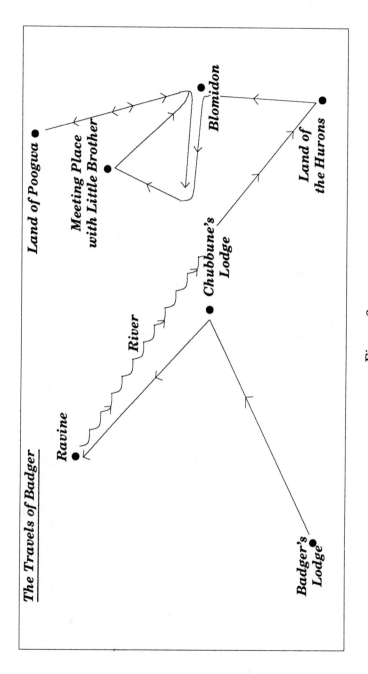

Figure 3
Students locate specific episodes
on map and illustrate these

necessary to note on the map the various locations as Badger visits them. Later, the class can be divided into small groups, with each group responsible for studying a specific episode, showing how the nature and motivation of Badger's trick reveals a positive or negative character development. The groups can then share the results of their examinations with the entire class and can be responsible for illustrating the part of the map at which "their" episode occurs. This activity not only enables each group to understand more fully a limited part of the novel, it also enables the group to contribute to a general understanding of the developing pattern of the complete story.

L. M. Montgomery's *Anne of Green Gables* is suitable for study in the higher elementary and junior high school grades. Although Anne enters the Cuthbert household at the beginning of Chapter 3, it is only after several years that she psychologically completes her journey. She has changed from an insecure, daydreaming, and sometimes tempestuous child to a poised, self-confident, and mature young woman. Remembering in proper sequence the many events that bring about these changes is a difficult task for many readers. One method of assisting students in this task is to keep a time line (see Figure 4). The time line can take the form of a long banner or streamer. Across the top line appears the chapter number. The second line lists the approximate date or the age of the heroine. On the bottom line, students briefly list the key events of the chapter they have just completed.

A second chart can help students to see more fully the pattern of Anne's character development. Titled "Anne's Marvellous Mistakes" (see Figure 5), it is designed to reveal how Anne learns from such "disasters" as speaking angrily to Rachel Lynde, dying her hair green, and getting Diana drunk on what she thinks is Marilla's cordial. As each mistake occurs, it is listed in the first column of the chart. In the second column, students note what they think Anne learns from the mistake.

Finally, *Anne of Green Gables* can be used to introduce an important structural principle of stories: an author's use of recurrent motifs or linking patterns to indicate development. At strategic points of the novel, Montgomery describes Anne's bedroom. At first, it is a bleak place, reflecting both Marilla's and Anne's basic loneliness. However, subsequent descriptions show the room becoming brighter and more cheerful, reflecting both Anne's increasing happiness and the influence she has on the lives of both Matthew and Marilla. This is particularly evident when Marilla, who had at first objected to Anne's decorating the room with leaves, places roses in the room to welcome Anne back from college. By comparing the descriptions in the order in which they occur, students should be able to notice not only the physical changes, but also the emotional changes these symbolize. Students who have studied Montgomery's descriptive technique can imitate it in describing a room in their own homes — a bedroom, kitchen, basement study or workshop — in such a way that the reader sees how the room reflects the personality of the principal occupant or user.

| Chapter | Date or Anne's Age | Main Events | |
|---|---|---|---|
| | | | |
| | | | |
| | | | |
| | | | |

Figure 4 — Anne of Green Gables

# Anne's Marvellous Mistakes

| What Anne Did | What She Learned |
| --- | --- |
|  |  |

Figure 5 — Anne of Green Gables

Creating Story Sequences: Introducing Children
    to the Family of Stories

It has been said that the best way to understand how to read stories is
to read large numbers of them. That is because literature is written according to conventions and patterns; individual stories imitate other
stories and follow the characteristics of a particular type of story. If
readers know what to expect from a western, a detective novel, or a spy
thriller, they will find it relatively easy to read a new book from one of
these categories because they will have frameworks of literary experience on which to base their present reading. As the literary critic
Northrop Frye stated in *The Educated Imagination*, "All themes and
characters and stories that you encounter in literature belong to one
big interlocking family.... You keep associating your literary experiences together: you're always being reminded of some other story
you read or movie you saw or character that impressed you."

People who read widely generally perform this linking operation
unconsciously. In the classroom, however, many students have not read
as widely as their teachers could desire, and the teachers do not have
time to read a large body of stories to them. Thus, children may not
have the literary background or the reading techniques necessary to
interact fully with each new story.

One way of overcoming this difficulty is to create literary units in
which selected stories are read in a predetermined sequence so that the

reading of a work draws on and reinforces reading skills introduced in the study of earlier works. By relating the themes, characters, situations, and techniques of a story they are reading to ones they already know, young readers will gradually become conscious of the ways in which stories work. They can then use this awareness to increase understanding and enjoyment of the story in front of them. Such awareness will assist them in reading all new stories they encounter.

Let us create story sequences in which a group of picture books, folktales, and short stories precedes the study of the novels discussed above. These stories need not all be Canadian; in fact, it is important to include stories from a variety of countries and cultures so that students can see Canadian children's literature within an international framework.

As we have seen, in reading *Jacob Two-Two Meets the Hooded Fang* children are not only studying the development of the hero's character, but they are also noticing the relationship between Jacob's waking life and his dream. The following sequence of stories can be used to introduce the various elements in the novel. Ron Berg's illustrations to Eugene Field's lullaby *Wynken, Blynken and Nod* show how the child's father and the physical objects in the child's room become part of the dream about Wynken, Blynken, and Nod. Similarly, in Marie-Louise Gay's *Rainy-Day Magic*, the children daydream themselves into a fantasy land that contains objects from their own house. These simple stories can introduce the literary convention of including elements from the waking world in dreams. Maurice Sendak's *Where the Wild Things Are* and Anthony Browne's *Gorilla*, in addition to linking the waking and dream worlds, show how the conflicts experienced before the dream are resolved through the events of the dream.

After reading and discussing these elements in the four picture books, children can then read Jacques de Roussan's *Au-delà du soleil / Beyond the Sun*, the account of a small boy's dream that he is an astronaut, travelling through space and returning home at sunrise. The simple text describes neither his thoughts nor his emotions. Children could divide into small groups to discuss these, with each group developing a fuller text for one of the illustrations. More adventurous students might wish to create dialogue and narration for some of the illustrations in Martha Alexander's wordless picture book *Bobo's Dream*.

Because moving — to new neighbourhoods, cities, or even countries — is an increasingly common Canadian experience, the problems of Lucy Bell in *Lost and Found* will be familiar to many children. However, in stories about relocating, the trauma of the move is only one significant element. Characters have inner conflicts to resolve and, often, many external obstacles to overcome before they feel at home in their new houses. Stories about moving thus invite considerations about the differences in the main characters' attitudes and situations at the beginning and the end of their stories, and about the major obstacles and the learning experiences in the middle of the stories. Shirley Hughes' *Moving Molly* and Betty Waterton's *Pettranella* are simple introductions to the theme and to the main emotions of such characters; they provide the basis for general discussions of the subject. "The River Bank," from Kenneth Grahame's *The Wind in the Willows*, and John Steptoe's retelling of the Native American legend *The Story of Jumping Mouse* are more complex and encourage more detailed analysis by readers. In the former, children must consider Mole's incredible naiveté and inexperience so that they can better understand the learning processes he undergoes before he finds a new friend and a new home. *The Story of Jumping Mouse* also describes a growing experience as the diminutive hero makes a long journey to a supernatural world. By noticing the character strengths he displays or develops as he encounters a variety of tests, readers will better understand how he has earned the right to his new and better home. With these patterns and conflicts firmly in mind, children can more fully understand the events and feelings depicted in *Lost and Found*. After reading *Lost and Found*, better students can enjoy reading Betty Waterton's *Quincy Rumpel*, another book about moving, but this one about a very zany family. Either of these books can be used as a starting point for student writing in which students who have relocated can describe their emotions or an event, humorous or sad, associated with the move.

As noted earlier, the trickster figure appears in Native cultures across Canada. As an irony-maker, one who is constantly doing what is not expected, he creates conflicts that are sometimes happily, sometimes unhappily resolved for himself and others. As a prelude to a study of *Badger, the Mischief Maker*, trickster stories can be selected from such collections as Fran Martin's *Raven-Who-Sets-Things-Right*, Fran Fraser's *The Bear Who Stole the Chinook*, Eleanor Brass's *Medicine Boy and Other Cree Tales*, and Dorothy Reid's *Tales of Nanabozho*. Readers should be encouraged to focus on the ironic situations and to consider the motivations for the tricks, the methods used to make them work, and the justness or unjustness of the conclusions. This approach will help students to understand the complexity of the trickster's character. To place these Native stories within a larger multicultural context, students can compare them to stories of the Black American trickster Br'er Rabbit and the English trickster Robin Hood, both of whose adventures are available in several books. With the shorter tales in mind, students will better appreciate the individual escapades of Badger and will have a stronger basis for relating these to each other as parts of a developing novel.

Using their knowledge of the structures and conventions of the trickster stories, students could try writing one of their own, either about Badger or a Native trickster from their own part of the country. To assist them in writing, it would be useful for them to keep the following patterns in mind: trickster wants something, for either selfish or unselfish reasons; the object is difficult to obtain; trickster invents a strategy to deceive the possessor of the object; trickster then obtains the object or fails.

As a feisty orphan, Anne Shirley must learn how to regulate her character so that she can become a full member of the new society in which she finds herself. Not surprisingly, Anne frequently finds herself in conflict with others. Her relationships with Rachel Lynde, Gilbert Blythe, and Diana Berry's aunt are three notable examples. In many ways, Anne is like Pippi Longstocking, the central character in several books by Astrid Lindgren. "Pippi Goes to the Circus" and "Pippi is Invited to Tea," both from *Pippi Longstocking*, can be used to introduce the idea of conflict between a highly individualistic person and a very settled community. A love-hate, competitive relationship between a girl and a boy is found in many of the stories in Bette Greene's *Philip Hall likes me, I reckon maybe*. Any one of these could be examined, with students discussing the underlying motives for the heroine's apparent attitudes to the boy. Finally, the difficulties created by Anne Shirley's love of daydreaming can be introduced by considering Evaline Ness's *Sam, Bangs, and Moonshine*. Although this is a picture book primarily intended for younger readers, it does examine the reasons for the central character's wild imaginings and the lessons she learns because of the problems that result from her "stories." Anne Shirley's imaginative excursions are delightfully humorous. However, an awareness of the reasons behind them is essential for an understanding of her developing character. As a follow-up to a reading of *Anne*, students would enjoy reading Suzanne Martel's *The King's Daughter*, comparing the seventeenth-century French orphan's character with Anne's.

Conclusion
We have seen that authors use public conventions of language and storytelling to communicate their stories to readers, and that readers use their awareness of these conventions to help make the stories part of their personal, private experiences. In a sense, classroom teachers are public mediators between the private worlds and experiences of authors and readers. Through a careful selection of books, teachers help young readers understand the conventions and thus provide them with keys that will open the doors to new and wonderful worlds of reading. We have presented the ideas above because they have been thoroughly tested in classrooms and because they can be adapted to work with a large number of stories. They are not, of course, the only devices teachers can use to introduce students to the process of noticing and interpreting details. In designing their own devices, however, teachers should keep in mind that, unless a device draws attention to signifi-

cant details, makes patterns clearer, or compels students to examine reasons for character actions, they do not achieve literary goals.

By using Canadian books extensively, although not exclusively, teachers can achieve two goals: they can start children down the road to life-long enjoyment of reading, and they can introduce them to the tremendously rich and ever-increasing literary heritage of our country.

# *R*ecommended Canadian Books for Elementary and Junior High: A Graded Reading List

"The right book for the right child." This is an often quoted rule of thumb for selecting literature for younger readers. Children's reading levels and interests, levels of maturity, and backgrounds are all different. Therefore, reading lists categorized by grades are, at best, very general. Individuals in the same grade at school will respond differently to a specific title. Different classes will vary in their reactions; what works wonderfully one year may fall flat the next.

In compiling the following list, we have kept these points in mind, recognizing the impossibility of creating anything closely resembling a definitive and completely accurate list. Instead, for the teacher or librarian confronted with the task of selecting from the rapidly growing number of Canadian children's books we have compiled a list intended as a starting point — a core group of titles to be shared with a specific group.

We have made our selections from works discussed in the entries on individual authors and illustrators in Part I, from works by these authors and illustrators that have been published since the completion of the bio-critical articles, and from recent books by authors and illustrators whose achievements to date have not been of sufficient magnitude for them to be included in Part I. Titles are arranged alphabetically within each grade level. Following each title and the names of authors, illustrators, and translators, we have indicated the publishers of hardcover (indicated by "hc") and paperback (indicated by "pb") editions and the International Standard Book Number (ISBN) of those titles currently in print. The letters "OP" following the letters "hc" or "pb" signify that the edition is now out of print. We have made every effort to be completely accurate. However, because books go out of print very quickly and because publishers must change ISBNs when issuing new editions of a title, readers wishing to order books should consult the most recent edition of the appropriate publisher's catalogue.

## KINDERGARTEN

*ABC*, by Elizabeth Cleaver (Oxford, 0-19-540466-1 hc)

*Alligator Pie*, by Dennis Lee, ill. Frank Newfeld (Macmillan, 0-7715-9591-3 hc; 0-7715-9566-2 pb)

*Anna's Pet*, by Margaret Atwood and Joyce Barkhouse, ill. Ann Blades (James Lorimer, 0-88862-249-X hc; 0-88862-250-3 pb)

*Big or Little?*, by Kathy Stinson, ill. Robin Baird Lewis (Annick, 0-920236-30-8 hc; 0-920236-32-4 pb)

*Big Sarah's Little Boots*, by Paulette Bourgeois, ill. Brenda Clark (Kids Can, 0-921103-11-5 hc)

*By the Sea: An Alphabet Book*, by Ann Blades (Kids Can, 0-919964-74-5 hc; 0-919964-64-8 pb)

*Cake That Mack Ate, The*, by Rose Robart, ill. Maryann Kovalski (Kids Can, 0-919964-96-6 hc)

*Elephant's New Bicycle, The*, by Mark Thurman (rev. ed. NC Press, 0-920053-90-4 hc; 0-920053-66-1 pb)

*Franklin in the Dark*, by Paulette Bourgeois, ill. Brenda Clark (Kids Can, 0-919964-93-1 hc)

*Have You Seen Birds?*, by Joanne Oppenheim, ill. Barbara Reid (North Winds, 0-590-71596-8 hc)

*If I Were a Cat I Would Sit in a Tree*, by Ebbitt Cutler, ill. Rist Arnold (Tundra, 0-88776-177-1 hc)

*Jillian Jiggs*, by Phoebe Gilman (North Winds, 0-590-71548-8 hc; 0-590-71515-1 pb)

*Lie that Grew and Grew, The*, by Mark Thurman (rev. ed. NC Press, 0-920053-54-8 hc; 0-920053-86-6 pb)

*New Baby Calf, The*, by Edith Chase, ill. Barbara Reid (North Winds, 0-590-71405-8 hc)

*ONCE: A Lullaby*, by bp Nichol, ill. Ed Roach (Black Moss, 0-88753-109-1 hc; 0-88753-105-9 pb)

*Red is Best*, by Kathy Stinson, ill. Robin Baird Lewis (Annick, 0-920236-24-3 hc; 0-920236-26-X pb)

*Sharon, Lois & Bram's Mother Goose*, ill. Maryann Kovalski (Douglas & McIntyre, 0-88894-487-X pb)

*Thomas' Snowsuit*, by Robert Munsch, ill. Michael Martchenko (Annick, 0-920303-32-3 hc; 0-920303-32-1 pb)

*To the End of the Block*, by bp Nichol, ill. Shirley Day (Black Moss, 0-88753-119-0 pb)

*Wheels on the Bus, The*, by Maryann Kovalski (Kids Can, 0-921103-09-3 hc)

## GRADE 1

*ABC/123: The Canadian Alphabet and Counting Book*, by Vlasta van Kampen (Hurtig, 0-88830-223-1 hc)

*Bonnie McSmithers You're Driving Me Dithers*, by Sue Ann Alderson, ill. Fiona Garrick (Tree Frog, hc OP; 0-88967-008-0 pb)

*Can You Catch Josephine?* by Stéphane Poulin (Tundra, 0-88776-198-4 hc)

*Difficult Day, A*, by Eugenie Fernandes (rev. ed. Kids Can, 0-921103-17-4 hc)

*Down by Jim Long's Stage: Rhymes for Children and Young Fish*, by Al Pittman, ill. Pam Hall (Breakwater, 0-920911-24-2 hc)

*Fire Stealer, The*, by William Toye, ill. Elizabeth Cleaver (Oxford, hc OP; 0-19-540515-3 pb)

*Garbage Delight*, by Dennis Lee, ill. Frank Newfeld (Macmillan, 0-7715-9592-1 hc)

*How Summer Came to Canada*, by William Toye, ill. Elizabeth Cleaver (Oxford, hc OP; 0-19-540-290-1 pb)

*Hurry Up, Bonnie!* by Sue Ann Alderson, ill. Fiona Garrick (Tree Frog, 0-88967-024-8 hc; 0-88967-023-4 pb)

*I Want a Dog*, by Dayal Kaur Khalsa (Tundra, 0-88776-196-8 hc)

*Moonbeam on a Cat's Ear*, by Marie-Louise Gay (Stoddart, 0-7737-2053-7 hc)

*Mud Puddle*, by Robert Munsch, ill. Sami Suomalainen (Annick, hc OP; 0-920236-47-2 pb)

*Ragtail*, by Patricia Sillers, ill. Karen Patkau (Oxford, 0-19-54585-4 hc)

*Salmon for Simon, A*, by Betty Waterton, ill. Ann Blades (Douglas & McIntyre, 0-88894-168-4 hc; 0-88894-533-7 pb)

*Spaghetti Word Race, The*, by Frank Etherington, ill. Gina Calleja (Annick, 0-920236-11-1 pb)

*There's a Dragon in My Closet*, by John Green, ill. Linda Hendry (North Winds, 0-590-71705-7 hc)

*Those Green Things*, by Kathy Stinson, ill. Mary McLoughlin (Annick, 0-920303-40-4 hc; 0-920303-41-2 pb)

*Two Stupid Dummies*, by Mark Thurman (NC Press, hc OP; 0-920053-94-7 pb)

*Who Hides in the Park*, by Warabé Aska (Tundra, 0-88776-162-3 hc; 0-88776-187-9 pb)

*Wynken, Blynken and Nod*, by Eugene Field, ill. Ron Berg (North Winds, 0-570-71597-6 hc; 0-570-71589-5 pb)

*Zoom at Sea*, by Tim Wynne-Jones, ill. Ken Nutt (Groundwood, 0-88899-021-9 hc)

*Zoom Away*, by Tim Wynne-Jones, ill. Ken Nutt (Groundwood, 0-88899-042-1 hc)

## GRADE 2

*Au-delà du soleil/Beyond the Sun*, by Jacques de Roussan (Tundra, hc OP)

*Candle for Christmas, A*, by Jean Speare, ill. Ann Blades (Douglas & McIntyre, 0-88894-050-2 hc)

*Clyde*, by Lindee Climo (Tundra, 0-88776-185-2 hc)

*Don't Eat Spiders*, by Robert Heidbreder, ill. Karen Patkau (Oxford, 0-19-540497-1 hc)

*Ida and the Wool Smugglers*, by Sue Ann Alderson, ill. Ann Blades (Douglas & McIntyre, 0-88894-790-9 hc)

*Jacob Two-Two Meets the Hooded Fang*, by Mordecai Richler (McClelland and Stewart, 0-7710-7482-4 hc; Seal, 0-7704-2109-1 pb)

*Jelly Belly*, by Dennis Lee, ill. Juan Wijngaard (Macmillan, 0-7715-9776-2 hc)

*Johann's Gift to Christmas*, by Jack Richards, ill. Len Norris (Douglas & McIntyre, 0-88894-289-3 pb)

*Jonathan Cleaned Up, Then He Heard a Sound, or Blackberry Subway Jam*, by Robert Munsch, ill. Michael Martchenko (Annick, 0-920236-22-7 hc; 0-920236-20-0 pb)

*Little Badger and the Fire Spirit*, by Maria Campbell, ill. David Maclagen (McClelland and Stewart, hc OP; pb OP)

*Lobster in My Pocket*, by Deirdre Kessler, ill. Brenda Jones (Ragweed, 0-920304-73-7 pb)

*Mandy and the Flying Map*, by Beverley Allinson, ill. Ann Powell (Scholastic-TAB, 0-590-71045-1 pb)

*Mary of Mile 18*, by Ann Blades (Tundra, 0-370-01804-4 hc; 0-88776-059-7 pb)

*Matthew and the Midnight Tow Truck*, by Allen Morgan, ill. Michael Martchenko (Annick, 0-920303-00-5 hc; 0-920303-01-3 pb)

*Matthew and the Midnight Turkeys*, by Allen Morgan, ill. Michael Martchenko (Annick, 0-920303-36-6 hc; 0-920303-37-4 pb)

*Mischief City*, by Tim Wynne-Jones, ill. Victor Gad (Groundwood, 0-88899-049-9 hc)

*Mountain Goats of Temlaham, The*, by William Toye, ill. Elizabeth Cleaver (Oxford, hc OP; 0-19-540320-7 pb)

*Murdo's Story: A Legend from Northern Manitoba*, by Murdo Scribe, ill. Terry Gallagher (Pemmican, 0-919143-07-5 small format pb; 0-919143-09-1 large format pb)

*My Kind of Pup*, by Meguido Zola, ill. Wendy Wolsak (Pemmican, 0-919143-19-9 pb)

*Pillow, The*, by Rosemary Allison, ill. Charles Hilder (James Lorimer, 0-88862-944-3 pb)

*Prairie Boy's Winter, A*, by William Kurelek (Tundra, 0-88776-022-8 hc; 0-88776-102-X pb)

*Queen Who Stole the Sky, The*, by Jennifer Garnett, ill. Linda Hendry (North Winds, 0-590-71524-0 hc; 0-590-71523-2 pb)

*Rainy Day Magic*, by Marie-Louise Gay (Stoddart, 0-7737-2112-6 hc)

*Sandwich, The*, by Ian Wallace, ill. Angela Wood (Kids Can, 0-919964-02-8 pb)

*Short Tree and the Bird that Could Not Sing, The*, by Dennis Foon, ill. John Bianchi (Groundwood, 0-88899-046-4 hc)

*Six Darn Cows*, by Margaret Laurence, ill. Ann Blades (James Lorimer, hc OP; 0-88862-942-7 pb)

## GRADE 3

*Akavak*, by James Houston (Longman, hc OP)

*Boy of Taché, A*, by Ann Blades (Tundra, 0-88776-023-6 hc; 0-88776-034-1 pb)

*Chester's Barn*, by Lindee Climo (Tundra, 0-88776-132-1 hc; 0-88776-155-0 pb)

*Children of the Yukon,* by Ted Harrison (Tundra, 0-88776-092-9 hc)

*Different Dragons,* by Jean Little (Viking Kestrel, 0-670-80836-9 hc; Penguin, 0-14-031998-1 pb)

*Hockey Sweater, The,* by Roch Carrier, trans. Sheila Fischman, ill. Sheldon Cohen (Tundra, 0-88776-169-0 hc; 0-88776-174-7 pb)

*Hug Me,* by Patti Stren (Fitzhenry and Whiteside, hc OP; 0-88902-974-1 pb)

*I'll Make You Small,* by Tim Wynne-Jones, ill. Maryann Kovalski (Groundwood, 0-88899-045-6 hc)

*Jenny Greenteeth,* by Mary Alice Downie, ill. Barbara Reid (Kids Can, 0-919964-58-3 pb)

*Last Ship, The,* by Mary Alice Downie, ill. Lissa Calvert (Irwin, 0-88778-201-9 hc)

*Lizzy's Lion,* by Dennis Lee, ill. Marie-Louise Gay (Stoddart, 0-7737-0078-1 hc)

*Long Claws,* by James Houston (McClelland and Stewart, 0-7710-4256-6 hc)

*Loon's Necklace, The,* by William Toye, ill. Elizabeth Cleaver (Oxford, 0-19-540278-2 hc)

*Lost and Found,* by Jean Little (Viking Kestrel, 0-670-80835-0 hc; Penguin 0-14-031997-2 pb)

*Mumbles and Snits,* by Beverley Allinson, ill. Ann Powell (Women's Press, 0-88961-023-1 hc)

*Pettranella,* by Betty Waterton, ill. Ann Blades (Douglas & McIntyre, hc OP; 0-88894-406-3 pb)

*Prairie Boy's Summer, A,* by William Kurelek (Tundra, 0-88776-058-9 hc; 0-88776-116-X pb)

*Sorcerer's Apprentice, The,* by Robin Muller (Kids Can, 0-919964-80-X hc; 0-919964-84-2 pb)

*Tales of a Gambling Grandma,* by Dayal Kaur Khalsa (Tundra, 0-88776-179-8 hc)

*Very Last First Time,* by Jan Andrews, ill. Ian Wallace (Groundwood, 0-88899-043-X hc)

*Violin, The,* by Robert Thomas Allen, photos by George Pastic (McGraw-Hill Ryerson, hc OP; 0-07-082620-X pb)

*Wish Wind, The,* by Peter Eyvindson, ill. Wendy Wolsak (Pemmican, 0-921827-03-2 pb)

## GRADE 4

*Auntie's Knitting a Baby,* by Lois Simmie, ill. Anne Simmie (Western Producer Prairie Books, 0-88833-160-6 hc; 0-88833-123-1 pb)

*Chin Chiang and the Dragon's Dance,* by Ian Wallace (Groundwood, 0-88899-020-0 hc)

*Christmas Wolf, The,* by Claude Aubry (Irwin, 0-7720-1439-6 pb)

*Comet's Tale,* by Sue Ann Alderson, ill. Georgia Pow Graham (Tree Frog, 0-88967-047-1 pb)

*Courage in the Storm*, by Thomas H. Raddall, ill. Are Gjesdal (Potters-field Press, 0-919001-424 pb)

*Enchanted Caribou, The*, by Elizabeth Cleaver (Oxford, 0-19-540492-0 hc)

*Enchanted Tapestry, The*, by Robert San Souci, ill. Laszlo Gal (Ground-wood, 0-88899-050-2 hc)

*Glooscap and His Magic*, by Kay Hill (McClelland and Stewart, 0-7710-4117-9 pb)

*Golden Phoenix, and Other Fairy Tales from Quebec, The*, by Marius Barbeau and Michael Hornyansky (Oxford, 0-19-540345-2 pb)

*Goldie and the Sea*, by Judith Saltman, ill. Kim La Fave (Groundwood, 0-88899-060-X hc)

*Jacob's Little Giant*, by Barbara Smucker (Viking Kestrel, 0-670-81651-5 hc)

*Mollie Whuppie and the Giant*, by Robin Muller (North Winds, 0-570-71106-7 hc; 0-570-71170-9 pb)

*Murder on the Canadian*, by Eric Wilson (Irwin, 0-370-11013-7 hc; Totem, 0-00-222632-4 pb)

*Northern Alphabet, A*, by Ted Harrison (Tundra, 0-88776-209-3 hc)

*Olden Days Coat, The*, by Margaret Laurence, ill. Muriel Wood (McClelland and Stewart, 0-7710-4742-8 hc)

*On the Edge of the Eastern Ocean*, by Pam Hall (GLC, 0-88874-055-7 hc)

*Paper Bag Princess, The*, by Robert Munsch, ill. Michael Martchenko (Annick 0-920236-82-0 hc; 0-920236-16-2 pb)

*Quincy Rumpel*, by Betty Waterton (Groundwood, 0-88899-036-7 pb)

*Sleighs, The Gentle Transportation* [original title, *Sleighs of My Child-hood*], by Carlo Italiano (Tundra, 0-88776-105-4 hc)

*This Can't Be Happening at McDonald Hall!* by Gordon Korman (Scholastic-TAB, 0-590-71046-X pb)

*Tikta'liktak*, by James Houston (Longman, hc OP)

*Toothpaste Genie, The*, by Frances Duncan (Scholastic-TAB, 0-590-71090-7 pb)

*Twelve Dancing Princesses, The*, by Janet Lunn, ill. Laszlo Gal (Methuen, 0-458-93890-4 hc; 0-458-98540-6 pb)

*Violin-Maker's Gift, The*, by Donn Kushner (Macmillan, 0-7715-9735-5 hc)

*Walk Out of the World, A*, by Ruth Nichols (Harcourt, Brace, Jovano-vich, 0-7747-0110-2 hc)

## GRADE 5

*Baby Project, The*, by Sarah Ellis (Groundwood, 0-88899-047-2 pb)

*Badger, the Mischief Maker*, by Kay Hill (McClelland and Stewart, 0-7710-4109-8 pb)

*Camels Can Make You Homesick and Other Stories*, by Nazneen Sadiq, ill. Mary Cserepy (James Lorimer, 0-88862-913-3 pb)

*Cartier Discovers the St. Lawrence*, by William Toye, ill. Laszlo Gal (Oxford, hc OP; 0-19-540290-1 pb)

*Dragon Children, The,* by Bryan Buchan (Scholastic-TAB, 0-590-71089-3 pb)

*Fusion Factor, The,* by Carol Matas (Fifth House, 0-920079-25-3 pb)

*Galahad Schwartz and the Cockroach Army,* by Morgan Nyberg (Groundwood, 0-88899-037-5 pb)

*Here She Is, Ms Teeny-Wonderful!* by Martyn Godfrey (Scholastic-TAB, 0-590-71482-1 pb)

*Hey, Dad!* by Brian Doyle (Groundwood, 0-88899-004-9, pb)

*Incredible Journey, The,* by Sheila Burnford (Atlantic Little Brown, 0-316-11714-5 hc; Bantam, 0-553-26218-1 pb)

*Joanie's Magic Boots,* by Brenda Bellingham (Tree Frog, 0-88967-031-5 hc; 0-88967-026-9 pb)

*Jory's Cove: A Story of Nova Scotia,* by Clare Bice (Macmillan, hc OP)

*King of the Thousand Islands, The,* by Claude Aubry (Irwin, 0-7720-1441-8 pb)

*Little Mermaid, The,* by Margaret Crawford Maloney, ill. Laszlo Gal (Methuen, 0-458-95110-2 hc)

*Lost in the Barrens,* by Farley Mowat (McClelland and Stewart, 0-7710-6553-1 hc; 0-7710-6639-2 ed. pb; 0-7710-6640-6 pb)

*Lost Treasure of Casa Loma,* by Eric Wilson (General, 0-7736-7044-0 pb)

*Medicine Boy and Other Cree Tales,* by Eleanor Brass, ill. Henry Nanooch (Glenbow Museum, 0-919224-04-0 pb)

*Morgan the Magnificent,* by Ian Wallace (Groundwood, 0-88899-056-1 hc)

*My Name Is Not Odessa Yarker,* by Marian Engel, ill. Laszlo Gal (Kids Can, hc OP)

*Naomi's Road,* by Joy Kogawa, ill. Matt Gould (Oxford, 0-19-540547-1 pb)

*Not Impossible Summer, The,* by Sue Ann Alderson (Irwin, 0-7720-1432-9 pb)

*Once Upon a Totem,* by Christie Harris (McClelland and Stewart, 0-7710-3995-6 pb)

*Our Man Weston,* by Gordon Korman (Scholastic-TAB, 0-590-71123-7 pb)

*Red Fox,* by Sir Charles G. D. Roberts (Scholastic-TAB, 0-590-71604-2 pb)

*Robot Alert,* by Suzanne Martel, tr. Patricia Sillers (Kids Can, 0-919964-82-6 hc)

*Scrubs on Skates,* by Scott Young (McClelland and Stewart, 0-7710-9088-9 pb)

*Secret World of Og, The,* by Pierre Berton, ill. Patsy Berton (McClelland and Stewart, 0-7710-1386-8 pb)

*Simon and the Golden Sword,* by Frank Newfeld (Oxford, hc OP)

*Son of Raven, Son of Deer,* by George Clutesi (Gray's, 0-88826-060-1 pb)

*Spirit of the White Bison,* by Beatrice Culleton (Pemmican, 0-919143-40-7 pb)

*Sun Horse, The,* by Catherine Anthony Clark, ill. Clare Bice (Macmillan, hc OP)

*Tales of Nanabozho,* by Dorothy Reid (Oxford, pb OP)

*Tales the Elders Told: Ojibway Legends,* by Basil Johnston, ill. Shirley Cheechoo (Royal Ontario Museum, 0-88854-261-5 hc)

*Tatterhood,* by Robin Muller (North Winds, 0-590-71411-2 hc; 0-590-71446-5 pb)

*Terror in Winnipeg,* by Eric Wilson (Bodley Head/Clark Irwin, 0-370-30232-X hc; 0-7736-7043-2 pb)

*That Scatterbrain Booky,* by Bernice Thurman Hunter (Scholastic-TAB, 0-590-71082-6 pb)

*Tom Penny,* by Tony German (McClelland and Stewart, 0-7710-3265-X pb)

*Underground to Canada,* by Barbara Smucker (Clark Irwin, 0-7720-111-7 hc; Penguin, 0-14-031122-X pb)

*White Archer, The,* by James Houston (Longman, hc OP)

*Who Is Bugs Potter?* by Gordon Korman (Scholastic-TAB, 0-590-71036-2 pb)

*Witch of the North, The,* by Mary Alice Downie (Oberon, hc OP)

*You Can Pick Me Up at Peggy's Cove,* by Brian Doyle (Groundwood, 0-88899-001-4 pb)

## GRADE 6

*Boy with an R in His Hand, The,* by James Reaney (Porcupine's Quill, 0-88984-059-8 pb)

*Canadian Fairy Tales,* by Eva Martin, ill. Laszlo Gal (Groundwood, 0-88899-030-8 hc)

*Child in Prison Camp, A,* by Shizuye Takashima (Tundra, 0-688-30113-4 hc; 0-88776-074-0 pb)

*City Under Ground, The,* by Suzanne Martel (Groundwood, 0-88899-019-7 pb)

*Cremation of Sam McGee, The,* by Robert W. Service, ill. Ted Harrison (Kids Can, 0-919964-2-3 hc)

*Curses of the Third Uncle, The,* by Paul Yee (James Lorimer, 0-88862-910-9 hc; 0-88862-909-5 pb)

*Death Over Montreal,* by Geoffrey Bilson (Kids Can, 0-919964-45-1 pb)

*Exit Barney McGee,* by Claire Mackay (Scholastic-TAB, 0-590-71002-8 pb)

*Harpoon of the Hunter,* by Markoosie (McGill-Queen's U. Press, 0-7735-0102-9 hc; 0-7735-0232-7 pb)

*Honor Bound,* by Mary Alice Downie (Oxford, 0-19-540331-2 pb)

*Magic Fiddler and Other Legends of French Canada, The,* by Claude Aubry, tr. Alice E. Kane (Irwin, 0-7720-1440-X pb)

*Marrow of the World, The,* by Ruth Nichols (Gage, 0-7715-1663-0 ed. pb)

*Mini-Bike Hero,* by Claire Mackay (Scholastic-TAB, 0-590-71413-9 pb)

*Mouse Woman and the Vanished Princesses,* by Christie Harris, ill. Douglas Tait (McClelland and Stewart, 0-7710-4023-7 hc)

*My Name is Paula Popowich!* by Monica Hughes (James Lorimer, 0-88862-690-8 hc; 0-88862-689-4 pb)

*Nicholas Knock and Other People,* by Dennis Lee, ill. Frank Newfeld (Macmillan, hc OP)

*Nkwala,* by Edith Sharp (Little, Brown, hc OP; McClelland and Stewart, 0-7710-8124-3 pb)

*Northern Nativity, A,* by William Kurelek (Tundra, 0-88776-071-6 hc; 0-88776-099-6 pb)

*Olden Days Coat, The,* by Margaret Laurence (McClelland and Stewart, 0-7710-4742-8 hc)

*Other Elizabeth, The,* by Karleen Bradford (Gage, 0-7715-7004-X ed. pb; 0-7715-9667-7 pb)

*Plan B Is Total Panic,* by Martyn Godfrey (James Lorimer, 0-88862-851-X hc; 0-88862-850-1 pb)

*River Runners: A Tale of Hardship and Bravery,* by James Houston (McClelland and Stewart, hc OP; Penguin, 0-14-031430-X pb)

*Slave of the Haida,* by Doris Andersen (Macmillan, hc OP; pb OP)

*Starbuck Valley Winter,* by Roderick Haig-Brown (McClelland and Stewart, hc OP)

*Storm Child,* by Brenda Bellingham (James Lorimer, 0-88862-794-7 hc; 0-88862-793-9 pb)

*Take a Giant Step,* by Myra Paperny (Overlea, 0-7172-2158-X hc; 0-7172-2157-1 pb)

*Teach Me To Fly, Skyfighter! and Other Stories,* by Paul Yee (James Lorimer, 0-88862-646-0 hc; 0-88862-645-2 pb)

*Very Small Rebellion, A,* by Jan Truss (J. M. LeBel, hc OP; pb OP)

*Willow Maiden, The,* by Megan Collins, ill. Laszlo Gal (Groundwood, 0-88899-039-1 hc)

*Wooden People, The,* by Myra Paperny (Little, Brown, hc and pb OP; Overlea, 0-7172-2272-1 pb)

### GRADE 7

*Alien Wargames,* by Martyn Godfrey (Scholastic-TAB, 0-590-71224-1 pb)

*Amish Adventure,* by Barbara Smucker (Irwin, hc OP; Penguin, 0-14-031702-3 pb)

*Anne of Green Gables,* by L. M. Montgomery (McGraw, 0-7700-0006-1 hc; 0-7700-0008-8 pb; Seal, 0-7704-211-3 pb)

*Beyond the Dark River,* by Monica Hughes (Nelson, hc OP)

*Bluenose Ghosts,* by Helen Creighton (McGraw-Hill Ryerson, 0-7700-0022-3 pb)

*Copper Sunrise,* by Bryan Buchan (Scholastic-TAB, 0-590-71059-1 pb)

*Ghost Dance Caper, The,* by Monica Hughes (Nelson, hc OP; Methuen 0-458-80240-9 pb)

*Hockeybat Harris,* by Geoffrey Bilson (Kids Can, 0-919964-57-5 pb)

*Julie,* by Cora Taylor (Western Producer Prairie Books, 0-88833-172-X pb)

*King's Daughter, The,* by Suzanne Martel, tr. David Homel (Groundwood, 0-88899-007-3 hc; 0-88899-006-5 pb)

*Last Voyage of the Scotian, The,* by Bill Freeman (James Lorimer,
0-88862-133-2 hc; 0-88862-112-4 pb)

*Listen for the Singing,* by Jean Little (Irwin, hc OP; 0-7720-1326-8 pb)

*Magic Fiddler, The,* by Claude Aubry, tr. Alice E. Kane (Peter Martin,
hc OP; Irwin, 0-7720-1440-X pb)

*Moons of Madeleine, The,* by Joan Clark (Viking Kestrel, 0-670-81284-6
hc; Penguin 0-14-032182-9 pb)

*Never Cry Wolf,* by Farley Mowat (Atlantic Monthly Press, 0-316-
58639-0 hc; Bantam, 0-553-26624-1 pb)

*New Wind Has Wings: Poems from Canada, The,* comp. by Mary Alice
Downie and Barbara Robertson, ill. Elizabeth Cleaver (Oxford,
0-19-540431-9 hc; 0-19-540432-7 pb)

*Payment in Death: A Susan George Mystery,* by Marion Crook (Overlea, 0-7172-1610-1 pb)

*Root Cellar, The,* by Janet Lunn (Lester & Orpen Dennys, hc OP;
0-919630-78-2 pb; Penguin, 0-14-031835-6 pb)

*Secret in the Stlalakum Wild, The,* by Christie Harris, ill. Douglas Tait
(McClelland and Stewart, hc OP)

*Shantymen of Cache Lake,* by Bill Freeman (James Lorimer, 0-88862-
091-8 hc; 0-88862-090-X pb)

*Summer the Whales Sang,* by Gloria Montero (James Lorimer,
0-88862-904-4 hc; 0-88862-903-6 pb)

*Sweetgrass,* by Jan Hudson (Tree Frog, 0-88967-076-5 pb)

*Trouble with Princesses, The,* by Christie Harris (McClelland and
Stewart, hc OP)

*Up to Low,* by Brian Doyle (Groundwood, 0-88899-017-0 pb)

*Whale People, The,* by Roderick Haig-Brown (Totem Books, 0-00-
222197-7 pb)

*Who is Frances Rain?* by Margaret Buffie (Kids Can, 0-919964-83-4 pb)

*Wild Animals I Have Known,* by Ernest Thompson Seton (McClelland
and Stewart, 0-7710-9254-7 pb)

*Witchery Hill,* by Welwyn Katz (Groundwood, 0-88899-031-6 pb)

GRADE 8

*Angel Square,* by Brian Doyle (Groundwood, 0-88899-070-7 pb)

*April Raintree* [rev. ed. of *In Search of April Raintree,* pb OP], by
Beatrice Culleton (Pemmican, 0-919143-030-2 pb)

*Book Dragon, A,* by Donn Kushner (Macmillan, 0-7715-9515-8 hc)

*Cowboys Don't Cry,* by Marilyn Halvorson (Irwin, 0-7720-1445-0 pb;
Dell, 0-440-91303-9 pb)

*Daring Game, The,* by Kit Pearson (Viking Kestrel, 0-670-80751-6 hc;
Penguin 0-14-031932-8 pb)

*Dear Bruce Springsteen,* by Kevin Major (Doubleday, 0-385-29584-7 hc)

*Emily of New Moon,* by L. M. Montgomery (McClelland and Stewart,
0-7710-6238-9 pb; Seal, 0-7704-1798-1 pb)

*False Face*, by Welwyn Katz (Groundwood, 0-88899-063-4 hc)

*Ghost Horse of the Mounties, The*, by sean o huigin (Black Moss, pb OP)

*Hold Fast*, by Kevin Major (Delacorte, 0-440-03506-6 hc; Irwin, 0-7720-1314-4 pb; Dell, 0-440-93756-6 pb)

*Hunter in the Dark*, by Monica Hughes (Clark Irwin, 0-7720-1372-1 hc; Avon Flare, 0-380-67702-4 pb)

*Jasmin*, by Jan Truss (Groundwood, 0-88899-014-6 pb)

*Keeper of the Isis Light, The*, by Monica Hughes (Atheneum, 0-689-30847-7 hc; Magnet, 0-416-21030-9 pb)

*Last of the Curlews*, by Fred Bodsworth (McClelland and Stewart, 0-7710-9137-0 pb; Scholastic-TAB, 0-590-71603-4 pb)

*Let It Go*, Marilyn Halvorson (Irwin, 0-7725-1523-9 pb; Dell, 0-440-20053-9 pb)

*Long Return, The*, by John Craig (Bobbs-Merrill, hc OP)

*Mama's Going to Buy You a Mockingbird*, by Jean Little (Penguin, 0-670-80346-4 hc; 0-14-031737-6 pb)

*Nine Days Queen, The*, by Karleen Bradford (Scholastic-TAB, 0-590-71617-4 pb)

*Nobody Asked Me*, by Elizabeth Brochmann (James Lorimer, 0-88862-753-X hc; 0-88862-752-1 pb)

*No Word for Good-bye*, by John Craig (Irwin, 0-7725-9006-0 hc)

*Raven's Cry*, by Christie Harris (McClelland and Stewart, hc OP; 0-7710-4033-4 pb)

*Sandwriter*, by Monica Hughes (Julia MacCrae Books, 0-86203-198-2 hc; Magnet, 0-416-95520-7 pb)

*Shadow in Hawthorn Bay*, by Janet Lunn (Lester & Orpen Dennys, 0-88619-134-3 hc; 0-88619-136-X pb)

*Susie-Q*, by Eric Wilson (Scholastic-TAB, 0-590-67042-7 pb)

*Thirty-six Exposures*, by Kevin Major (Doubleday, 0-385-29347-X hc)

*Winners*, by Mary-Ellen Lang Collura (Western Producer Prairie Books, 0-8883-116-9 pb)

# Part III:
# Major English-Language
# Children's Book Awards

# *M*ajor English-Language Children's Book Awards

*The Amelia Frances Howard-Gibbon Illustrator's Award*

The Canadian Association of Children's Librarians presents a silver medal annually to the best illustrated children's book published in Canada. The illustrator must be a Canadian citizen, and the book must be on a Canadian subject.

1971 Elizabeth Cleaver. *The Wind Has Wings,* compiled by Mary Alice Downie and Barbara Robertson

1972 Shizuye Takashima. *A Child in Prison Camp*

1973 Jacques de Roussan. *Au-delà du soleil/Beyond the Sun*

1974 William Kurelek. *A Prairie Boy's Winter*

1975 Carlo Italiano. *Sleighs of My Childhood/Les traîneaux de mon enfance*

1976 William Kurelek. *A Prairie Boy's Summer*

1977 Pam Hall. *Down by Jim Long's Stage* by Al Pittman

1978 Elizabeth Cleaver. *The Loon's Necklace* by William Toye

1979 Ann Blades. *A Salmon for Simon* by Betty Waterton

1980 Lazlo Gal. *The Twelve Dancing Princesses* by Janet Lunn

1981 Douglas Tait. *The Trouble with Princesses* by Christie Harris

1982 Heather Woodall. *Ytek and the Arctic Orchid* by Garnet Hewitt

1983 Lindee Climo. *Chester's Barn*

1984 Ken Nutt. *Zoom at Sea* by Tim Wynne-Jones

1985 Ian Wallace. *Chin Chiang and the Dragon's Dance*

1986 Ken Nutt. *Zoom Away* by Tim Wynne-Jones

1987 Marie-Louise Gay. *Moonbeam on a Cat's Ear*

*Canadian Library Association Book of the Year Award for Children*

The Canadian Library Association presents a bronze medal to the author of the best Canadian children's book. The awards procedure changed in 1966, resulting in the presentation of two awards that year.

1947 Roderick Haig-Brown. *Starbuck Valley Winter*

1948 Mabel Dunham. *Kristli's Trees*

1949 No Award

1950 Richard S. Lambert. *Franklin of the Arctic*

1951 No Award

1952 Catherine Anthony Clark. *The Sun Horse*

1953 No Award

1954 No Award

1955 No Award

1956  Louise Riley. *Train for Tiger Lily*
1957  Cyrus Macmillan. *Glooscap's Country and Other Indian Tales*
1958  Farley Mowat. *Lost in the Barrens*
1959  John F. Hayes. *The Dangerous Cove*
1960  Marius Barbeau and Michael Hornyansky. *The Golden Phoenix and Other Fairy Tales from Quebec*
1961  William Toye. *The St. Lawrence*
1962  No Award
1963  Sheila Burnford. *The Incredible Journey*
1964  Roderick Haig-Brown. *The Whale People*
1965  Dorothy M. Reid. *Tales of Nanabozho*
1966  James McNeill. *The Double Knights: More Tales from Round the World*
1966  James Houston. *Tikta'liktak: An Eskimo Legend*
1967  Christie Harris. *Raven's Cry*
1968  James Houston. *The White Archer: An Eskimo Legend*
1969  Kay Hill. *And Tomorrow the Stars: The Story of John Cabot*
1970  Edith Fowke. *Sally Go Round the Sun*
1971  William Toye. *Cartier Discovers the St. Lawrence*
1972  Ann Blades. *Mary of Mile 18*
1973  Ruth Nichols. *The Marrow of the World*
1974  Elizabeth Cleaver. *The Miraculous Hind*
1975  Dennis Lee. *Alligator Pie*
1976  Mordecai Richler. *Jacob Two-Two Meets the Hooded Fang*
1977  Christie Harris. *Mouse Woman and the Vanished Princesses*
1978  Dennis Lee. *Garbage Delight*
1979  Kevin Major. *Hold Fast*
1980  James Houston. *River Runners*
1981  Donn Kushner. *The Violin-Maker's Gift*
1982  Janet Lunn. *The Root Cellar*
1983  Brian Doyle. *Up to Low*
1984  Jan Hudson. *Sweetgrass*
1985  Jean Little. *Mama's Going to Buy You a Mockingbird*
1986  Cora Taylor. *Julie*
1987  Janet Lunn. *Shadow in Hawthorn Bay*

*The Canada Council Children's Literature Prizes*

In 1975, the Canada Council established English- and French-language prizes of $5000 for the best books by Canadian writers and illustrators. A prize is not necessarily awarded in each category every year.

*The Canada Council Children's Literature Prize for English-Language Writing*

1975  Bill Freeman. *Shantymen of Cache Lake*
1976  Myra Paperny. *The Wooden People*

1977   Jean Little. *Listen for the Singing*
1978   Kevin Major. *Hold Fast*
1979   Barbara Smucker. *Days of Terror*
1980   Christie Harris. *The Trouble with Princesses*
1981   Monica Hughes. *The Guardian of Isis*
1982   Monica Hughes. *Hunter in the Dark*
1983   sean o huigin. *The Ghost Horse of the Mounties*
1984   Jan Hudson. *Sweetgrass*
1985   Cora Taylor. *Julie*
1986   Janet Lunn. *Shadow in Hawthorn Bay*

*The Canada Council Children's Literature Prize for English-Language Illustration*

1978   Ann Blades. *A Salmon for Simon* by Betty Waterton
1979   Laszlo Gal. *The Twelve Dancing Princesses* by Janet Lunn
1980   Elizabeth Cleaver. *Petrouchka*
1981   Heather Woodall. *Ytek and the Arctic Orchid* by Garnet Hewitt
1982   Vlasta van Kampen. *ABC/123: The Canadian Alphabet and Counting Book*
1983   Laszlo Gal. *The Little Mermaid* by Margaret Maloney
1984   Marie-Louise Gay. *Lizzy's Lion* by Dennis Lee
1985   Terry Gallagher. *Murdo's Story* by Murdo Scribe
1986   Barbara Reid. *Have You Seen Birds?* by Joanne Oppenheim

*The Governor General's Literary Awards*

The Governor General's Literary Awards for juvenile literature were discontinued after 1959. Beginning with the Awards for 1987, however, the Governor General's Literary Awards will replace the Canada Council Children's Literature Prizes. By restoring the Awards, the Canada Council, which administers them, hopes to accord writers for children the same respect given to writers for adults. Each winner receives $5000 and a specially bound copy of the winning book.

*The Governor General's Award for English-Language Children's Text*

1987   Morgan Nyberg. *Galahad Schwartz and the Cockroach Army*

*The Governor General's Award for English-Language Children's Illustration*

1987   Marie-Louise Gay. *Rainy Day Magic*

*The IODE Book Award (Toronto Chapter)*

The Imperial Order of the Daughters of the Empire, Toronto Chapter, annually presents an award of $1000 for the best book written or illustrated by a Canadian and intended for children between the ages of 6 and 12 years.

1974  Dennis Lee. *Alligator Pie*
1975  William Kurelek. *A Prairie Boy's Winter*
1976  Aviva Layton. *How the Kookaburra Got His Laugh*
1977  William Toye. *The Loon's Necklace*
1978  Laszlo Gal for illustration of three texts:
       *The Shirt of the Happy Man* by Mariella Bertelli
       *My Name Is Not Odessa Yarker* by Marian Engel
       *Why the Man in the Moon Is Happy* by Ronald Melzack
1979  Janet Lunn. *The Twelve Dancing Princesses*
1980  Olena Kassian for illustration of two texts:
       *The Hungry Time* by Selwyn Dewdney
       *Afraid of the Dark* by Barry Dickson
1981  Bernice Thurman Hunter. *That Scatterbrain Booky*
1982  Kathy Stinson. *Red Is Best*
1983  Tim Wynne-Jones. *Zoom at Sea*
1984  Ian Wallace. *Chin Chiang and the Dragon's Dance*
1985  Robin Muller. *The Sorcerer's Apprentice*
1986  Barbara Reid. *Have You Seen Birds?* by Joanne Oppenheim

*The National Chapter IODE Book Award*

The National Chapter of the Imperial Order of the Daughters of the Empire has established an annual award of $3000 for the best English-language book containing at least 300 words of text and suitable for children aged 13 or younger.

1985  Mary-Ellen Lang Collura. *Winners*
1986  Marianne Brandis. *The Quarter Pie Window*
1987  Janet Lunn. *Shadow in Hawthorn Bay*

*The Ruth Schwartz Children's Book Award*

The Canadian Booksellers' Association annually presents a prize of $2000 to the writer or creative source of an outstanding children's work written by a Canadian and published in Canada.

1976  Mordecai Richler. *Jacob Two-Two Meets the Hooded Fang*
1977  Robert Thomas Allen. *The Violin*
1978  Dennis Lee. *Garbage Delight*
1979  Kevin Major. *Hold Fast*
1980  Barbara Smucker. *Days of Terror*
1981  Suzanne Martel. *The King's Daughter*
1982  Marsha Hewitt and Claire Mackay. *One Proud Summer*
1983  Jan Truss. *Jasmin*

1984  Tim Wynne-Jones. *Zoom at Sea*
1985  Jean Little. *Mama's Going to Buy You a Mockingbird*
1986  Robert Munsch. *Thomas' Snowsuit*
1987  Barbara Reid. *Have You Seen Birds?*

## *The Vicky Metcalf Award*

The Canadian Authors' Association presents an award of $1000 to the Canadian writer who has produced a body of work consisting of at least three books appealing to children between 7 and 17 years of age.

1963  Kerry Wood
1964  John F. Hayes
1965  Roderick Haig-Brown
1966  Fred Swayze
1967  John Patrick Gillese
1968  Lorraine McLaughlin
1969  Audry McKim
1970  Farley Mowat
1971  Kay Hill
1972  William Toye
1973  Christie Harris
1974  Jean Little
1975  Lyn Harrington
1976  Suzanne Martel
1977  James Houston
1978  Lyn Cook
1979  Cliff Faulknor
1980  John Craig
1981  Monica Hughes
1982  Janet Lunn
1983  Claire Mackay
1984  Bill Freeman
1985  Edith Fowke
1986  Dennis Lee
1987  Robert Munsch

## *The Young Adult Canadian Book Award*

The Saskatchewan Library Association presents an annual award for the best Canadian English-language work of creative literature for young adults.

1981  Kevin Major. *Far from Shore*
1982  Jamie Brown. *Superbike!*
1983  Monica Hughes. *Hunter in the Dark*
1984  O. R. Melling. *The Druid's Tune*
1985  Mary Ellen Lang-Collura. *Winners*

1986  Marianne Brandis. *The Quarter Pie Window*
1987  Janet Lunn. *Shadow in Hawthorn Bay*

*The Max and Greta Ebel Memorial Award for Children's Writing*

The Canadian Society of Children's Authors, Illustrators, and Performers (CANSCAIP) administers an annual prize of $100 for the Canadian children's book that most contributes to a greater understanding among people of differing backgrounds, cultures, or generations.

1986  Mary-Ellen Lang Collura. *Winners*

*The Elizabeth Mrazik-Cleaver Canadian Picture Book Award*

The Canadian Section of IBBY, the International Board on Books for Young People, offers an award in memory of Elizabeth Cleaver for the best Canadian picture book.

1986  Anne Blades. *By the Sea*

# *I*ndex

Alphabetized according to the letter-by-letter system, this index includes references to all three parts of *Canadian Books for Children*. **Bold** numerals indicate pages of the bio-critical entry on that author or illustrator in Part I. The abbreviation (ill.) following a numeral indicates that the page contains an illustration from the listed title or from a work by the listed author or illustrator. The abbreviation (fig.) following a numeral indicates that the page contains a figure related to the classroom presentation of the title or the work of the listed author or illustrator.